Esther Tusquets' Novelistic Tetralogy

Juan de la Cuesta
Hispanic Monographs

EDITOR
Tom Lathrop
University of Delaware

ASSOCIATE EDITOR
Alexander R. Selimov
University of Delaware

EDITORIAL BOARD
Samuel G. Armistead
University of California, Davis

Annette G. Cash
Georgia State University

Alan Deyermond
Queen Mary and Westfield College of the University of London

Daniel Eisenberg
Regents College

John E. Keller
University of Kentucky

Steven D. Kirby
Eastern Michigan University

Joël Rini
University of Virginia

Donna M. Rogers
Middlebury College

Noël Valis
Yale University

Amy Williamsen
University of Arizona

Squaring the Circle:
Esther Tusquets' Novelistic Tetralogy
(A Jungian Analysis)

by

STACEY DOLGIN CASADO

Juan de la Cuesta
Newark, Delaware

On the cover:
   Mandala image © 2002 Erik Wrenholt.
   www.timestretch.com

Cover design by Michael Bolan.
   www.michaelmade.com

Copyright © 2002 by Juan de la Cuesta—Hispanic Monographs
270 Indian Road
Newark, Delaware 19711
(302) 453-8695
Fax: (302) 453-8601
www.JuandelaCuesta.com

MANUFACTURED IN THE UNITED STATES OF AMERICA

ISBN: 1-58871-023-8

*To PABLO
and his anima, with whom my animus
and I form a perfect marriage quaternity
and to
ALEX, MARC and SHANA,
who round out our world with so much joy*

Table of Contents

PREFACE 9

I. THEORETICAL INTRODUCTION
   1. Esther Tusquets' Novels and their
      Jungian Implications 11
   2. The Make-Up of the Psyche
      According to Jung 38
   3. The Psyche as Work of Art:
      A Creation Story 45
   4. Symbolism: Bridging the
      Psychological and the Physical 52
   5. *Mandala*: Symbol of the
      Self and Structure of the Tetralogy 66
   6. Squaring the Circle:
      Individuation as Thematic Structure 73
   7. Synchronicity: Psyche and
      Tetralogy as *Unus Mundus* 82

II. ANALYSIS
   1. *El mismo mar de todos los veranos*:
      One as the Beginning and the End 89
   2. *El amor es un juego solitario*:
      The Oscillating Duality of Binary Oppositions 126
   3. *Varada tras el último naufragio*:
      Three as Synthesis and Transcendence 148
   4. *Para no volver*: From the Four Comes the One 172

III. CONCLUSION 191

BIBLIOGRAPHY 197

Preface

My onerous investigation into the *Collected Works* of Carl Jung followed multiple readings of Tusquets' four novels in their chronological order of publication. With each successive reading, I became aware of myself mentally visualizing a square-framed circle within which was contained a variety of numerical and geometric symbols, along with other symbolically endowed shapes: squares, circles, triangles, spirals, crosses, and the like. The relationship between the first and the fourth novels seemed reminiscent of a circle with no single identifiable beginning or ending point. At times, the first novel seemed to close the circular structure of the tetralogy while, paradoxically, functioning as its overture. Similarly, the fourth novel signified the culmination of the theme of individuation in one sense, while synchronously harking its incipience from another vantage point. The second novel seemed to set into motion the individuation process, while at the same time being a "natural" sequel to the first novel with which the individuation process both begins and ends. And the opening of the third novel—like that of the first and last—set the stage for the entire process of psychological transformation that was to take place in both the preceding and following novels. It occurred to me that the structural relationship of the four novels constituted a circle in the truest sense of the word: there existed no easily identifiable point of origin or termination; the beginning and the end were simultaneously everywhere and nowhere.

The next most prominent aspect of the mental image were the innumerable sets of diametric pairings of contradictory, yet complementary, concepts bisecting the framed circle: conscious/unconscious, male/female, child/adult; innocence/experience, fragmentation/wholeness, Apollonian/Dionysian, idealism/disillusionment, progression/regression-repetition, lightness/darkness, aggression/passivity, and countless others. Furthermore, each of the four titles conveyed a dualism from whose paradox emerged a third synthetic meaning that did not cancel out the mutually exclusive concepts but, rather, endowed them with a transcendent meaning. The role of paradox as a necessary prelude to the transcendence of conflict (in this case, psychological), and the recognition that Tusquets' four novels are patterned in accordance with this and many other Jungian principles, pointed me in the direction of Jungian theory. I could not think of any literary work or group of works that had ever carried me to the breadth and depth of fictional self-discovery, nor could I think of anyone who had written more extensively and eloquently on the human journey toward self-knowledge than had Carl Jung. It seemed inevitable to me that Esther Tusquets and Carl Jung had much to illuminate about each other's work. Indeed they have.

Since the function of literary criticism is—or should be—the elucidation of literary works of art for the purpose of heightening and deepening readers' understanding of their meaning, as well as for the purpose of enhancing their ability to experience the text as an esthetic object, a determination of the nature of the text necessarily must precede the selection of a theoretical approach. If indeed our mission is to illuminate obscurity, then we must be able to explain in the most direct, coherent manner possible the form/content relationship of a single literary work of art, or of a body of literary texts, provided that they constitute a meaningful unity. The most valuable instrument we have to assist us in accomplishing our goal as literary critics is over two thousand years worth of theoretical approaches to literary works of art. The literary text should drive the selection of the theory used to explain it; that is to say, the theory should be subordinated to the literary work of art and not—as we so often see—the other way around. We are, after all, critics of literature, so it is not to the emergence of the latest theory that to which we owe our allegiance but, rather, it is to the ontological status of the literary text that we owe our utmost loyalty and deference.

STACEY DOLGIN CASADO
University of Georgia, Athens

I. Theoretical Introduction

1. Esther Tusquets' Novels and Their Jungian Implications

> I should like to emphasize that the integration of the shadow, or the realization of the personal unconscious, marks the first stage in the analytic process, and that without it a recognition of *anima* and *animus* is impossible. The shadow can be realized only through a relationship to a partner, and *anima* and *animus* only through a relationship to a partner of the opposite sex, because only in such a relation do their projections become operative. The recognition of the *anima* gives rise, in a man, to a triad, one third of which is transcendent: the masculine subject, the opposing feminine subject, and the transcendent *anima*. With a woman the situation is reversed. The missing fourth element that would make the triad a quaternity is, in a man, the archetype of the Wise Old Man, and in a woman the Chthonic Mother. These four constitute a half immanent and half transcendent quaternity, an archetype which I have called the *marriage quaternio*. The marriage quaternio provides a schema not only for the Self but also for the structure of primitive society with its cross-cousin marriage, marriage classes, and division of settlements into quarters. The Self, on the other hand, is a God-image, or at least cannot be distinguished from one. Of this the early Christian spirit was not ignorant, otherwise Clement of Alexandria could never have said that he who knows himself knows God.
>
> JUNG, *Aspects of the Feminine* 179

THE PRESENT STUDY DESCRIBES and analyzes the implications of a four-part psycho-narrative journey toward wholeness that is undertaken by a woman and literary artist, Esther Tusquets, as she stands at the threshold of the second half of her life. The four novels to be considered in this study, *El mismo mar de todos los veranos* (1978), *El amor es un juego solitario* (1979), *Varada tras el último naufragio* (1980), and *Para no volver* (1985), reveal a process of psychological transformation that at once is autobiographical and fictional, individual and universal. The psycho-literary act of creation that they encompass on a symbolic level of interpretation, spans a seven-year period that began when the author was forty-two years old, and was completed on the eve of her fiftieth birthday. Not coincidentally, the latter corresponds to the ages of the anonymous female protagonist[1] autobiographically disclosing the contents of her psyche in the first-person in the opening novel of the series, as well as that of Elena who is the protagonist of the fourth, appearing seven years later, which is told from the third-person omniscient point of view.

Throughout the course of this study, it will become clear how and why this shift in narrative perspective is one among a vast array of narrative elements bringing to light the collective theme of the four novels: psychological transformation. As a unified novelistic *opus*, they reveal perceivable development and change, resulting from an increasing familiarity with one's personal and collective unconscious, ultimately leading to a more conscious awareness not only of one's specific individuality, but of one's universality as well. Throughout the eighteen volumes of his writings, the Swiss psychiatrist and founder of analytical psychology,[2] Carl Jung (1875-1961), referred to this numinous evolution of the psyche as "individuation."[3]

The four novels published within a seven-year period constitute a hermetically-sealed literary microcosm whose structure is circular and whose content is at least partially autobiographical in the traditional sense of the word, if not wholly autobiographical within the context of the psychological

---

[1] When Anagrama re-edited *El mismo mar...*, Tusquets made some modifications to the original edition published by Lumen, among them a single mention of the name "Elia" as that belonging to the autobiographical narrator. When the author was interviewed by Mercedes M. de Rodríguez in 2000, the interviewer asked her why she had done so, if it was to more clearly establish the three novels as constituting a trilogy, Tusquets replied: "Sí, porque me divierten mucho los guiños y los juegos. Cuando escribí *El mismo mar...* no pensaba en una trilogía; luego me pareció que los personajes de las tres novelas simbolizan lo mismo, aunque no sean idénticos, y esa mujer mayor de *El mismo mar...* puede ser Elia" ("Entrevista..." 614).

[2] I am employing Jung's definition of the term "analytical" as "a procedure that takes account of the existence of the unconscious" (*Aion* 275).

[3] Although the term "individuation process" does not appear until the 1921 publication of Jung's *Psychological Types*, Jacobi informs us that its conceptualization can be found as early as 1902 in Jung's doctoral dissertation entitled *On the Psychology and Pathology of So-called Occult Phenomena*. The most elaborate explanation of the concept reaches its culmination in Jung's last major work, *Mysterium Coniunctionis*, published in 1955-56 (Jacobi, *The Way...* 12).

development of its creator as it is portrayed (consciously, unconsciously, or both) in her fictional rendition of the same. It is our intention to show that the four novels comprise a meaningfully integrated whole—a tetralogy—in which all paired opposites have transcended their differences and merged into an indivisible wholeness of One. Esther Tusquets' novelistic tetralogy might thus be described as an autobiographical (factual) projection (fictional) of the author's female psyche in particular, and of the universal female psyche in general, insofar as each and every unique woman simultaneously contributes to the make-up of a collective female psyche, remnants of which each individual has inherited from the previous generation since the early origins of the human race. According to Jung, each individual psyche comprises, at its lowest stratum, a common collective unconscious housed by primary, inborn *imagos*, which he termed universal archetypes. Throughout his long, illustrious career as both a practicing psychoanalyst and scholarly theorist of the profoundest inner workings of the human psyche, the depth psychologist came to describe archetypes as innate releasing mechanisms with which the psyche, when in a state of emotional arousal, somehow is predisposed to construct coherent images. Around the universal images of the shadow, the contra-sexual *anima* inhabiting the masculine psyche, the contra-sexual *animus* dwelling within the feminine psyche, the Great Mother, the Terrible Mother, the Father, the Wise Old Man, etc., there develop psychological complexes which constitute the primary building blocks of the human personality. Each complex is an emotionally charged cluster of images and/or ideas that acts as an autonomous "splinter" personality, often in opposition to, and undermining, the ego consciousness of the individual. Jung believed that at the core of each complex there is to be found an emotionally powerful archetype, which the individual unconsciously projects[4] onto others whenever it is activated by a real-life situation. First and foremost, it is the withdrawal of such projections, followed by the passage of these complexes into conscious awareness, that which defines the primary goal of individuation. Jung considered this most arduous phase of the lifelong, ongoing individuation process to be a distinctly mid-life task. As a matter of fact, the depth psychologist believed that it was an ensuing neurosis brought about by irreconcilable differences between the conscious mind and an unconsciously activated complex in an individual, to be that which characterizes the requisite *sine qua non* of the individuation process. Tusquets' four novels thematically structure the individuation process; that is,

---

[4] A projection is an "unconscious, that is, unperceived and unintentional, transfer of subjective psychic elements onto an outer object" (Franz, *Projection*... 3).

they *are* and *are about* the recognition of one's divided conscious/unconscious nature, leading to the ultimate dissolution of the unconscious complexes and the corresponding expansion of consciousness within an individual female psyche constituted by four female protagonists at different stages of the individuation process.

Throughout the first half of our lives, most women are so consumed with carving out a niche for ourselves in the world while tending to our homes, husbands and children, that we remain relatively unaware of the existence of our collective, or even personal, unconscious, that are harbored within each and every human being. As all of us, men and women alike, approach the waning years of the first half of our lives and must cross the threshold to the second half of life, the priorities of the psyche tend to become inverted. We become less interested in meeting the demands of the outer world as a pronounced need to get to know our inner world better demands more and more of our attention. Like the ebb and flow of the ocean tides, the personal unconscious increasingly spills over into consciousness, often interfering with our daily functioning and making a restful night of sleep a rare occurrence. Suddenly, for some unexplained reason, we find ourselves feeling lost, insecure, unsure of who we are and how we wish to proceed, questioning the meaning of life and becoming painfully aware of our mortality. If we are able to remember our dreams and take the time to reconstruct and analyze them, we soon discover their archetypal structure and meaning, wherein lie the most profound truths about the human condition in general, as well as the individuality that is unique to each of us.

Born in Barcelona on August 30, 1935, it is astonishing, although readily explainable, that as skilled a literary artist as is Esther Tusquets did not publish her first novel until the age of forty-two. This factor is germane to the appropriateness of a Jungian analytical approach to her novelistic production[5] because it corresponds to the incipience of the second half of life when the human psyche seems to undergo the natural process of reorganization to which we alluded earlier. The Jungian scholar, David L. Hart, explains the nature of this mid-life reorientation of the psyche as a

---

[5] The four novels being considered in this study are not Tusquets' only novels. Her other three novels, *Siete miradas en un mismo paisaje* (1982), *Con la miel en los labios* (1997) and *Correspondencia privada* (2001) have not been included in this study because they are unrelated both in content as well as in form to those comprising her novelistic tetralogy.

gradual emergence out of the ego's control and into the realm of the Self—out of merely personal values and into those of more impersonal and collective meaning. The first half of life is normally devoted to establishing a secure base in the world: education, profession, family, a personal identity. But at mid-life that crisis threatens, whose ubiquity and importance Jung helped to clarify in the public mind. It is at bottom a spiritual crisis, the challenge to seek and discover the meaning of life. To meet this challenge, none of the tools of the first half of life are adequate. It is not a question of further conquests or acquisitions; it is more a question of exploration of the soul, for its own sake, letting go of the familiar demands of the ego to be fed and gratified. Therefore, it is often felt as a loss, and is often powerfully resisted; and yet the psyche, with its own powerful demand to be realized, will persist in confronting consciousness with new and unheard-of views of life's meanings and possibilities. (99)

Unconscious contents, both personal and archetypal, that had been lying dormant for decades suddenly make their presence known. The inner stirrings of the lesser known and unknown realms of the psyche often precipitate what commonly is referred to as a mid-life crisis. Many individuals attempt to assuage the internal discomfort with a make-over of their physical appearance, an extra-marital affair, the purchase of a sports car, or a change in job, career, or lifestyle, only to discover that the psychological rumblings become increasingly louder in protest of being ignored. If not attended to, they wreak havoc upon the psyche, and internal warfare in the form of neuroses results. If, however, they are recognized for what they are, confronted, struggled with long enough, and eventually accepted and incorporated into consciousness, the individual is able to settle into the waning sun of the second half of life with greater maturity and fortitude.

Our author was at this very crossroad when her career as a writer of narrative fiction began. The same year that she published her first novel, *El mismo mar...*, she ended a fourteen-year relationship with Esteban, with whom she was not legally married, but with whom she maintained a marital relationship and had two children (Rodríguez 616-17). Nor should it go unnoticed that, from a sociological perspective, the publication of *El mismo mar...* in 1978 coincides with the waning years of artistic censorship and the transition from the autocratic theocracy of the Franco years to the advent of an egalitarian democracy which afforded Spanish women an unprecedented opportunity to forge a new identity for themselves. This dramatic reorientation of the author's life, both as an individual and as a social being, was bridged only by the continuity of motherhood and the ownership of Editorial Lumen in Barcelona, which she had inherited from her father in the 1960s and which continues in operation today. Due to feelings of insecurity and self-doubt about the quality of her fiction, the middle-aged writer was reluctant to send her work to a reputable publisher. Consequently, she elected to publish all of her novels and short story collections at Lumen, unbeknownst to her that within just a few years after the appearance of her first novel, she was to be considered one of the most widely read and respected writers of contemporary Spanish fiction.

Within the context of her literary production, the difficult psychological issues with which the fictional protagonists wrestle—and from which they emerge with greater self-knowledge—symbolize a death/rebirth rite of initiation, "a basic change in existential condition," an "ordeal" from which an individual emerges "endowed with a totally different being from that which he possessed before his initiation" (Beane 164). Symbolic rites of initiation are a concomitant of individuation. Since it is the individuation process that which constitutes the thematic structure of Tusquets' four novels, it comes as no surprise that symbolic acts of death/rebirth appear and reemerge time and again as structural and thematic *leitmotifs* interconnecting the four works. As a matter of fact, the tetralogy begins with a symbolic *regressus ad uterum* typical of rites of initiation: "Cruzo la puerta de hierro y cristal, pesada, chirriante, y me sumerjo en una atmósfera contradictoriamente más pura—menos luz, menos ruidos, menos sol" (Tusquets, *El mismo mar...* 7). As the narrator/protagonist of the first novel leaves the light of day and descends into the dark, musty, subterranean depths of the abandoned home of her childhood, we are reminded of the primitive stages of culture in which the initiation rites of adolescents entailed the novice's transformation into an embryonic state in order to be reborn. The symbolic return to the womb "is signified either by the neophyte's seclusion in a hut, or by his being symbolically swallowed by a monster, or by his entering a sacred spot identified with the uterus of Mother Earth" (Beane 174) for the purpose of being "born into a new mode of being." From a structural viewpoint, "the return to the womb corresponds to the reversion of the Universe to the 'chaotic' or embryonic state. prior to the birth of consciousness. The prenatal darkness corresponds to the Night before Creation and to the darkness of the initiation hut" (Beane 175).

Although not consciously determined at the outset of her creative enterprise, it is retrospectively evident that Tusquets' four novels collectively are goal–oriented and reaching, in accordance with many of the principles guiding and defining the psychoanalytic process.[6] The destination toward which

---

[6] Dr. Murray Stein, President of the Chicago Society of Jungian Analysts, has come

the author's psycho-literary odyssey develops, and reaches fruition, is a two-pronged quest for wholeness of being for herself and for her literary creation. As the rigidities of ego-consciousness dissolve and an increasingly greater portion of the unconscious is permitted to participate in the Self, the experience carries with it "an influx of energy and vitality, so that one common result of analysis is more creativity in one's responses to life and its challenges" (Stein 31).

Individually and collectively, the four novels are structured as death /rebirth rites of initiation, albeit psychological ones, consisting of difficult tasks that must be performed and obstacles that must be overcome by the four female protagonists collectively constituting four stages in the individuation process of one female psyche. Although there do exist insignificant differences among the four protagonists, of far greater relevance than the differences is that all of them are under the shared psychological dominance of a negative mother complex, coupled with an extreme case of *animus* possession, both of which have thwarted their psychological development and been the source of troubled, unsuccessful familial, hetero-, homo- and bi-sexual relationships throughout their adult lives. Healing the emotional scars left by an unsatisfactory mother-daughter relationship and breaking free of the *animus* stranglehold are the two primary tasks that the collective female psyche of Tusquets' protagonists must perform successfully in order to propel into motion the psychological development upon which crossing the threshold and meeting the challenges of the second half of life are so dependent.

It is in this pursuit and ultimate achievement of an integrated psycho-literary totality that the four novels constituting the subject matter of this study symbolize the culmination of modernity in the arts. According to Jean-François Lyotard, modern art is the technique of presenting the unpresentable, of making visible what can be conceived but neither seen nor made to be seen (21). From an artistic standpoint, Tusquets achieves the near-impossible: through the medium of a language rich in universal symbolism, she renders visible the synchronous development of the individuation and creative processes by virtue

---

up with the clearest, most succinct definition of psychoanalysis that we have encountered. "Jungian analysis takes place within a dialectical relationship between two persons, analyst and analysand, and has for its goal the analysand's coming to terms with the unconscious: the analysand is meant to gain insight into the specific unconscious structures and dynamics that emerge during analysis, and the structures underlying ego-consciousness are meant to change in their dynamic relationship to other, more unconscious structures and dynamics" (29).

of the symbol of the *mandala*[7] that symbolically depicts each as one-and-the-same. At the close of the circular tetralogy, the reader experiences the sublime perception of the indivisibility of psyche and matter in the theme-content oneness of the æsthetic microcosm. In cultural terms, it would seem that when creator and creation, psyche and cosmos, spirit and matter, merge into a single self-contained circular entity as they do at the close/incipience of Tusquets' fourth/first novels, thereby constituting an undifferentiated *unus mundus*, then the ultimate state of perfection—the goal of modernity—has been attained.

As indicated by the title that we have given this study, we regard *El mismo mar de todos los veranos*, *El amor es un juego solitario*, *Varada tras el último naufragio* and *Para no volver* as constituting a novelistic tetralogy by virtue of their symbolically meaningful integration. In the most general sense, a tetralogy is a series or group of four related works, although the manner by which the four works are related need not conform to any regulating principle. In its most specific context, a tetralogy is a group of four dramas, three tragic and one satiric, performed consecutively at the festival of Dionysus in ancient Athens. Compelling arguments may be made on behalf of the applicability of each of these definitions to the aforementioned four novels. Turning to the first definition, although a perfunctory reading of the four novels might well create the impression that each exists independently of the other three, they are, in fact, distinct, yet intrinsically and mutually related manifestations of movement

---

[7] Of the *mandala*, Cirlot writes the following: "This is a Hindu term for circle. It is a kind of *yantra* (instrument, means, or emblem), in the form of a ritual geometric diagram, sometimes corresponding to a specific, divine attribute or to some form of enchantment (*mantra*) which is thus given visual expression." *Mandalas* are to be found all over the Orient, "always as a means toward contemplation and concentration—as an aid in inducing certain mental states and in encouraging the spirit to move forward along its path of evolution from the biological to the geometric, from the realm of corporeal forms to the spiritual." Cirlot provides further insight into how Jung came to incorporate the symbol of the *mandala* into his extensive clinical practice and writings centered around the paradoxically universal and, at the same time, highly individualized individuation process. Cirlot informs us that "one of the members of the Lamaist convent of Bhutia Busty, Lingdam Gomehen," personally told Jung that "no one *mandala* is the same as another, that all are different because each is a projected image of the psychic condition of its author, or in other words, an expression of the modification brought by this psychic content to the traditional idea of the *mandala*. Thus, the *mandala* is a synthesis of a traditional structure plus free interpretation. Its basic components are geometric figures, counterbalanced and concentric. Hence it has been said that 'the *mandala* is always a squaring of the circle'" (190-91).

towards psychic wholeness. The depth psychologist's theory of the individuation process, when and how it takes place and what its manifestations are, provides a coherent explanation as to the nature of the thematic as well as structural interrelationship of our novelist's four works. When considered from a Jungian perspective, the successive reading of each component of the narrative tetrad contributes to a progressive enlargement and deepening of a whole that transcends the mere sum of its four parts. It is a tetralogy encompassing a/the search for, and discovery of, a/the female Self.

With respect to the second definition of a tetralogy as four works performed in succession at the Dionysia in Athens, it exhibits some curious points of contact with Tusquets' four novels. Although these similarities may be purely coincidental, they are worth mentioning. It is from the Dionysia that we owe the birth of Greek tragedy and comedy as prototypes of the peaceful coexistence of binary oppositions within a single culture. Leaving aside differences of genre, the tragic trilogy followed by a single contrapuntal satiric work, accurately describes the rhythmic configuration of Tusquets' tetralogy as a trilogy whose parts were published in 1978, 1979, and 1980, followed by a four year hiatus, after which a single contrapuntal fourth novel appeared. As a matter of fact, the editorial bio-bibliographies printed on the back jacket cover of her books refer to *El mismo mar...*, *El amor...* and *Varada...* as a trilogy, and to *Para no volver* as an isolated novel. Although the fourth novel indeed is contrapuntal, within the framework of the psycho-literary tetralogy it is an integral part of the growth toward psychic wholeness that the tetramerous totality encompasses. The ostensible narrative disassociation between the so-called trilogy (point) and *Para no volver* (counterpoint), constitutes the essential dialectic that produces the tension enabling a transcendental synthesis of oppositional forces within the psyche.

The conflicting conclusions reached as to whether the four novels constitute a trilogy plus a fourth unrelated novel, or a tetralogy, undoubtedly are due to the critics' strictly numerical interpretation of the prefixes "tri-" and "tetra-" when they are in fact inseparably numerical *and* configurational. "Tri-," meaning "three," and "tetra-," meaning "four," are combining forms revealing the number of parts constituting the *single total structure* to which they refer. Hence, a "triad" is *a group* of three or *a musical chord* consisting in three tones; a "triangle" is *a geometrical figure* measuring one hundred eighty degrees, having three identical sides and angles of sixty degrees each; a "triarchy" is *a government* by three rulers; a "tetragon" is *a plane figure* with four angles and four sides; a "tetrahedron" is *a solid figure* with four triangular faces; a "tetrastich" is *a poem or stanza* of four lines, and so on. In none of the examples listed above may the designated number of parts be understood without an *a priori* comprehension of the *single structural configuration* to whose composition they are contributing. In other words, it is neither the number of parts *per se*, nor the contents of the parts, that which results in a meaningful unity. It is, rather, whether the parts are arranged in such a way so that their unified wholeness is of greater transcendental significance than the mere sum of the parts. Thus, a trilogy is not merely a group of three, nor is a tetralogy simply a set of four, related works. It is a great deal more. In order for three works to constitute a trilogy, or four a tetralogy, the sum of the parts—each of which *must* constitute a unity unto itself—*must form* an extended, unified work. The implications of the total work always will be more far-reaching than the sum of the parts by virtue of the fact that the wholeness will not be derived exclusively from relationships of similarity shared among the parts but, more significantly, from the fact that they will be structurally interrelated. Just as the sum total of correct building materials do not add up to a house unless they are arranged and combined in accordance with certain architectural principles, so is the case in the construction of a (literary) trilogy or a (literary) tetralogy where the nature of the individual components are subordinated to the collective structuring of those elements.

Our study sets out to explore the seven-year process by which Esther Tusquets' creative psyche constructs a coherent, self-contained fictional microcosm—a literary universe—whose coming into being would seem to run parallel to the psychic journey toward wholeness that she has projected onto her fictional personæ. The finished literary *corpus* configurationally depicts the integrated psyche that came into being while simultaneously creating an image of totality that was in the process of unfolding. To understand this paradox, which for Jung is a synonym for transcendence, requires paying particularly close attention to the nature of the interrelationship of the four texts. Although such a phenomenon could never be proven empirically, there is every reason to postulate the following with respect to Tusquets' novelistic tetralogy: since both the individuation and the creative processes may be symbolized as an identical rite of initiation, and since both reach closure at the same point in time and space when the closing words of the fourth novel coincide structurally and thematically with the opening sentence of the first, conceptually rendering visible a *mandala* (squared circle) configuration, there is every reason to assume that the two processes unfolded following an identical rhythmic pattern. This supposition is supported by the fact that the *mandala* is at once a universal symbol of the Self (microcosm) and of the Universe (macrocosm) by virtue of the essential structural properties inherent in all cosmogonies. This "meaningful coincidence" (Jung, *Mysterium*... 464), which forms the basis for our classification of Tusquets' four novels as constituting a psycho-literary cosmos, has been defined by Jung as "synchronicity." Among the Swiss analytical psychologist's major contributions to our understanding of the relationship between psyche and matter is his extensive exploration into synchronistic events, in which a material and a psychic phenomenon temporally coincide and are linked by a common meaning. When Jung created the concept, he laid a foundation for what might allow us to perceive the complementary realms of psyche and matter as one reality. At the close of Tusquets' fourth novel, psyche (as manifested throughout the individuation process whose structure thematically runs through the four texts) and matter (the esthetic object resulting from the formed content of the four works) are indistinguishable the one from the other. The finished literary *opus* is the image of the psychic wholeness of being that conceived it at its outset and developed it to its meaningful conclusion.

While the general tendency, including initially by the author herself, has been to classify the texts as a trilogy plus a fourth unrelated novel,[8] a few critics have taken the position that the first three novels do not comprise a trilogy at all, thereby implying that all four novels should be considered as separate entities.[9] More recently, two notable critics of Tusquets' fiction have referred to the four texts as comprising a novelistic tetralogy and indeed have touched upon some of the relevant arguments for categorizing them as such from the thematic perspective of female psychological development.[10]

---

[8] The back cover of *Para no volver*, presumably written by the author herself (or approved by her at the very least) since it was published by her own Editorial Lumen, reads as follows: "Se inicia como escritora tardíamente, con la publicación de *El mismo mar de todos los veranos* (1978), primera parte de una trilogía que se completaría con *El amor es un juego solitario* (Premio Ciudad de Barcelona, 1979), y *Varada tras el último naufragio* (1980). *Siete miradas en un mismo paisaje* (1981) cierra provisionalmente un ciclo narrativo que se reabre, desde un punto de mira más amplio, si cabe, con *Para no volver.*"

[9] In her article, "Esther Tusquets and the Trilogy Which Isn't," Mary S. Vásquez rejects classifying *El mismo mar...*, *El amor...* and *Varada...* as a trilogy for reasons of theme, characterization, and parity of parts. The critic contends that the three female Elias should be regarded as distinct figures, as opposed to one-and-the-same at different stages of female development as purported in the present study. She also notes that the commonalities shared by the three protagonists, the most psychologically damaging of which is their having been emotionally deprived of parental bonding, is true of nearly all of Tusquets' female characters appearing in all of her works of fiction.

[10] Pablo Gil Casado classifies the four texts as a tetralogy by virtue of their shared theme of individuation: "La tetralogía de Esther Tusquets integrada por *El mismo mar de todos los veranos, El amor es un juego solitario, Varada tras el último naufragio* y

In truth, a comparison of the plots, characters, and themes of the four novels leads to nothing but chaos and confusion as evidenced by the different, sometimes contradictory, conclusions to which critics have arrived in an attempt to explain the (dis)unity of the *corpus* of Tusquets' novelistic fiction. The same holds true if one attempts to determine to what extent fiction and autobiography overlap and/or intermingle, a question to which the author and her critics have failed to provide a satisfactory answer. It is indeed a complex issue, for while the fictional search for identity is narrated in the process of unfolding, it would seem that there must have existed an *a priori* autobiographical search for identity serving as a model for the fictional construct. This is not to imply that Tusquets could not have animated more complexes and merged them into a more expansive self-consciousness during her seven-year creative odyssey. It is meant to suggest that either the author knowingly, and paradoxically, is creating (in the sense of inventing) her own psychic autobiography as though it were coming into existence for the first time, or that Jung was correct in his theory that there exists an archetypal world plan in the collective unconscious of all individuals, what might be understood as residual material that each one of us has inherited from the pre-existing mental plan for the creation of the Universe.[11] This primordial cosmic background, which Jung referred to as the *unus mundus*, sporadically manifests itself in synchronistic phenomena as a *creatio continua*, "as the continuous creation of a pattern that exists from all eternity, repeats itself sporadically, and is not derivable from any known antecedents" (Jung, *The Structure and Dynamics...* 518). Is it possible that Tusquets' novelistic tetralogy is an example of the latter? Either scenario would explain the literal meaninglessness of both physical space and chrono-

---

Para no volver, responde en conjunto a una temática de carácter psicopático. Sin embargo, el tema que presta unidad a los cuatro libros se pierde de vista en el segundo y tercer volumen a causa del asunto erótico que, al particularizarse fuertemente, da la impresión de responder a unas motivaciones hedonistas, ajenas al tema psicopático... Así pues, *El amor...* y *Varada...* pueden leerse por separado como novelas eróticas. No obstante, los cuatro libros forman una unidad predicada por el proceso de individuación de la protagonista y a ese vínculo primordial nos ajustamos" (223-24). Barbara Ichiishi shares a similar view which serves as the thematic *motif* of her impressive study dealing with all of Tusquets' fiction. The reader may also consult my articles on Esther Tusquets, all of which argue for the structural and thematic unity of the four novels.

[11] All references to the biblical rendition of God's creation of the Universe should be understood strictly within the context of Jungian theory and should not, under any circumstances, be interpreted as an attempt on our part to impose or interject religious points of view in this study.

logical time permeating the tetralogy, where spatial references and temporal coordinates play the dual role of foregrounding the plot and of depicting mental states. For example, the ocean setting around which the development of the first and third novels revolve—and which is adumbrated by the respective titles of each, *El mismo mar de todos los veranos* and *Varada tras el último naufragio*—sets the stage for the psychological transformation, or rebirth, that is symbolically enacted at the end of each. The ocean connotes not only a physical space associated with escape from the mundane and quotidian by virtue of the regenerative effects of its seemingly infinite expanse, ceaseless movement and the formlessness of the waters, but is equally symbolic "of dynamic forces and of transitional states," "of woman or the mother (in both her benevolent and terrible aspects)," and "of the collective unconscious out of which arises the sun of the spirit" (Cirlot, *passim* 241-42). With regard to time, all four novels are enclosed temporally within the three-four month period from late spring to early fall, thereby encompassing two periods of seasonal transition within which the entire summer is contained: from late spring to early summer (May to June) and from late summer to early fall (August to September). Psychologically speaking, the summer months during which the four-part individuation process unfolds, span the transition between the first half of life (symbolized by the end of the spring) and the second (symbolized by the beginning of the fall). The passing of one season yields the birth of another just as letting go of the past signifies embracing a new beginning that is oriented toward a more positive outlook for the future. Furthermore, the August 30th birthday that the four fictional protagonists share with the author, reinforces the death/rebirth initiation theme serving as a structural-thematic link between the individuation and creative processes, the former emerging out of the darkness of the unconscious and the latter out of the Darkness preceding the Creation of the Universe according to biblical depiction. Not coincidentally, as the collective female psyche discovers her divine spirit at the close of the tetralogy, Tusquets synchronously acquires the identity of demiurge of her self-contained narrative cosmos. Just as the Creator is to be found everywhere in the Universe but nowhere in particular, Tusquets permeates her fictional cosmos while at the same time being unidentifiable at any given time or place. From a Jungian theoretical perspective, she, like the divine Creator, is both omnipresent and invisible, existing outside of the cosmos as its creator while spiritually embodying her object of creation. For example, in each of the four novels, the female protagonist unequivocally: is a member of the privileged Catalonian bourgeoisie; laments profusely a lifetime of longing for the maternal love and bonding from which she has felt deprived since early childhood; suffers from an intense void resulting from the absence of a meaningful relationship with a father who spent little time at home; is saddened by the recognition that she has unintentionally, but nonetheless tragically, passed the emotional legacy left to her by her parents on to her own children; is disillusioned with a failing or failed marriage; yearns to be able to love another and to experience the love of another for her; is sexually uninhibited and experimental; and is in search of a lost object for which she travels far and wide, only to learn that it lies within herself: it is her own selfhood. Since many of these factors are relevant to Tusquets' personal life, and being that the narrative point of view of the first novel, *El mismo mar...*, is the first-person autobiographical, the temptation to assume that the author has written a fictional autobiography indeed is great. Problems with this theory quickly arise, however, when the reader moves to the second, third, and fourth novels, all of which are narrated predominantly from a third-person omniscient point of view. To make a confusing situation even more convoluted, the autobiographical narrator/protagonist in the first novel—although she does disclose the fact that she has a two-syllable first name—remains nameless throughout,[12] while the female protagonists appearing in the second and third are named Elia, and Elena in the fourth. Furthermore, both the anonymous narrator in the first novel and Elena in the fourth novel are approaching the occasion of their fiftieth birthday—as was Tusquets when she published *Para no volver* in 1985—are married to a promiscuous cinematographer named Julio, and are wrestling with the typical fears and insecurities associated with crossing over into the second half of life. By most accounts, not only would they appear to be the same character, but they also would seem to be thinly veiled disguises for the author herself.

Nevertheless, the autobiographical theory is not as airtight as it might appear at first glance, at least not as the term "autobiography" is commonly understood, for the unnamed storyteller in the first novel has a two-syllable name and a daughter named Guiomar, while Elena has a three-syllable name and two sons named Pablo and Jorge, the former being the same name as Eva's husband in *Varada...*, and the latter corresponding to the name of Elia's husband in the third novel and the narrator's adolescent lover who had committed suicide when she was but seventeen years old in the first novel. Tusquets' personal life corresponds to neither, as she is the mother of one daughter and one son. Furthermore, and at the risk of stating the obvious, if Tusquets was the same age as Elena when she published *Para no volver*, then

---

[12] I am referring to the Lumen edition and not to the later Anagrama edition in which Tusquets edited the text to include one mention of the autobiographical narrator's name as "Elia."

she was only forty-two years old when she published *El mismo mar...*, whose narrator/protagonist, like Elena and Esther, was to turn fifty at the end of the summer. It thus becomes impossible to argue forcefully in favor of an autobiographical connection between the author and her fictional characters—at least from a circumstantial point of view—for it defies all laws of logic for a forty-two year old author to construct her own fictionally disguised autobiography as a woman of fifty.

Turning to the second and third novels, the Elia who appears in *El amor...* is in her thirties, while the Elia who serves as the projecting unconscious in the following novel is in her forties. Although the female protagonists in all four novels are married, those in the first two novels engage in bi-sexual activity, while those in the third and forth novels appear to be heterosexual in practice although they do fantasize about lesbian relationships. The young Clara who appears in the first three novels is nowhere to be found in the fourth, while the protagonists' cat, Muslina, either appears or is referred to in all four texts. The unnerving tension between chronology and discontinuity, similarity and difference, self-revelation and self-disguise, with regard to plot, characters, and recurring *leitmotifs* and themes, renders the content of these four novels an unreliable source for determining whether or not they share an exclusive unity of design. From the sole vantage point of their content, it could as easily be argued that they do as that they do not.

When an obvious relationship between an author and certain aspects of his/her fictional creation exists, we immediately are confronted with the question of the extent to which fiction and autobiography can coexist—if indeed they can at all—within a single text or meaningfully related body of works. If, by virtue of being a product of the writer's imagination, fiction is "untrue," and if, by definition, autobiography offers a factual and, therefore "true" account of an individual's life told by that very individual, then are fiction and autobiography not mutually exclusive? Can a work of fiction be autobiographical? Can an account of a person's life be presented fictitiously and still be autobiographical? And if a co-presence of fiction and autobiography is possible, then what are the points of convergence and/or complementation? Inasmuch as it is evident that Tusquets' four novels require a critical vantage point other than a plot-oriented one if a meaningful analysis of the relationship among them and between creator and creation is to be undertaken, to our knowledge none exists at the present time. Despite the classificatory differences posed by critics of Tusquets' fiction, there does exist a single commonality shared by them all: whatever conclusion has been reached has been based unilaterally on the content of the four novels at almost the complete exclusion of their formal composition or structural design. The twenty years of scholarship dealing with Esther Tusquets' four aforementioned novels has focused almost entirely on their plot and/or character development, often to the complete exclusion of formal aspects such as structure, internal dynamics, narrative style and techniques, etc. We hope to have demonstrated that, from the point of view of plots and characters, an argument against the interrelationship of the four novels just as readily could be made as one in support of such unity. If, however, we cast our glance beyond what is immediately and easily apprehended, the four novels do indeed constitute a meaningful whole, not by virtue of a relationship among their characters and what befalls them, but as the result of a coherent unity of design to which their plots and characters are subordinated.

The originality of the present study resides in the contention that the unity-in-diversity characterizing the four novels is configurative, conforming to certain predictable structural patterns of psychic development which, as stated earlier, Jung called "individuation." The analytical psychologist employs the term "individuation" to denote "the process by which a person becomes a psychological 'in-dividual,' that is, a separate, indivisible unity or 'whole'" (*Aion* 275). From the theoretical perspective of the quest for self-knowledge, the cumulative and integrative structure of the four novels reveals a unified pattern of meaningful psychic activity leading to the "attainment of the Self," whose point of departure, according to Jung, is entrance into "the realm of the syzygies, the paired opposites, where the One is never separated from the other, its antithesis" (*Aion* 106). The sum total of the content is equivalent to the structural process of differentiation, integration, and ultimate transcendence to a higher plane of consciousness, of the many sets of paired opposites that constitute a/the Self. In his commentary on *The Secret of the Golden Flower*, Jung explains symbolism as the key to grasping expressions of psychological transformation:

> The union of opposites on a higher level of consciousness is not a rational thing, nor is it a matter of will; it is a process of psychic development that expresses itself in symbols. Historically, this process has always been represented in symbols, and today the development of personality is still depicted in symbolic form. I discovered this fact in the following way. The spontaneous fantasy products I discussed earlier became more profound and gradually concentrate into abstract structures that apparently represent 'principles' in the sense of Gnostic *archai*. When the fantasies take the form chiefly as thoughts, intuitive formulations of dimly felt laws or principles emerge, which at first tend to be dramatized or personified. If

the fantasies are drawn, symbols appear that are chiefly of the *mandala* type. (*On Active Imagination* 77-78)

Within this context, the Tusquets' characters are symbolic personified projections of the differentiated, contrasting parts of *a* personal and *the* feminine collective unconscious. As the author herself clarified when asked to what extent she identified with her fictional characters, she is all of her characters—male and female alike—in general, while at the same time not being identified with any single one of them in particular: "Hay muchas cosas mías en Clara (la adolescente que yo fui tiene muchas cosas de Clara), quizás un poco en todos los personajes. Lo que pasa es que el lector sólo se guía por el sexo y por la edad. Buscan y piensan que yo me tengo que identificar con una mujer mayor, cuando a lo mejor me estoy identificando con uno de los hombres o con Clara" (Rodríguez, "Entrevista..." 617). The contents of the personal and collective unconscious, in conjunction with the ego-consciousness of the individual, comprise a whole Self in its process of coming into being. The plot of each of the four novels functions archetypically as a rhythmic, dialectical pattern involving the confrontation of oppositional aspects of the Self which also is laden with positive psychological meaning in that each phase of psychic development, as we shall demonstrate in the analytical section of this study, represents a transcendence of its previous state. Ultimately, the numinous condition of psychic wholeness is rendered attainable by the reader, for the interrelationship of the four novels stimulates the mental concretization of a *mandala*-like structure in the imagination of any reader who receives the texts symbolically (as opposed to literally) *and* who is endowed with the ability to interpret the symbols correctly. The so-called "New Novel" is not for everyone, least of all for the passive, impatient, untrained reader.

The repeated content-oriented pattern of critical analysis with regard to Tusquets' fiction fails to acknowledge the dramatic change witnessed in the Spanish novel in the 1960s when objectivist, socio-critical realism was supplanted by the so-called "New Novel." The leading theoretician was Alain Robbe-Grillet, whose battle cry for the continued innovation of the form of the novel was heard and practiced by international novelists who, like the French novelist and critic, were seeking to invent new forms for the novel. In Spain, the New Novel was ushered in by Juan Benet with the publication of *Volverás a Región* in 1967. Dozens of Spanish novelists followed suit: Luis Goytisolo, Gonzalo Torrente Ballester, Carlos Rojas, Carmen Martín Gaite, and Ana María Moix, just to mention a handful. Among such a prestigious group of writers prominently figures Esther Tusquets.

The elusive, deceptive quality of Tusquets' unassuming tetralogy is consistent with the tenets of the French *nouveau roman* as reflected upon by Alain Robbe-Grillet in his collection of essays entitled *Pour un nouveau roman*, which appeared in France in 1963 and in Spanish translation two years later. In the introductory pages, Robbe-Grillet admonishes the critic not to define the term "New Novel" too narrowly, for it is not meant "to designate a school, nor even a specific and constituted group of writers working in the same direction; the expression is merely a convenient label applicable to all those seeking new forms for the novel, forms capable of expressing (or of creating) new relations between man and the world, to all those who have determined to invent the novel, in other words, to invent man" (9). As previously mentioned, the "New Novel" as *praxis* was "introduced" in Spain in 1967 by Juan Benet. Far from being "new" to the Spanish novel, however, Benet's novel quickly was recognized for being what it was: namely the re-introduction of dehumanized art as theorized by José Ortega y Gasset in *La deshumanización del arte* (1925) and *Ideas sobre la novela* (1925), and subsequently practiced by a dozen or so of his followers between 1926-1934.[13] Two of Ortega's most loyal disciples, Francisco Ayala and Rosa Chacel, resumed the writing of dehumanized novels in the decades following the Spanish Civil War with texts such as *Muertes de perro* (1958) and *La sinrazón* (1960), respectively.

Such classifications of novels as "Formalist," "Vanguard," "Avant-Garde," "*Orteguista*," or "New," share a single invariable trait: a commitment to the future evolution of the genre, for which formal innovation is a *conditio sine qua non*: "There are not, for a writer, two possible ways to write the same book. When he thinks of a future novel, it is always a *way of writing* which first of all occupies his mind, and commands his hand. He has in mind certain rhythms of sentences, certain architectures, a vocabulary, certain grammatical constructions, exactly as a painter has in mind certain lines and colors. What will happen in the book comes afterward, as though secreted by the style itself" (Robbe-Grillet 44, Robbe-Grillet's italics). Thus, not only is the content subordinated to the formal aspects of the New Novel; it actually is determined and consumed by it, for it is "in their form that their meaning resides, their 'profound signification,' that is, their content" (43-44). No longer are plot, characters, and themes ends unto themselves as in the traditional nineteenth-century Realist novel, or its numerous vanguard reformulations and advancements throughout the course of the twentieth century. Quite to the contrary, in the New Novel they are mere "devices" or "artifices" that are manipulated in

---

[13] We have appropriated these dates from the title of Pérez Firmat's book.

whatever ways most effectively serve the interests of the creative process, the mechanics and nuances of which constitute the underlying theme of the text.

For Robbe-Grillet, the most essential aspect of the New Novel is the uncompromising commitment of the writer to bring something "new," never before seen, into the world. This preoccupation with the future of the novel implies that the writer must not be enslaved by pre-existing models or forms. (S)He must look ahead, not backward; imagine, not remember; invent, not reproduce; create, not imitate. The mere ontological existence of the work of art will be its own justification and reward: "If art is something, it is *everything*, which means that it must be self-sufficient, and that there is nothing *beyond*" (43, Robbe-Grillet's italics). The finished esthetic object has neither a past nor a future, neither a transcendental value nor meaning; "it is based on no truth that exists before it; and one may say that it expresses nothing but itself. It creates its own equilibrium and its own meaning" (45). The process of creating a novel is a journey of its own self-discovery as it comes into being, "an exploration which itself creates its own significations, as it proceeds" (141).

This shared perspective on art invariably has yielded novels that are hermetic, periphrastic, self-reflective, and solipsistic. Due to the fact that plot, characters, time, and space serve the exclusive interests of innovative formalist concerns, they are not at all what they appear to be when viewed from outside the realm of the creative enterprise. The playfully deceptive quality of the New Novel, what Robbe-Grillet has classified as a "game, imposture, dilettantism" (45), is consistent with its refusal to propagate any meaning outside its own internal network of self-created relationships. Therefore, a New Novel must be scrutinized from the inside out, for the reverse yields a distorted perception of its *raison d'être*.

The emergence of the New Novel reflects a shift in cultural sensibility that began to be perceived in Spain between 1962 and 1967 when consumerism, and its concomitant economic pressures, were starting to be felt. As luxuries came to be regarded as necessities and as the consumer market became increasingly inundated with products that were bigger, better, newer, and faster, rendering obsolete what one already owned, there came a corresponding demand for individuals to earn a great deal more money at an ever-increasing rate of speed. The economic pressure to keep up with the most recent electronic or telecommunication advancement, or with the latest middle-class fad, created a more competitive workplace in which employees were constantly looking over their shoulders to see who was after their job. The underlying tension and mistrust with which employees were living at work, coupled with economic pressures at home, resulted in a breakdown of human relations and the increased isolation of the individual. As workers felt more and more alienated at their jobs and inept at meeting the increasing demands of their families, they found themselves turning to the credit system, not only as immediate relief from the tension of the moment, but also as a source of instant pleasure and gratification. At least temporarily, their feelings of inadequacy were assuaged. He soon discovered, however, that rather than solving his problems, his economic difficulties were just beginning. He found himself more and more tightly squeezed economically, and less and less able to earn enough money to keep up with a standard of living that appeared to be socially mandated, but which clearly was beyond his financial means. As feelings of personal failure grew, so did the statistics for divorce, alcoholism, violence, drug abuse, and suicide.

Art is not created in a vacuum. It can always be culturally contextualized, for it invariably reflects in some way the prevailing political and economic extra-textual dynamics. The acquisition frenzy, in conjunction with the keen feeling of uncertainty and insecurity about Spain's future during these waning years of the Franco regime, manifested themselves in the novel not only with the reappearance of dehumanized themes, but also with a baroque esthetics. As Pablo Gil Casado explains, baroque art and its characteristic forms of indirect, convoluted expression at which the theme of a work is subtly hinted while at the same time being well concealed ("formas de expresión indirectas, retorcidas, mediante las que se sugiere y se oculta el tema"—22), are indicative of a society whose social institutions are in crisis, where personal insecurity is more the rule than the exception, and for whom the future is viewed with skepticism and fear: "La psicología que condiciona el gusto barroco es peculiar de épocas de quiebra de las instituciones, de colapso de las relaciones humanas, de desasosiego personal, de malestar colectivo, de desconfianza en el futuro" (22). In the early years of the Spanish democracy following the dictator's death in 1975, it became increasingly obvious that "reality" was anything but what it had appeared to be: "la época franquista ya no es lo que aparentó ser" (23). The economic prosperity in the forms of real estate and industrial development that had been sold to the public as "reality" turned out to be a mere barrage of false appearances concealing bankruptcies, swindles, ecological ruin, and unemployment: "El milagro económico es un conjunto de bancarrotas o, aún peor, de estafas; el desarrollo mobilario e industrial es una ruina ecológica; la emigración se repatria para integrarse al paro. Los pantanos que se llenan de arena son una fiel imagen de las maravillas de la dictadura. La superabundancia se ha convertido en carestía y, para mayor confusión, coexisten las dos" (23).

The esthetics of the Spanish New Novel reflects a similarly confusing, complex, contradictory nature of an almost impenetrable reality. Due to the mistrust that these texts inspire on the part of the reader, resulting at times from the narrator coming to be perceived by the reader as unreliable, and in other cases from contradictions or inconsistencies pervading the text, they require numerous readings in order to be penetrated beneath the veneer of their literal meaning to their innermost core where the key to their internal coherence is to be found. Such fiction is not designed for the casual, passive reader seeking an interesting plot that is acted out by well-developed characters and neatly brought to closure in the final pages. Quite to the contrary, the purpose of this type of fiction is to engage the reader's intellect and esthetic sensibility. The author employs any device at his/her disposal that will challenge the patient, motivated, qualified reader to fine-tune his analytical skills so that (s)he can recognize that the text is not what it appears to be at first, second, or even third reading. Every conceivable tactic is put into play for the purpose of taunting the reader to plunge beneath the surface in order to decipher its "true" hidden meaning. More often than not, once the reader is able to bypass the deceptive surface layer of the text, the descent into its multi-layered depths is guided by a centripetal force which turns out to be none other that the identical centrifugal force that had guided the author in the elaboration of his/her work of art: the creative process.

Consistent with the nature of baroque esthetics is the supremacy of form—the mechanics of narration—over content, this latter unequivocally playing a subordinate role to the former. In the same way that Velázquez's renowned baroque painting, "Las meninas," has little to do with the chambermaids attending to the young princess, in the four novels to be considered in this study, form not only takes precedence over their individual as well as collective content, it *is* the content. Just as the significance of Velázquez's baroque masterpiece has to do neither with its title nor with the figures illuminated in the foreground but, quite deceptively, to the royal couple who are exogenous to the spatial confines of the painting and obscured in the background as a reflection in a mirror, plot and characters in Tusquets' novels cannot be taken at face value when they in fact constitute an allegory of the numinous process of becoming a person. As is the case with all allegories, a mere literal reading of Tusquets' novels falls well short of grasping the depth and magnitude of the author's narrative project. When the plot and characters of a New Novel are taken for what they are from the point of view of the author, namely as strategems by means of which (s)he may exhibit an exuberant narrative style or an inventive fictional construct, or perhaps as allegorical embodiments of the creative process itself or some other type of psychic process, then the act of reading for the reader, like the act of writing for the writer, crosses over into the realm of the sublime. The satisfaction that comes from "getting through" the multiple readings required by most "new" novels is the reader's discovery that the literal layer of meaning (the characters, their actions, the setting of the story, etc.) is emblematic of a meaning, or multiple meanings, that exist independently of the plot. And to complicate matters even further where Tusquets' four novels are concerned, within the allegorical structuring of their totality the author makes extensive use of geometric, numerical, color, and other types of universal symbolism, not to mention of universal myths and archetypes inhabiting the collective unconscious, all of which tap into the intellectual and cultural sophistication of the reader who must "interpret" them both individually and within the context of the whole. In this sense, the reader participates in the mechanics of creation of the work of art in reverse, for the end of his/her textual journey is identical to the point of departure for the literary artist. The rewards for the reader are many: the sublime experience of perceiving the integrative wholeness of the esthetic object; an appreciation of its structural, technical and/or linguistic originality and ingeniousness; and last, but certainly not least, comes the self-indulgent recognition that one is intellectually, linguistically, and culturally sophisticated enough to uncover the hidden theme that binds the parts of the whole together.

In contrast to nineteenth-century Realism, or its more condensed, synthetic twentieth-century modifications (the New Romanticism of the Generation of 1927, the historical Realism of the Civil War generation, and the objectivist, socio-critical Realism of the Generation of 1954) which placed form in a subservient role with respect to content, the New Novels published in the 1960s, '70s, and '80s reveal a utilization of the content as a mere vehicle by means of and upon which an unprecedented form is elaborated. Pablo Gil Casado succinctly expresses the overturning of the form/content relationship of the Spanish dehumanized novel when he writes of the priority of form over content, where what matters are not the events, but rather, the manner in which they are narrated ("la prioridad de la forma sobre el fondo. Lo que importa no son las peripecias sino el modo de contarlas"—14). Referring to this type of fiction, Terry Eagleton writes that "man is stripped of his history and has no reality beyond the self; character is dissolved in mental states. The dialectical unit between inner and outer worlds is destroyed and both individual and society consequently emptied of meaning" (31). Although at times appearing to be mimetic, the content in fact is referential only to itself, generally either to the mechanics of its own creation or to its own unique system of interrelated images and concepts. The plot almost invariably conceals an abstract, metaphoric—often symbolic—layer of meaning that requires a sophisticated level of interpretation on the part of the literary critic. More often than not, a competent interpretation demands of the reader secondary expertise in a related field such as critical theory, literary ontology, esthetics, history, mythology, psychology, the symbolic knowledge required to interpret dreams, fantasies, and the like.

The descriptive plot of each novel is a second-order reality emanating synchronously from the unconscious creative archetype of the novelist and from the unconscious archetype of the self in the collective female protagonist. The plot, or unfolding of events in their cause-and-effect relationship, consists of a series of symbolically meaningful constellations of unconsciously projected images. It cannot be over-emphasized that an intra-psychic interpretation of each of the four novels and an inter-psychic interpretation of the four novels as a tetralogy entails treating what *appears* to be a first-order reality as a mere pretext for a more significant—but far less conspicuous—reality. It involves treating the plot as a second-order reality that is subordinated to a series of events that, although giving every indication of being insignificant, in fact foreground the perspective from which we must read and interpret the text if we are to arrive at the universal truth buried at its depths. Ironically, what appears to be trite and trivial in fact constitutes the first-order reality of the work. In order to illustrate this point, we will use the well-known example of *The Wizard of Oz*, whose psycho-narrative structure is analogous to that of Tusquets' tetralogy. In the 1939 film classic, the first-order reality is nothing more than the story of a pre-teenage girl who gets caught in a twister, is rendered unconscious (or semi-unconscious) by a piece of lumber that hits her on the head, has a fantastic dream about a journey to and within a far-away land "somewhere over the rainbow," and eventually regains consciousness only to find that she has returned "home" to a destination that she had never left to begin with. This is all that the film (or the book) is about if the story is apprehended literally. And if asked why it is a classic, we can only respond that it is a colorful, exciting (and musical in the case of the film) adventure that has never lost its appeal.

However, is this the real reason why *The Wizard of Oz* has withstood the test of time and become not only a North American classic, but an international one as well? We would suggest that the answer to this questions is the same as if we applied them to the timeless attraction of fairy tales: they stir up in the profoundest recesses of our collective unconscious the most basic truths about the human condition. When interpreted symbolically, the plot structure of Dorothy's psychic transposition from Kansas to "somewhere over the rainbow," and all of the adventures and mishaps that befall her there, reveal fundamental essences about the human processes of psychic development that move each and every one of us at the core of our being. Like a fairy tale, *The Wizard of Oz* reveals an archetypal process of psychic growth and maturation. Let's see what a symbolic interpretation yields.

Muddled and dazed upon awakening, Dorothy is unable to distinguish first-order reality (consciousness) from second-order reality (her dream as a manifestation of unconscious psychic activity). Such mental confusion is typical when contents of the collective unconscious are actively interfacing with an individual's personal unconscious, as well as when the unconscious and consciousness are engaged in dialogue as is the case with Dorothy's psyche during the final few minutes of the film. From a psychological standpoint, we are meant to interpret Dorothy's befuddlement metaphorically as the psychological integration of consciousness and the contents of her unconscious that were made manifest in her dream. A number of technical strategies are used to achieve the fusion of multiple layers of the psyche, the most effective of which are the dual or multiple roles played by the same characters in the primary text (first-order reality) and the meta-textual dream (second-order reality): Ms. Gulch / the Wicked Witch of the West; farmhand #1 / the Scarecrow; farmhand #2 / the Tin Man; farmhand #3 / the Cowardly Lion; Professor Marvel / the doorkeeper, horse-and-buggy driver, and Wizard of Oz. The closing line of the first-order reality, "there is no place like home," which also were the same magical words that, together with the clicking of the heels of the ruby slippers, ended her dream and returned her home to Kansas, further serves as a technique of integration of the multiple layers of psychic activity. Although the work is circular in structure, suggesting that the end and the beginning are one-and-the-same point, there is little doubt that Dorothy possesses greater insight and a wider expanse of consciousness after her dream than before it. Inasmuch as everyone and everything around her is the same when she awakens as it was before her dream, Dorothy is not the same person. Psychological change has taken place.

The Wizard of Oz gives the impression of being everything but what it is: a coming-of-age story that symbolically depicts that difficult rite-of-passage from the simplicity of childhood innocence to the painful complexity of adolescence. The first-order reality merely sets the stage for the catalytic second-order reality—Dorothy's dream—which is not just any ordinary dream, but a symbolic quest throughout which a naïve girl's one-dimensional consciousness undergoes profound psychological restructuring as she confronts evil for the first time and must come to terms with the fact that it co-exists with good. The psychological development undergone by Dorothy comes at an enormous price: not only must she come to terms with the fact that she has ended two lives (albeit unintentionally)—that of the Wicked Witch of the East when the protagonist's house fell on her, and that of the Wicked Witch of the West when Dorothy unknowingly liquidated her in an attempt to save the life of the burning Scarecrow—but she must make the conscious decision to forsake her dearest friends, the Scarecrow, the Tin Man, and the Cowardly Lion, in order to return home to Aunt Em and Uncle Henry. Achieving one's goals entails painful sacrifice: in order to reach the Land of Oz, Dorothy must survive the obstacles that the Witch of West places along the path; in order to get the Wizard to grant her wish and that of her three male companions, she must take possession of the witch's broomstick (which can only mean killing her); once inside the Witch's castle, she must relinquish the ruby slippers in order to save Toto's life; and in order to return home, she must forever part with her dearest friends. In psychological terms, in order to mature (transcend her present psychological level) as a result of her symbolic journey in search of the "lost" object (her home in Kansas = the Self), she must learn one of life's most difficult lessons: everything an individual needs to be complete is within the individual. This is precisely what Glenda, the Good Witch of the North, meant when she told Dorothy that she always had the power to return home, but had to discover that truth for herself.

We have taken this detour in the hope that it will serve as a useful model for understanding the need to and how to read Tusquets' tetralogy as an allegorical system of meaningfully related symbols. In *El mismo mar de todos los veranos*, for example, the lesbian relationship between the middle-aged protagonist and Clara is but a projection of a psychic process undergone by the former. The descriptions of their physical and emotional relationship, and ultimately the protagonist's abandonment and betrayal of Clara at the end of the novel, is not intended to be taken literally. Everything that "happens" between the protagonist and Clara is symbolic of an invisible, but nonetheless "real" (within the framework of the presented fictional reality of the novel) process of psychological transformation within the psychic complexity of the fifty-year-old protagonist. The first-order reality of the novel consists of nothing more than the protagonist's psycho-emotional crisis precipitated by her husband's infidelity, propelling an extensive psycho-graphic incursion into her mental make-up (consisting of an interpenetration of conscious, personal unconscious, and collective unconscious layers) within which is contained her relationship with Clara, and ending with the termination of the lesbian affair and a reconciliation between her and her husband, suggesting a return to the *status quo*. This, however, is the case only if we take the narrative "happenings" literally, as constituting a first-order reality, rather than as images depicting a series of internal psychic "happenings." A symbolic reading of the unfolding of events tells quite a different story, one that is wholly consistent with Jung's theory of the psychological process of individuation, whereby psychic transformation occurs only when an individual is courageous enough to let go of what is comfortable and take on the struggles and responsibilities of life, however challenging that may be, with a broader, more mature level of consciousness. Contrary to the prevailing critical opinion that *El mismo mar...* ends pessimistically with the protagonist's return to the unhappy *status quo* with which the novel begins, a symbolic reading of the final pages of the novel, when read within the context of the symbolically-rendered individuation process that constitutes the theme of the novel, yields a positive, "happy" ending from the point of view of psychological development as confirmed by the closing words of the novel: "...Y Wendy creció" (229).

Like *The Wizard of Oz*, Esther Tusquets' tetralogy is a symbolic quest for the Self. A metaphysical revelation such as the constituent nature of the Self cannot be depicted by any means other than symbolically. The art of conveying meaning through images is precisely what links fiction to reality. Although an invisible transformation has taken place within the collective psyche of Tusquets' female protagonists, as well as within Dorothy's psyche, the architectural design of both works of art is circular insofar as both end at the same place where they began. In both instances, the circular structure conveys the theme of both: the passage from one stage of psychic life to the next.

In order for a reader to perceive in a particular configuration or structure a meaning that is at once distinct and of greater significance than the obvious literal one, (s)he must first be able to perceive it as a symbol representing something that is more far-reaching, however abstract and numinous that something may be. Due to the fact that symbolic meaning is latent, it is easily overlooked. Intuiting its presence is necessary, but it is only a small first step when compared to what follows: the task of correctly interpreting each individual symbol followed by all of them as a meaningfully interrelated system of symbols. The latter requires the guiding light of some kind of "systematic" theoretical approach, be it mythological, philosophical, psychological, sociological, or some other type. As a general rule, the writer is following, or is at the very least guided by, a theoretical orientation, whether by intuition, by conscious design, or by some indeterminate combination of the two. It always serves the critic well in his/her analysis to identify that system or principle of coherence. Should the reader/critic discovers that the system does not hold together, (s)he must then question whether his/her interpretative approach is flawed and, if that turns out to be the case, make the changes or adjustments necessary to acquire the correct analytical vantage point. If, on the other hand, the reader/critic discovers that his/her analytical perspective is the appropriate one, (s)he must then assume that the author simply has not succeeded in creating a coherent work of art, in which case it is up to the critic to explain how and why the work is defective.

When a text, or group of texts, has been conceived symbolically (either by conscious intention, unconscious, but nonetheless meaningful design, or some blending of the two) by the author as we believe to be the case with Tusquets' four novels, then failure to interpret the text(s) from that same symbolic perspective inevitably will result in the critic falling short or totally off the mark. In other words, the method of textual analysis should be appropriate to the nature of the object(s) under scrutiny. Should (s)he remain at the level of literal meaning when confronted with an allegory, then it is unlikely that the more obtuse implications that are concealed beneath the surface layer will be gleaned from the text.

Yet another deficiency in the existing criticism on Esther Tusquets' novels is its disequilibrium: much has been written about *El mismo mar...*; relatively little has been published on *El amor...* and *Para no volver*; and virtually nothing except a section in a handful of comprehensive studies has been said about *Varada...* Finally, the third deficit with respect to Esther Tusquets' four novels is that there does not exist at the present time an in-depth analysis of them as constituting a structurally-driven tetralogy in accordance with the principles governing the New Novel. To our knowledge, there exist only three instances where a critic has even referred to the four novels as a tetralogy dealing with the structural dynamics of the individuation process as described by Jung throughout his extensive writings: myself (1987, 1988 1999, 2000), Pablo Gil Casado (1990), and Barbara Ichiishi (1994), the latter borrowing from the former two. Due to the nature of the three studies, articles in the first case, a typology of the novel in the second, and the general theme of female development in the third, none has done justice either to the integrated quality or complexity of Tusquets' four novels published between 1978 and 1985. This present study is an attempt to accomplish just that.

In summing up the point of departure of the present study, Esther Tusquets' novelistic tetralogy is a quest for self-knowledge that carries us unexpectedly far and deep, encompassing a single journey of self-discovery and of its concomitant psychological healing. The four texts deal individually and collectively with a female consciousness that is her parents' daughter, her husband's wife, her children's mother, her lovers' sexual partner, no one to the world and, most tragically of all, no one to herself. Through her fictional characters, the author plummets the uncharted waters of their, her own, and the universal feminine unconscious for the purpose of raising to consciousness the macrocosmic correlatives of the feminine principles governing the universe, the collective attributes of all female psyches and, ultimately, the uniqueness of an/her own individual female identity. The payoff is tremendous: the resolution of the mother-daughter conflict of which the omnipresent negative mother complex is symptomatic, and the discovery and integration both of the *animus* archetype and of the archetype of divinity tucked away within each and every one of us. This is the demiurge within that enabled Esther Tusquets to create the literary cosmos that is the subject of this study.

2. The Make-Up of the Psyche According to Jung

> In addition to our immediate consciousness, which is of a thoroughly personal nature and which we believe to be the only empirical psyche (even if we tack on the personal unconscious as an appendix), there exists a second psychic system of a collective, universal, and impersonal nature which is identical in all individuals. This collective unconscious does not develop individually but is inherited. It consists of pre-existent forms, the archetypes, which can only become conscious secondarily and which give definite form to certain psychic contents.
> JUNG, *Aion* 43

No one has written more extensively on the subjective path to objective awareness than has Jung. In his revolutionary book, *Psychology and the Unconscious* (1912), the publication of which ended his five-year professional and personal relationship with Sigmund Freud, Jung postulated the existence of a universal archetype that he called the shadow that was comprised of two dimensions of the unconscious. The first is uniquely personal to each individual, consisting of repressed or forgotten contents of the individual's life experiences. The Jungian scholar, Josef Goldbrunner, describes the relationship between consciousness and the personal unconscious by effectively employing the simile of an island projecting above the surface of the sea (consciousness) "with the waters of forgetfulness washing lightly against its threshold, sometimes receding and laying bare an inch of land and suggesting that the solid land is not yet at an end" (13). All that is repressed or forgotten by an individual constitutes a storehouse of psychic energy which Jung called "libido,"[14] and forms the uppermost layer of the unconscious. The contents of

---

[14] It should be noted that the concept of "libido" acquires a more generalized meaning in Jungian terminology than its Freudian usage. Whereas Freud employed the term to refer exclusively to sexual impulses, Jung generalized the concept to refer to all psychic energy, sexual and otherwise.

the personal unconscious cannot be known directly, for at the moment that we become consciously aware of them, they no longer are unconscious. All that can be observed are the psychic and physical symptoms that become manifest when the unconscious invades consciousness: slips of the tongue, stuttering, pain in a particular part of the body, involuntary actions, an inexplicable overreaction to something, and the like.

The second realm of the unconscious lies deeper and is rarely accessible to consciousness. It is collective and described by Jung as archetypal in nature, consisting of mental patterns and structures shared by all members of a particular cultural group, or universally by the human race. The founder of analytical psychology understood archetypes to be universal symbols that possess the greatest potentiality for psychic development. They are numinous, structural elements of the psyche that act as autonomous energy forces. Their universality is corroborated by the repeated pattern of behavior that psychoanalysts such as Jung were able to observe in countless individual cases, which allowed him to arrive to the conclusion that an archetype was the mythical and merely human aspect of the symbol. The interpretative work that Jung underwent with his clients consisted of identifying the objective, universal truth of the symbol with the particular circumstances influencing the individual who was experiencing the symbol. In other words, uncovering one's individuality curiously entailed the recognition of the individual's universality. It is this very paradox that which allows the literary analyst to siphon out universal "truths" from the particulars of a fictional literary work.

Archetypes recurrently manifest themselves in dreams and fantasies as figures, images, or situations that are endowed with a powerful emotional impetus, or libido. As we will discuss at length in the next section, godliness is one such archetype inhabiting the collective unconscious. It is driven by the libidinal urge to create a self-contained universe. Throughout the history of the human race, demiurges have been inspired by the emotional thrust of the creative archetype. In this manner, "the great poets provide us with information about the depths of the soul. Their figures are real images of the world and at the same time condensations of inner images which express the life and being of the soul itself" (Goldbrunner 140). According to Jung, it is due to the inconspicuous presence of the collective unconscious that we are able to identify the truly great works of art by virtue of the fact that they have withstood the test of place and time, thereby confirming the universal, atemporal quality of their message. Referring to the effect of a great dramatic work of art on the audience, Jung had the following to say:

When a 'typical situation' is represented it takes hold of the audience, they suddenly feel themselves liberated or upheld, or transported by an overwhelming force. In these moments man is addressed not as a single being but as a generic being. The voice of humanity sounds inside him. It is like the bed of a spring of water dug deeply into the soul where the life that formerly spread with groping uncertainty over wide but shallow surfaces suddenly plunges into a mighty flood when it reaches that particular concatenation of circumstances which have contributed from time immemorial to the producing of the primordial image. The moment in which the mythological situation enters is always characterized by a special emotional intensity; it is as though strings in us were being touched which had never sounded before, or forces were being unleashed of whose existence we had no inkling. (Cited in Goldbrunner, 139)

If asked why Tusquets' novels, particularly *El mismo mar...* and *Varada...*, have enjoyed the popularity that their numerous reprints and translations would indicate, we would refer them to Jung's account quoted above of what constitutes a great work of art. Tusquets' novels have enormous appeal for women because they stir within each and every one of us, irrespective of age or national origin, the timeless, universal female experience.

According to the depth psychologist, the psychoanalytic process consists of an individual's uncovering of his/her personal history, paying particular attention to the unresolved complexes inhabiting the personal unconscious. Jung was convinced that any serious probing into an individual's personal history inevitably would lead to the collective unconscious, that is, the universal archetypal level of the individual's objective psyche. Jung distinguishes between the personal and the collective unconscious in the following manner:

The collective unconscious is a part of the psyche which can be negatively distinguished from a personal unconscious by the fact that it does not, like the latter, owe its existence to personal experience and consequently is not a personal acquisition. While the personal unconscious is made up essentially of contents which have at one time been conscious but which have disappeared from consciousness through having been forgotten or repressed, the contents of the collective unconscious have never been in consciousness, and therefore have never been individually acquired, but owe their existence exclusively to heredity. Whereas the personal unconscious consists for the most part of *complexes*, the content of the collective unconscious is made up essentially of *archetypes*. (*Aion* 42, Jung's italics)

This predictable pattern of psychological probing, ultimately resulting in an expansion of consciousness, is to be found in each of the four novels individually and in Tusquets' tetralogy as a unified totality whose individual parts are meaningfully interrelated. As in the traditional psychoanalytic setting, the answers to the psychological problems posed in Tusquets' works of fiction are sought by means of an exploration into the fictional protagonists' personal history. Sooner or later, but inevitably, the retroactive scrutiny of the individual's past taps into forgotten or repressed contents of her personal unconscious that explain the origin of the complexes causing the psychic disturbances. As the previously unknown shadow components of the personal unconscious dialogue with consciousness, universal archetypal images, that is, patterns of behavior that had been lying dormant in the abyss of the unconscious, are exhumed and begin to intermingle with the personal unconscious.

Although one never can experience archetypes directly since they are housed within the remotest layers of the collective unconscious, all individuals do experience these biologically based patterns of feeling and behavior as they emanate from the collective depths and enter his/her personal unconscious as images laden with universal symbolic meaning. However solipsistic the mode of presentation of the four novels may be, the present study offers tangible proof that Tusquets has tapped into the female objective psyche. If this were not the case, then the perception of a novelistic coherence equally encompassing and encompassed by a search for a/the female, Self motivated and guided by the archetype of the self,[15] could not possibly take place.

Throughout his professional career, Jung maintained that the goal of human existence was for each individual to become all that (s)he could become. This involved a commitment to a process of bringing as much of one's potential psychic being into actualization (consciousness) as was possible in a lifetime. Psychoanalytically, this meant undergoing a process of discrimination, or differentiation, of the parts of the psyche: consciousness versus the unconscious, the subjective versus the objective, the individual versus the universal, etc., which, once distinguished from each other, then could be merged to form a transcendent, undivided whole. The analytical psychologist referred to this psychic phenomenon as the transcendent function. It arose out of his efforts to comprehend, come to terms with, and describe, the complex relationship

---

[15] The term "self" possesses two distinct meanings in Jungian analytical psychology. One meaning—the one that we have been using up to this juncture—refers to the totality of the psyche, including all conscious and unconscious *strata*. The second meaning refers to a specific archetype that acts as a guiding and regulating force for the individuation process. In order to avoid confusion, I will use an upper-case "S" when referring to the entire psyche, and a lower-case "s" when referring to the archetype.

between consciousness and the unconscious. In his 1958 re-working of *The Structure and Dynamics of the Psyche*, originally published in 1916, Jung explains that

> Experience in analytical psychology has amply shown that the conscious and the unconscious seldom agree as to their contents and their tendencies. This lack of parallelism is not just accidental or purposeless, but is due to the fact that the unconscious behaves in a compensatory or complementary manner toward the conscious. We can also put it the other way around and say that the conscious behaves in a complementary manner towards the unconscious. (Jung, *Jung on Active Imagination* 43)

Dr. Joan Chodorow, an analyst member of the C.G. Jung Institute of San Francisco and editor of *Jung on Active Imagination*, explains that among the depth psychologist's most invaluable contributions to our understanding of the working of the psyche was his discovery of "an inborn dynamic process that unites opposite positions within the psyche" which "draws polarized energies into a common channel, resulting in a new symbolic position which contains both perspectives" (4). This transcendent function is at work throughout Tusquets' tetralogy as either/or choices related primarily to gender issues, become both/and as vital possibilities for enriching the quality of life. If we compare, for example, the Clara/Ricardo incompatibility as projected by the thirty-year-old consciousness of Elia in *El amor*...,—the first novel in the series from the point of view of the chronological ages of the four female consciousnesses projecting the individuation drama in the tetralogy—with the harmoniously bi-sexual protagonist in the opening/closing novel of the series, *El mismo mar*..., the one-or-the-other in the former has evolved throughout the tetralogy into an all-encompassing, versatile gender identity. Whereas the *animus*-possessed Elia of *El amor*... experiences her masculine traits as wholly disruptive—both incompatible with her neglected inner child and at odds with her archetypal maternal instincts—the pronounced dichotomous conflicts of feminine/ masculine, mother/child, prey/predator, passive/aggressive, etc., merge into an indivisible entity of oneness as symbolized by the royal/common marriage quaternity at the close of *El mismo mar*... This is explained by the fact that the once incomplete middle-aged neophyte has become connected with the universal feminine principle via the Demeter/Kore archetype, in addition to having integrated into consciousness her contra-sexual *animus*. As the Jungian psychoanalyst, Dr. Katherine Bradway, explains:

As is true with many other archetypes, the *anima* and *animus* tend to function in negative ways as long as they remain wholly in the unconscious and therefore function only autonomously. When a man becomes aware of and accepts his contra-sexual part, he no longer has to deny it, and its disruptive aspects are diminished. Furthermore, as he discovers the positive quality of the *anima*—the principle of relatedness—he finds he can use it to understand himself better, as well as those around him. Likewise, as a woman familiarizes herself with her *animus*, she learns how to monitor its outbursts and let it help her focus, throw light as a torch does, and become a creative power. (277-78)

After Jung's death in 1961, a great many sociological changes took place in the western hemisphere with respect to cultural definitions and expectations of "male" and "female." Not only did an increasingly large number of women assume many of the roles traditionally attributed to men, such as carving out a professional niche for themselves and becoming the primary source of family income, but men equally were displaying their domestic talents, as well as their ability to be the primary caregiver and nurturer of their children. Jung was not enslaved to the terms "male" and "female" as were most of his contemporaries. This is readily explained by the fact that he regarded men and women to be innately androgynous, partaking of traits belonging to both genders in accordance with each individual's unique relationship between his/her conscious, on the one hand, and his/her contra-sexual archetype on the other. In recent decades, the field of psychology has made great strides in increasing the flexibility and elasticity of the terms "masculine" and "feminine":

Although the terms *male* and *female* are used in a single sense that is readily understood, the terms *masculine* and *feminine* are used in two overlapping senses: to identify the psychological traits and the range of behavior associated with being a male or a female, and to denote principles or patterns that are experienced as opposing or complementary sides of individuals irrespective of their gender. If we can separate the terms *masculinity* and *femininity* from being male or female, we can reserve them for reference to principles that function in either sex. (Bradway 279, Bradway's italics)

Bradway elaborates further by explaining the increasing popularity of the Greek word *androgyny* (*andro* = "male" and *gyn* = "female"), which merges male and female into a single concept. For the Jungian analyst, "becoming androgynous means overcoming stereotypical attitudes about what is appropriate for males and females, so that one develops more flexible behavior appropriate to a given situation: an assertive or aggressive behavior if that is required; a caring or nurturing attitude if that is required" (282). As we shall see in our analysis of *El mismo mar...*, the androgynous Mercurius, who appears in statuesque form in the opening pages of the novel, performs the paradoxical task of orienting the tetralogy toward the hermaphroditic goal that is propelled by the bi-sexual, regulating nature of the archetype of the self.

If it is not already obvious, we must drive home the point that the entire contents of the collective unconscious cannot ever be known to consciousness. Therefore, when Jung speaks of psychic wholeness—the Self—he is referring to an ongoing dialogue between the conscious ego and the remainder of the psyche, comprised of the personal unconscious and the collective unconscious, all of which is guided and controlled by the archetype of the self. An integrated psyche is a perpetual goal driven by the self, not a destination; therefore, it is to be understood as a lifelong process to which no final arrival point exists. In defining the psychic goal of wholeness of being—actualization of the Self—toward which the archetype of the self propels the psyche, he had the following to say:

> I use the term 'individuation' to denote the process by which a person becomes a psychological 'in-dividual,' that is, a separate, indivisible unity or 'whole.' It is generally assumed that consciousness is the whole of the psychological individual. But knowledge of the phenomena that can only be explained on the hypothesis of unconscious psychic processes makes it doubtful whether the ego and its contents are in fact identical with the 'whole.' If unconscious processes exist at all, they must surely belong to the totality of the individual, even though they are not components of the conscious ego. (*Aion* 275)

The individuation process may best be understood as the dynamics of the interaction between the ego and the self, the archetypal centralizing energy field of the Self, the latter being synonymous with the constitutional make-up of the entire psyche, of which the ego is but one aspect. As the *mandala* therapist, Susanne Fincher, explains, the relationship between the ego and the self alternates between alignment and alienation in the different stages of life:

> We find within the individuation process a dynamic relationship between self and ego that displays a natural rhythm of alternating closeness and separation. The close alignment of ego and self is revealed when young children create *mandala* drawings. Their *mandalas* reflect the fact that the

ego is developing within the matrix of the self. As we mature into young adults, the ego achieves a separation from the archetypal structure of the self. We encounter the self again in midlife, often as the urge to express our untapped potential, to live the life unlived, and to complete the pattern of wholeness ordained by the self. (145)

Tusquets' tetralogy is an exploration into the mid-life re-connection of the ego with the archetype of the self, and the manner by which this alignment fosters the expansion and maturation of the autobiographical Self of the author and of its fictional literary projection in the form of a novelistic tetralogy.

3. The Psyche as Work of Art: A Creation Story

> Understandably enough, the creative principle that brings the world into being is derived from the creative nature of man himself. Just as man—our figures of speech say the same thing today—brings forth his creation from his own depths and 'expresses' himself, so do the gods.
> NEUMANN, *The Origins and History of Consciousness* 21

Esther Tusquets' four novels attest to the fact that psychoanalysis and artistic creation share an astonishingly large number of traits in common, not the least of which is a quest for self-knowledge and its concomitant confrontation with the unconscious. Creative formulation (the medium of art) and understanding (the medium of psychoanalysis) are two intrinsic aspects of one reality: self knowledge, for which Tusquets' novelistic tetralogy is a symbol both of the method and of the attainment of the goal. Psychoanalysis and artistic creation alike express themselves as discursive texts, verbal in the case of former and written in the case of the latter, that are expressed by their "creator" by means of a variety of modes of consciousness and representation. This implies the existence of a recipient—an analyst or a reader, as the case may be—who brings to the encounter his or her own intelligence, understanding, ignorance, experiences, limitations, beliefs, prejudices, observations, feelings, interpretative skills, etc., all of which in turn determine his or her mode of textual interpretation. Furthermore, psychoanalysis and creativity are processes that move toward the unequivocal goal of wholeness of being for the psyche and the esthetic object, respectively. For the analysand, completion of the process requires uniting two distinct, often contradictory, parts of the psyche: the conscious and the unconscious. Generally speaking, it is when the demands of conscious life and obscure, primordial stirrings within the unconscious wind up in irreconcilable conflict with one another that an individual enters into the psychoanalytic process. The primary task of the analytical psychologist is to tap into the unconscious of his/her client for the purpose of helping him/her to identify those aspects of the psyche that are, or have been in the case of trauma, splintered from consciousness and now are engaged in an adverse relationship with it. In the course of psychoanalysis, the mysterious realm of the personal and collective unconscious, wherein are housed the complexes and universal archetypes, respectively, unfolds. The analyst and analysand work together to identify these psychic forces and to discover ways that they might be integrated into consciousness so that the original symptoms of neuroses can be obliterated.

The common goal of self-knowledge that is shared by psychoanalysis and artistic creativity, recalls Jung's discovery of active imagination during the years 1913-16 following his traumatic break with his mentor, Sigmund Freud. At that significant juncture in his life, he sunk into deep despair and depression. Not unlike Tusquets' fictional personæ, he was overcome by fears and insecurities about the meaning of his life up until that point, and was riddled with uncertainties about its future direction. He was in desperate need of a way out of his psychological stagnation, and found it in a therapeutic method that eventually he was to name "active imagination." Beginning with his rediscovery of the symbolic play of childhood, Jung allowed his unconscious to arise, while at the same time consciously coming to terms with the unconscious contents. He accomplished this by permitting himself to fully experience his emotions and then "to find the images that are concealed in the emotions," for which he employed "a number of expressive techniques (mainly writing, drawing and painting) to give symbolic form to his experience" (Chodorow 2). Out of the confrontation between the conscious and the unconscious arose a new symbolic position that contained both perspectives. To this third symbolically expressed synthesis, he ascribed the term "transcendent function." Jung described it as "a movement out of the suspension between two opposites, a living birth that leads to a new level of being, a new situation" (*The Structure...* 210).

Of particular relevance to Tusquets' tetralogy are the two tendencies that arise as the inner experience of active imagination is given tangible, artistic form: the first is the esthetic way of formulation, and the second is the scientific way of understanding (Chodorow 12). Returning to the point/counterpoint structure of a tetralogy as elaborated upon earlier, as well as the distinction that the novelist herself made between her first three novels (the 1978, 1979, 1980 trilogy) on the one hand, and *Para no volver* on the other, the 1985 novel is, in fact, the so-called scientific understanding of the esthetic form of the trilogy. The fourth novel methodologically elucidates how the novelistic tetralogy—the trilogy plus itself—came into being as an esthetic creation. Chodorow explains the mutual dependency of creative formulation and scientific understanding in order for active imagination to have a healing, therapeutic effect, and for the psychological transformation to take place by means of the transcendent function:

> Each tendency seems to be the regulating principle of the other. For active imagination, a balance of both is needed. If the first tendency predominates, a person may lose the goal of psychological development and instead get fascinated with the artistic elaboration of a theme. If the second tendency predominates, there is the danger of so much analysis and interpretation that the transformative power of the symbol is lost. The important thing is to develop a self-reflective, psychological attitude that draws from both the esthetic passion for beauty and the scientific passion to understand. The task is to express both, yet not be consumed by either. (12)

In our analysis of *Para no volver*, we will demonstrate how the closure of the tetralogy is identified with the contrapuntal "understanding" of the esthetic "formulation" of the trilogy along with the contents of the unconscious that emerge from its discourse. If the trilogy is unmistakably "Jungian" in its "irrational" mythological and archetypal approach to the inner workings of the protagonists' psyche, *Para no volver* contrastingly narrates its protagonist's two month, four times weekly, sessions of "lie-down-on-the-couch-with-your-back-to-the-analyst oriented" "Freudian" psychoanalysis. The nature of the relationship of the fourth novel with the trilogy is complementary (from an esthetic standpoint) and compensatory (from a psychological one), for it is from the transcendental synthesis of the three plus the one that the oneness of the four is achieved.

According to Jung, the creative process is an autonomous archetype that has been tucked away within the collective unconscious of mankind since the origin of his existence. It is "a detached portion of the psyche that leads an independent psychic life withdrawn from the hierarchy of consciousness, and in proportion to its energetic value or force, may appear as a mere disturbance of the voluntarily directed process of consciousness, or as a superordinated authority which may take the ego bodily into its service" (*Contributions...* 238). Perhaps this is in part what is meant when we say that man is created in the image of God, the supreme Creator. Creativity is a force emanating from the unconscious of us all. It is the artist, however, who consciously chooses to objectify his creative energy in a work of art. For him or her, "the unborn work in the soul of the artist is a force of nature that effects its purpose, either with tyrannical might, or with the subtle cunning which nature brings to the achievement of her end, quite regardless of the personal weal or woe of the man who is the vehicle of the creative force" (*Contributions*... 238). A numinous force indeed, the creative process is an unconscious awakening of the creative archetype that is responded to by a development of its image until it has been completed and represented musically, pictorially, sculpturally, as a literary text, etc. This is the process by which a work of art comes into being.

The psychoanalytic and creative processes rely heavily upon the contents of the unconscious and the manner by which those obscure contents make their existence known to the consciousness of the analysand or artist. The degree to which conscious awareness, acceptance and, ultimately, integration of those contents into consciousness is possible will determine the degree of success of the psychoanalytic client in achieving psychic wholeness, or of the literary creator in arriving at the ontological wholeness of the work of art.

At the very core of the tetralogy lies the theme of the parallel evolution and coming into being of the individual psyche and of the narrative microcosm, or stated more simply, individuation as creative process. Consistent with the symptoms of the transition from the first to the second half of life is the confrontation of the ego with "the creative background of the psyche" (Jacobi, *The Way*... 42). At this all-important juncture of life, the individuation process directs the psyche to summon up those aspects which have been neglected during the first half of life. For those individuals for whom the transition to mid-life is laden with crisis, serious efforts to confront the contents of the unconscious not only "can result not only in the removal of the crisis but also in an activation of the creative powers of the unconscious psyche" (Jacobi, *The Way*... 43). These creative powers are inextricably linked to the androgynous constitution of the human psyche and help us explain the profuse bi-sexual content of Tusquets' novelistic tetralogy.

The novelistic tetralogy as finished product yields the discovery of the unique Self that one always had the potential of becoming and, concomitantly, the creation of a "new" universe of which the integrated Self is demiurge. When we asked Esther Tusquets in our 1988 interview with her, to what extent her novels were autobiographical, her reply was so revealing that we decided to use it as the point of departure for our analysis of the psychodynamics of autobiography and fiction that permeate all of her narrative works, but most notably the novelistic tetralogy. She responded that she was to be found not in the *what*, but in the *how*; that is to say, she associates the autobiographical quality of her fiction not with what happens in her novels, but with how what happens in her novels is narrated: "Creo que lo que soy se ve más por el modo en que están escritas las novelas que por lo que pasa. Mi modo de escribir es barroco, envolvente, volviendo sobre unas y otras cosas, muy obsesivo, muy de puntualizar, muy de repetir, muy esteticista. Creo que es más esto que no lo que les pasa a los protagonistas" (401). Her observation is easily substantiated by a reading of her texts, for it hardly can be disputed that Tusquets' highly estheticized, self-conscious style of writing commands the reader's attention to a much greater extent than that about which she writes. Plots and characters seem to emanate naturally from her painstakingly crafted style. Just as the author sees her own personality reflected in her narrative style, her fictional characters' self-obsessive behavior and thought process, their psychological neuroses, their erotic adventures, their continuous self-scrutiny, their penchant for fantasizing and daydreaming, their insecurities, conflicts, and disillusionment with life, love, the future, and themselves, all are indistinguishable from a sensuous, sensorial narrative style that is riddled with evasiveness, circumlocutions, contradictions, and uncertainty. From the author was born a style that depicts her own psychological self-portrait, and from that style were born characters and plots that reverberate not only Esther Tusquets' inimitable style of writing, but her composite psychological make-up as well.

As elaborated upon extensively in the previous section, since Esther Tusquets' novelistic tetralogy conforms to the tenets of the New Novel on all accounts, any meaningful analysis must operate from the vantage point that formalist concerns justify the conception and determine the function of all aspects of their content. The same is applicable to autobiographical considerations. If the tetralogy possesses an autobiographical quality, as we believe to be the case, it does so at the formal level by a blending of intentional and intuitive design, and at the content level by structural exigency. For this reason, some portions of the content reflect factual events and circumstances pertaining to the author's life while other portions have no obvious relevance to it whatsoever. Consequently, we are not dealing with a case of fictional autobiography whereby an account of the events of the author's life narratologically are disguised as those pertaining to a fictional character. Quite to the contrary, Tusquets' novelistic tetralogy is what more accurately might be described as pseudo-autobiographical. Unlike the traditional autobiography in which the author writes his or her own life story, Esther Tusquets is portraying the psychodynamics of her inner life via the creative process by which her four novels came into being as a structurally integrated and stylistically interrelated totality. We have chosen to refer to the tetralogy as pseudo-autobiographical because neither in the incipient novel which is narrated in the first-person (point), nor in the following three, which are narrated in the third-person (counterpoint), are the characters and what happens to them "true" to Tusquets' life in the sense of being empirically verifiable. Consistent with the mission of the New Novel and of all those writers seeking new forms for the novel, Tusquets' tetralogy is autobiographical in an unprecedented "new" way: at the formal level of structure and style. If, as the *Old Testament* tells us, (wo)man was created in God's image, it logically follows that the human creative psyche would operate according to the same structural dynamics by which He created the universe. Hence, when He created (wo)man in His own image, it was with the capacity to create miniature replicas—microcosms—of the macrocosm. Following this argument, the tetralogy and the creative psyche of the literary demiurge, Esther Tusquets, to which it owes its existence, conform to the same structural principles by which the Cosmos was created: unity in diversity and the equilibrium of opposing forces. It is in this sense that creator and created, the individual and the universal, are one-and-the-same. Just as the Creator permeates the Universe, Esther Tusquets pervades her literary microcosm; she is embedded in its constitutional make-up. As a demiurge, she has created a novelistic cosmos in the image of the dynamic structure of her own psyche, a universe in which she is dispersed throughout so that a part of her resides in every fictional character—the young as well as the old, the male as well as the female, the heterosexual as well as the bisexual—in every anecdote, incident, fantasy, hope, and disillusionment that is narrated, and in every passion that is experienced, feared, or desired.

At the innermost core of Esther Tusquets' fiction resides the implicit belief that an intimate, integral relationship exists between the process of literary creation and the process of coming into being of the Self. In the words of Barbara Ichiishi," her novels constitute a series of attempts to 'work through' the fundamental psychic issues of her life story, to achieve a kind of catharsis in the act of artistic creation. She aims to achieve this by taking control of the events of her life in her writing, through the beauty and perfection of artistic form, and by gradually moving toward a more mature, forward-looking view of life in the characters and stories she creates" (19). The Self, as we know, can never be fully apprehended at the conscious level since so much of it remains eternally tucked away in the unfathomable depths of the collective unconscious. Self-knowledge, like writing, is a journey, not a destination, and the greater the awareness and appreciation an individual has of his/her uniqueness, the greater the proclivity (s)he has toward actualizing that uniqueness in a tangible way. This contention is supported by the American founder and theoretician of humanist, client-centered therapy, Carl R. Rogers, in his essay entitled: "Toward a Theory of Creativity." For Rogers, the creative process must produce "something observable, some product of creation" that is "symbolized in words, or written in a poem, or translated into a work of art, or fashioned into an invention" (349). Rogers goes on to say that the creative work of art, or invention, must be "novel," with the novelty emanating from "the unique qualities of the individual in his interaction with the materials of his experience." Although the finished object always bears the uniqueness of the individual, "the product is not the individual, nor his materials, but partakes of the relationship between the two" (349). Of particular interest in relation to the creative accomplishments of Esther Tusquets is the following statement made by Rogers: "The mainspring of creativity appears to be the same tendency which we discover so deeply as the curative force in psychotherapy—*man's tendency to actualize himself, to become his potentialities*. By this I mean the directional trend which is evident in all organic and human life—the urge to expand, extend, develop, mature—the tendency to express and activate all the capacities of the organism, or the self" (350-51, Roger's italics). No stranger to the therapist's couch by her own admission, Tusquets' debut as a writer seems to have been born out of enormous strides made in the decades she devoted to discovering, scrutinizing, reorganizing, and integrating the many disparate, often contradictory, selves making up her one unique Self. It would seem that writing was, at one-and-the-same-time, an outgrowth of the author's individuation journey and a facilitating tool for remaining on that same path of growth, expansion, maturity, and self-actualization throughout her lifetime. Since each process fuels the other, it is only natural for both creative endeavors—writing and becoming—to be co-present in all instances of self-expression. As Rogers tells us, no particular activity or content has a monopoly over creativity: "There is no fundamental difference in the creative process as it is evidenced in painting a picture, composing a symphony, devising new instruments of killing, developing a scientific theory, discovering new procedures in human relationships, or creating new formings of one's own personality as in psychotherapy" (349).

As the universe is a transcendental synthesis of heaven and earth, Tusquets' tetralogy is a transcendental synthesis of psyche (the non-linear, non-sequential creative process) and novel(s) (the linear, sequential writing process). In this sense, it is a creation story. It is the story of how dichotomous differences are patterned in a manner that yields undivided wholeness, a solidarity of oneness, whose integrated totality supercedes the value of the sum total of its parts. If not for the transcendental synthesis of heaven and earth, day and night, darkness and light, land and seas, sun and moon, fish and fowl, animal and man, work and rest, creation and contemplation, into one entity of harmonious wholeness, the universe that we inhabit could not have come into being. Tusquets' literary cosmos shares an analogous relationship with the manner of creation of the universe. Without the juxtaposition and ultimate integration of form and content, autobiography and fiction, conscious light and unconscious darkness, the feminine and the masculine, childhood and adulthood, mother and daughter, homosexuality and heterosexuality, thought and feeling, sensation and intuition, love and hatred, life and death, mortality and immortality, fear and courage, loss and triumph, the individual and the universal, literary creation and psychological individuation, into an ontologically whole work of literary art, we could not be arguing a case for the four-part totality of *El mismo mar de todos los veranos*, *El amor es un juego solitario*, *Varada tras el último naufragio* and *Para no volver*, which constitutes the thesis statement of the present study.

4. Symbolism: Bridging the Psychological and the Physical

> Given that every symbol 'echoes' throughout every plane of reality and that the spiritual ambience of a person is essentially one of these planes because of the relationship traditionally established between the macrocosm and the microcosm, a relationship which philosophy has verified by presenting Man as the 'messenger of being' (Heidegger): given this, then it follows that every symbol can be interpreted psychologically.
> CIRLOT, xlv-xlvi

In the last century, psychology has come to rely more and more on the use of symbols to explain psychic phenomena whose subject matter defies rational comprehension. Symbolic working models, or hypotheses, such as the archetypes were formulated by Jung in order to describe as adequately as possible occurrences that were known to take place empirically, but whose existence could not be proven scientifically. Edward Whitmont explains the difficulty of describing psychic happenings and the need for symbolic representation:

> We cannot speak of the psyche as a thing that *is* or *does* this or that. At best we can speak of it indirectly by describing human behavior—the behavior of others and also our own subjective experience—*as if* it expressed aspects of a hypothetical pattern of meaning, *as if* a potential, encompassing wholeness were ordering the action of the parts. For instance, we can recognize that an autonomous impulse or a hitherto hidden personality pattern has emerged and behaved as if it intended a certain action which was meaningful in relation to that total personality. The most basic

hypothesis about the human psyche with which we deal here, then, is that of a pattern of wholeness that can only be described symbolically. (15, Whitmont's italics)

Since individuation is a psychic process which, according to Jung and his disciples, follows a certain predictable structure or pattern of evolution leading to a wholeness which can be conceptualized as a result of observable change and development in human behavior, but neither seen nor scientifically proven per se, a symbolic interpretation of Tusquets' tetralogy is mandated by the very nature of its structural-thematic orientation. Jung defines a symbol as "the best description, or formula, of a relatively unknown fact; a fact, however, which is none-the-less recognized or postulated as existing" (*Psychological Types* 601). A view that interprets the symbolic expression as "the best possible formulation of a relatively *unknown* thing, which cannot for that reason be more clearly or characteristically represented, is *symbolic*" (601, Jung's italics). Symbolic interpretation, by definition, always extends beyond itself and surpasses what can be apprehended by the senses. A symbolic approach "is not abstract or rational, neither can it be regarded as irrational; rather it has laws and a structure of its own which correspond to the structural laws of emotion and intuitive realization" (Whitmont 19-20). All psychic processes are propelled by energy, or dynamism, which, in general, characterizes something that is in a state of flux or undergoing change. With specific reference to the field of psychology and, in particular, to the regressive/expansive dynamics characteristic of the individuation aspect of the analytic branch, the primary focus is on unconscious processes and their effects on the conscious life of the individual. In one of his earlier works, *Symbols of Transformation*, Jung postulated that all emotional, and therefore energy-laden, psychic processes evince a striking tendency to be expressed rhythmically by means of perseverance and repetition (219-20). The most celebrated of Jung's many disciples, Marie-Louise von Franz, supports her mentor's theory that "natural number remains the common ordering factor of both physical and psychic manifestations of energy (waves being an example of the former and rhythm an example of the latter) and is consequently the element that draws psyche and matter together" (*Number and Time* 166). She maintains that the human mind is able to grasp the phenomena of the outer world precisely because natural numbers appear to represent the typical, universally recurring, common motion patterns of psychic as well as physical energy: "The existence of such numerical nature constants in the outer world, on the one hand, and in the preconscious psyche, on the other (e.g., in the quaternary structure of the 'psychic center,' the triadic structure of dynamic processes, the dualistic structure of threshold phenomena, and so forth) is probably what finally makes all conscious knowledge of nature possible" (166-67).

In the study of literature, among the critic's primary concerns is the dynamic interplay among the various forces at work in the textual form as well as content, and the manner by which such forces shift and change throughout the author's process of thematic embedding. The act of reading Tusquets' four novels and experiencing their intertextual interaction at deeper numerically symbolic, archetypal levels, synchronously reveals a process of acquisition of a more complete awareness, acknowledgment and acceptance of the complexity of a/the whole psyche. The psyche is defined as the sum total of all psychic processes emanating from the conscious as well as unconscious strata of each individual, and including all of its personal as well as universal contents. These two parallel processes—the one literary and the other psychological—indiscriminately involve for the reader, protagonist, narrator, and author alike, wrestling with numerous psycho-narrative contradictions and conflicts between opposites. On the literary plane, these include a tension between autobiography and fiction, between narrative subject and object, and between the literal and the symbolic. Psychologically, these include an interaction between the subjective psyche, consisting of the conscious ego and the personal unconscious, and the objective psyche, which Jung defines as a universal archetypal blueprint existing in the unconscious of each and every individual psyche from its moment of conception.

In contrast to *logos*, which refers to the masculine conscious principle of rational discrimination, the *anima*, meaning "soul" in Latin, refers to a man's *eros*, that is, to the unconscious, "feminine" side of a man's personality that governs human relatedness and bonding. The female images that appear in a man's dreams and fantasies are symbolic representations of his emotional needs, desires, or fears. Typical *anima* figures include: goddesses, famous women, mother-figures, maidens, prostitutes, and witches. In contrast to *eros*, which refers to the feminine conscious principle of human bonding, the *animus*, meaning "spirit," is the unconscious male component of the female psyche and imparts the capacity for rational discrimination, clear thinking, deep understanding, creative energy, and serves to endow her life with a spiritual meaning. *Animus* figures appear in women's dreams and fantasies as a diverse group of figures. A good example of this are the multiple masculine figures appearing in *Para no volver* (Arturo, Eduardo, her husband Julio, and her Argentine analyst to whom she ambivalently refers as "the Wizard" (*el Mago*) or " Father Freud" (*Papá Freud)*, who collectively are embodiments of Elena's own *animus* projections. This factor perhaps may be as a compensation[16] for the essentially monogamous feminine ego-consciousness. According to Jung, "the conscious attitude of woman is in general far more exclusively personal than that of man" whose "world is the nation, the state, business concerns, etc." and for whom "family is simply a means to an end, one of the foundations of the state" (*Aspects of the Feminine* 98-99). Whatever the reason, "a passionate exclusiveness... attaches to the man's *anima*, and an infinite variety to the woman's *animus*" (99). Not only is the *animus* the repository of all of woman's primordial experiences of man, "he is also a creative and procreative being, not in the sense of masculine creativity, but in the sense that he brings forth something we might call the spermatic word. Just as a man brings forth his work as a complete creation out of his inner feminine nature, so the inner masculine side of a woman brings forth creative seeds which have the power to fertilize the feminine side of man" (Jung, *Aspects of the Feminine* 98).

The archetype of the self is a teleological force that, unless impeded by a past trauma or by a simple fear of taking necessary developmental steps, unconsciously drives each of us in the direction of fully becoming all of our psychological, emotional, creative, and intellectual human potential. In a word, it compels us to renounce perfection as a goal for the sake of achieving completion, that is to say, wholeness. It is from this vantage point that Jung considers Christ to be a symbol of the Self: "The Christ-image is as good as perfect (at least it is meant to be so), while the archetype (so far as known) denotes completeness but is far from being perfect" (*Aion* 68-9). Commenting on the paradoxical nature of the coming-into-being of the Self, he concludes by saying that "the realization of the Self, which would logically follow from a recognition of its supremacy, leads to a fundamental conflict, to a real

---

[16] According to Jungian theory, the role of the unconscious *anima* in males and of the unconscious *animus* in females is one of compensation. The Jungian scholar, Steven Walker, explains their compensatory role in the following manner: "The *anima*, the archetype of the feminine, and the *animus*, the archetype of the masculine, are psychic representations of the sexual instinct. In Jungian theory, their role is primarily one of *compensation*. The *animus*, the unconscious masculine element in a woman, compensates for her conscious femininity—the female elements of her *persona*—and the *anima*, the unconscious female element in a man, compensates for his conscious masculinity—the male elements of his *persona*. Typically, Jung *personifies* these contrasexual archetypal images. Thus the most macho male perhaps will harbor the figure of a shy little girl inside him; the most feminine woman may be cohabitating psychologically with the figure of a violent hoodlum. Whatever the conscious sexual *persona*, the figure inside will tend to compensate for its one-sidedness." (45, Walker's italics)

suspension between opposites (reminiscent of the crucified Christ hanging between two thieves), and to an approximate state of wholeness that lacks perfection" (*Aion* 68-9). Hence, wholeness of being, that is, the fullest, most complete actualization of the Self, implies the expansion of the horizon of consciousness, and it is towards this goal that the archetype of the self directs us regardless of forfeitures along the way. As abstract a notion as "wholeness" may appear to be, it is, in fact, empirical "in so far as it is anticipated by the psyche in the form of spontaneous or autonomous symbols" such as "the quaternity or *mandala* symbols, which occur not only in the dreams of modern people who have never heard of them, but are widely disseminated in the historical records of many peoples and many epochs. Their significance as *symbols of unity and totality* is amply confirmed by history as well as by empirical psychology" (*Aion* 31, Jung's italics). It is precisely from "the tension of opposites from which the divine child is born as the symbol of unity" (*Aion* 31).

Jung tells us that "the ways that lead to conscious realization are many, but they follow definite laws" beginning, generally, "with the onset of the second half of life" (*Aspects of the Feminine* 45). That which commonly is referred to as a mid-life crisis is, by definition, a spiritual one whose resolution requires that the individual seek and discover the true meaning of life in general and of his/her life in particular. Nothing of what the individual has acquired in the first half of life—family, professional success, economic status, the respect of peers, etc.—can be of any help, for the individual must turn inward, tap into his/her soul, and be willing to turn his/her back on all that serves to gratify the ego. Fundamentally, the type of introspection that is peculiar of the transition from the first to the second half of life, entails withdrawing one's contra-sexual projections and embracing this *Other*—the *anima* in males and the *animus* in females—not as an *Other*, but as something belonging to the *Self*:

> Expressed as emotionally-laden archetypal images which often are projected onto people of the opposite sex, these contra-sexual sub-personalities develop over a lifetime and come into play in a new way in midlife or after the reproductive period has ended. In midlife or later, we tend to question our earlier commitments and may begin to recognize the Other within and desire to realize its potential. Jung's theory of contra-sexuality is a contribution to depth psychology that problematizes our stereotypes about the 'opposite sex,' tracing the shadow of Otherness back to its owner. (Young-Eisendrath 32)

As the Jungian theorist, David Hart, writes, failure to let go of what is old and familiar, and to embrace what is new and challenging, carries tragic consequences for the individual: "Without a real sense that this change carries the true meaning of one's life, and a willingness to take on the inner voyage of discovery, one can fall into despair and a repetitive existence, which in effect only marks time until the end. The challenge of the second half of life is to prepare for death in a questioning, seeking, and *conscious* way, accepting both the pain of disillusionment and the wonder of growth into ever new views of spiritual and psychological reality" (99, Hart's italics).

The collective psyche narrating Tusquets' tetralogy teeters between the two options of comfortable despondency on the one hand, and painful, terrifying change on the other. Throughout her four novels, the author brings many of the unconscious archetypes to the forefront of female consciousness. Each novel follows a psychological trajectory that begins with the projection of the protagonist's unconscious shadow onto secondary characters. As Jung explains, projections have the effect of alienating the individual from his/her physical environment: "The effect of projection is to isolate the subject from the environment... Projections change the world into the replica of one's own unknown face... The resultant *sentiment d'incomplétude* and the still worse feeling of sterility are in their turn explained by projection as the malevolence of the environment, and by means of this vicious circle the isolation is intensified" (*Aion* 9). This reality is evidenced by the profound estrangement that each of Tusquets' protagonist experiences *vis-à-vis* the outer world. The anonymous protagonist in the first novel, the Elia who appears in the second and third, and Elena who is the main character in the fourth, all are trapped within an inner labyrinth of emotionally disturbing mental images. It is the task of each of them—as mandated by the transition from the first to the more reclusive, introspective second half of life—to embark upon an inner odyssey through the dense emotional forest of their unconscious psyche in the hope of eventually discovering a lighted opening from which they can emerge as a whole human being, at one with the world and with the Self.

As explained earlier, the shadow refers to all aspects of one's psyche—positive or negative, same-sex or contra-sexual, individual or universal—of which a person is not consciously aware. According to Jung, close examination of the dark, inferior aspects of the shadow "reveals that they have an *emotional* nature, a kind of autonomy, and accordingly an obsessive or, better, possessive quality" (*Aion* 8, Jung's italics). Each of the four novels ends with the protagonist's withdrawal of a portion of those projections as she confronts them and painstakingly comes to recognize and accept them as belonging to her own contradictory, but nonetheless, single Self. Throughout his writings, Jung repeatedly states that personality integration is a *sine qua non* of the psychoanalytic process, whose goal is mental health, and that it is only possible when an individual admits to and is accepting of his/her "undesirable" shadow traits and their inherently bisexual nature. The latter must be preceded by the former and may only be actualized, according to Jung, under the following conditions: "The integration of the shadow, or the realization of the personal unconscious, marks the first stage in the analytic process," without which "a recognition of the *anima* and *animus* is impossible. The shadow can be realized only through a relation to a partner, and *anima* and *animus* only through relation to the opposite sex, because only in such relations do their projections become operative" (*Aion* 22). The secondary characters in Tusquets' novels perform this function for the female protagonist; they are screens onto which her unconscious inner life is projected and made to interact with her consciousness. Such is the case with Clara in *El mismo mar...*, and Clara and Ricardo in *El amor...*, who serve as projections of the personal unconscious, and with Eva, Pablo, and Clara in *Varada...*, and Arturo, Eduardo, Julio, and the psychoanalyst in *Para no volver*, who function as projections of the archetypal collective unconscious, all of whom personify aspects of the single integrated female psyche whose configuration as a squared circle is visually intimated at the close of the tetralogy. The nature of projections and their withdrawal explains the reason why, by the end of each of the novels, the secondary characters seem to evaporate from the narrative and the female protagonist gives every indication of operating at a higher, broadened level of consciousness than at the onset of the narrative development. We are meant to interpret this vanishing act performed by the secondary characters as their assimilation into the conscious life of the protagonist. The sum total of the four undifferentiated, unified selves, one bringing each of the four novels to a close, is an/the integrated female Self. Hence, the conclusion of the tetralogy yields a symbolic form of wholeness that, at one-and-the-same-time, discloses the unique particularities of an individual female Self—that belonging to the author of whose psyche the four female protagonists served as projections—and the collective generalities of the universal female Self with which each and every female reader of the tetralogy can identify. Individuation, or the process of acquiring a deeper and more comprehensive understanding of the Self, "follows the natural course of life—a life in which the individual becomes what he always was" (Jung, *The Archetypes...* 40). Jung goes on to explain why this is a dialectical, spiral process as opposed to an progressive, uninterrupted linear one: "Because man has consciousness, a development of this kind does not run very smoothly; often it is varied and disturbed, because consciousness deviates again and again from its archetypal, instinctual foundation and finds itself in opposition to it. There then arises the need for a synthesis of the two positions" (40).

From a Jungian perspective, the systematic coherence of the innumerable symbols of individuation populating the four novels reveal a novelistic trilogy which, in accordance with Jung's theory of individuation, evolved quite naturally into a tetralogy within which it became subsumed. The fourth novel, as previously suggested, is a heightened, fully conscious understanding of the partly conscious, partly unconscious female developmental process experienced in the trilogy. *Para no volver* offers a rational, objective, theoretical perspective on the relational aspects of the novelistic whole, as symbolized by Elena's acknowledgement and admission of her contra-sexual *animus* into her female consciousness.

The symbolic significance of the numerical and geometrical factors defining the temporal and spatial configuration of Tusquets' four novels cannot be ignored. As Cirlot reminds us, numbers are not merely the expressions of quantities, "but idea-forces, each with a particular character of its own. The actual digits are, as it were, only the outer garments" (230). Modern symbolic logic and the theory of groupings postulate the quantitative as the basis for the qualitative. The numerical series possesses a "symbolic dynamism" founded on the idea that "one engenders two and two creates three" on the premise that "every entity tends to surpass its limits, or to confront itself with its opposite." When we interviewed Tusquets in 1988 and questioned her about the origin and development of her tetralogy (up until that time considered by her to be a trilogy plus a fourth "unrelated" novel), she had the following to say:

> Mira, eso de tetralogía no me lo han dicho nunca hasta que me lo dices tú, y me parece muy acertado. Yo no tenía ningún plan previo. Simplemente me puse a escribir una novela: *El mismo mar...* La escribí con mucho esfuerzo porque tuve que encontrar un tono narrativo, aunque las otras novelas no me costaron nada porque el tono fue el mismo. De todos los modos, cuando terminé *El mismo mar...* tenía una segunda parte que se parecía a lo que sería *El amor es un juego solitario*. Y luego escribí esta novela como un relato de tipo corto. Cuando estaba terminando *El amor...*, como me pareció muy duro, más cínico, más desagradable, creí que no acababa de dar mi imagen del mundo y que requería una tercera novela. Entonces pensé la tercera novela, *Varada tras el último naufragio* como cerrando una trilogía. Y supuse que ahí iba a terminar. Después quise hacer algo más sencillo, un paréntesis... Y después escribí *Para no volver*, que en realidad es como dar una vuelta a las tres primeras. Descolgándose desde otra altura, ¿no? O sea, mis tres primeras novelas tienen un sentido

de humor en algún punto, aunque me tomo la vida tremendamente en serio, grandilocuentemente en serio. Pero en *Para no volver* los valores absolutos y las grandes pasiones, se tratan con cierto aspecto irónico. Con lo cual viene a ser como el revés de la trilogía." (Dolgin, "Conversación..." 399-400)

In fact, the writer's second, third, and fourth novels either transcend the previous text(s) or represent(s) a confrontation with its opposite. *El amor...* is written in a cynical tone in contrast to the hermetically dense, profoundly sincere tone of *El mismo mar...*; *Varada...* is a transcendental synthesis of the first two novels, and *Para no volver*, published after a seven-year time lapse, recreates the theme of the trilogy from a related yet opposing vantage point, "como el revés de la trilogía," thereby making the difficult transition from three to four (which would explain why the first three novels were published between 1978-1980 while the fourth did not appear on the market until 1985) and changing its geometric configuration from a triangle to a square. As we know, the square is formed by joining an upward-pointing triangle with a downward-pointing one. It is therefore symbolically significant that the two father-mother-child archetypal triangles at work in *Varada...* (the literal one constituted by Jorge-Elia-Daniel and the projected one emanating from Elia's psyche comprised of Pablo-Eva-Clara), ultimately yields a fourth novel, *Para no volver*, which transcends the previously-existing trilogy while also squaring the circular structure of the tetralogy to which it gives closure as well as origin.

The four novels indeed are far more related as a single totality than the author apparently was aware. Each of the four female protagonists plays the dual function of being an unconscious projection of the autobiographical and creative psyche of Esther Tusquets, while at the same time functioning as a projecting, image-producing psyche of the contents—that is, of the secondary characters and the meaningful environmental setting in which they interact—of the novel in which she appears. In addition to the obvious quantitative progression of the texts (from the first to the second to the third to the fourth novels), there also exists a corresponding incremental expansion (or increasing discrimination) of the projected contents of the psyche that we witness as we move successively from one text to the next. In *El mismo mar...*, the seventeen-year-old Clara is a projection of the fifty-year-old female psyche who, in order to reinitiate her psychological development that had been arrested since she was seventeen years old, must relive the traumatic time when the love of her life, in whom she had invested all of her hopes and dreams for the future, opted to commit suicide; in *El amor...*, two seventeen-year-old classmates, Clara and Ricardo, are projections of the hedonistic Elia's recognition of the binary oppositions in conflict within her psyche; in *Varada*..., the tripartite father-mother-child archetypal triangle of Elia's troubled childhood is projected by her in the triangular image constituted by Pablo, Eva, and the "adopted" Clara; in *Para no volver*, Elena's *animus* is projected in the collective figures of Eduardo, Arturo, Julio, and her psychoanalyst. Furthermore and not coincidentally, the primary male projections appearing in each of the four novels—the statue of Mercurius in the first, Ricardo in the second, Pablo in the third, and the psychoanalyst in the fourth—correspond to the four progressive stages in which the *animus* typically makes its appearance in the female psyche.[17] Since Jung has pinpointed confrontation with the contra-sexual archetype as the most challenging stage of the individuation process, it seems only fitting that the fourth novel should tackle that very problem as its central theme.

It quickly becomes evident how quantitative progression assumes qualitative proportions, whereby psychological growth becomes a concomitant of a narrative sequence that has been meaningfully organized, albeit unconsciously.[18] As Cirlot writes, "where there are two elements, the third appears as the union of the first two and then as three, in turn giving rise to the fourth number as the link between the first three, and so on. Next to unity and duality (expressing conflict, echo and primordial duplication), the ternary and the quaternary are the principal groupings; from their sum comes the septenary; and from their multiplication the dodecanary" (231). The sum of Tusquets' trilogy (*El mismo mar*..., *El amor*... and *Varada*...) and the tetralogy (*El mismo mar*..., *El amor*..., *Varada*... and *Para no volver*) is seven (3 + 4 = 7), "symbolic of perfect order, a complete period or cycle" (Cirlot 231) and their multiplication yields twelve (3 × 4 = 12), "symbolic of cosmic order" (Cirlot 235). The usual

---

[17] In *Man and His Symbols*, Jung writes: "The *animus*, just like the *anima*, exhibits four stages of development. He first appears as a personification of mere physical power—for instance, as an athletic champion or 'muscle man.' In the next state he possesses initiative and the capacity for planned action. In the third phase, the *animus* becomes the 'word,' often appearing as a professor or clergyman. Finally, in the fourth manifestation, the *animus* is the incarnation of meaning... He gives the woman a spiritual firmness, an invisible inner support that compensates for her outer softness. The *animus* in his most developed form sometimes connects the woman's mind with the spiritual evolution of her age, and can thereby make her even more receptive than a man to new creative ideas" (194-95, Jung's italics).

[18] Since the author acknowledges originally not having considered her four novels as a tetralogy, and since they are described as a trilogy plus a fourth unrelated novel in the biographical sketch appearing on the back cover of the editions published by Lumen, then we assume that its symbolically meaningful structure unconsciously came into being.

symbolism of these numbers is as follows: "The ternary represents the intellectual or spiritual order; the quaternary the terrestrial order; the septenary the planetary and moral order; the dodecanary the universal order" to which are linked "the notions of space and time, and the wheel or circle" (Cirlot 231). We will return to the symbolic importance of the circle momentarily. Furthermore, if we add the sum of the four novels, one plus two plus three plus four, we arrive at the number ten which is "symbolic, in decimal systems, of the return to unity, while in the *Tetractys* (whose triangle of points—four, three, two, one—adds up to ten) it is related to four" (Cirlot 234).

It is neither arbitrary nor accidental that these very numbers appear as *leitmotifs* throughout the tetralogy, predominantly in the first text which serves as an overture to the entire *opus*. If we take the example of *El mismo mar...*, we find an astounding enumeration of numerical references that are highly symbolic of the process toward, and/or the achievement of, wholeness. References to triads, the number three being symbolic of flux, change, and transition, abound in the early pages of the text. Here is a limited number of examples: "tres balcones" (17, 27, 28, 30), "el mágico triángulo de mi infancia" (31), "tres días" (77, 78, 79), "tres pozos" (79, 82), "tres enanos" (81), "tres gotas de sangre maternal" (151). References to tetrads are fewer, but recurrent enough to be significant to the symbolic meaning of the novel as a progression towards quaternity wholeness: "cuatro sofás" (30), "somos cuatro en la barca" (105), "llegamos las cuatro" (174). Septenary references include "algún séptimo velo" (35) and "siete colchones de pluma fina" (93), while references to multiples of ten are countless and include: "las Mil y Una Noches" (20), "cien generaciones de princesas aztecas" (85), "cien disfraces" (106), "millones de años" (122), "hace más de cien años" (128), "mil eternidades" (132), "hace siglos" (133), "cien alfileres de diamante" (158), "mil años de soledad" (188).

In addition to symbolizing spiritual synthesis, the resolution of conflict posed by dualism, and the triangle, the number three "forms a half-circle comprising birth, zenith, and descent" (Cirlot 232). As will be demonstrated at the appropriate time, the first and fourth novels are two sides of the same coin, or meaningfully opposing versions of the same novel. Since *Para no volver* ends exactly where *El mismo mar...* begins, and the two intermediary novels, *El amor...* and *Varada...* , develop the process leading up to the indistinguishable beginning and end of the tetralogy, it can be said that the tetralogy is a squaring (the joining of two inverted triangles, or trilogies, the upward-pointing one made up of novels one, two, and three, and the downward-pointing one made up of novels four, three, and two) of the circle constituted by two half-circles comprising novels one, two, three and novels four, three, two. If we add the two half-circles from the point of view of the protagonists' approximate ages (50 in the first and fourth novels, thirty-five in the second, and forty-five in the third), plus the ages of the two female protagonists comprising the vertical bisection of novels one and four (50 + 50), an amazing thing occurs: we arrive at the number three hundred sixty (50 + 35 + 45 + 50 + 45 + 35), which corresponds to the number of degrees of a circle. Similarly, if we add the degrees of the two triangles geometrically configuring the square, we arrive at another astonishing revelation: the sum total of the degrees of the two triangles (180 + 180) equals the number of degrees making up a circle (360).

We may now begin to appreciate how the structuring of the four novels illuminates their meaning and not the other way around. Content is not merely subservient to form; it is determined by it if the structure of Tusquets' tetralogy is read symbolically. Symbolism is at once universal (transcending history) and particular (relating to a specific period in history). If we take, for example, the symbolic meaning of the circle, just as it is a symbol of the universe, it also is a symbol of the Self (Jung, *Man and His Symbols* 161). A logical conclusion follows: macrocosm and microcosm partake of certain innate characteristics, the most important of which is that both represent a self-contained and self-sufficient unity derived from multiplicity and the balancing of diametric oppositions. As Erich Neumann writes, "circle, sphere, and round are all aspects of the Self-contained, which is without beginning and end," with the round corresponding to the egg, "the philosophical World Egg, the nucleus of the beginning, and the germ from which, as humanity teaches us everywhere, the world arises. It is also the perfect state in which the opposites are united—the perfect beginning because the opposites have not yet flown apart and the world has not yet begun, the perfect end because in it the opposites have come together again in a synthesis and the world is once more at rest" (8). When read as an allegorical creation story, the reader can only marvel at the structural-thematic perfection of Tusquets' tetralogy when the closing words of *Para no volver* swings the four-part narrative full-circle to the opening of *El mismo mar...* and (s)he is able to experience what Nuemann refers to as a "perfect state of being in which the opposites are contained" whose "self-sufficiency, self-contentment, and independence of any 'you' or any 'other' are signs of its self-contained eternality" (9).

Symbolism, by definition, "is organized in its vast explanatory and creative function as a system of highly complex relations, one in which the dominant factor is always a polarity, linking the physical and metaphysical worlds" (Cirlot xvi). The four novels to be analyzed in this study illustrate this definition insofar as they function as a system of four meaningfully interrelated units whose structural-thematic whole transcends the sum of its parts. As previously stated, the common theme shared by the four texts is a quest for wholeness of being, or the Self. The circular structure and the discovery of the Self converge at the end of the fourth novel to form an indivisible *unus mundus* where the psycho-narrative multiplicity becomes One; the theme dissolves into the structure, the structure symbolizes the theme, and the four novels physically and materially, as well as psychologically and spiritually, come to experience an ontological Oneness of being. For this reason, we have classified the four novels as a tetralogy whose organizing, regulating principle is the search for the Self via the individuation process. The end of both the creative and the psychological journeys toward wholeness—of the work of art in the former and of the psyche in the latter—are realized when the conceptualization of self-knowledge occurring at end of the fourth novel takes us full-circle to the threshold of the first, the incipience of its creative formulation. This is what is meant by the title of the present study, *Squaring the Circle*, upon whose symbolic significance we subsequently will elaborate.

Tusquets' tetralogy probes the unfathomable depths of the female experience, revealing not only their complexities and contradictions within an individual female psyche, but within the human condition and universe in general. The strife and tension between and among the characters who personify the components of the total female psyche, create the kinetic energy necessary to mobilize the personality toward the transcendence of conflict. Psychological maturation indeed does occur, not in a readily visible, linear manner, but akin to the ebb and flow of the sea: spirally and ever so slowly, at times euphorically progressing and at others despairingly regressing, always the same, yet somehow is a state of continuous flux and change. While the characters personify abstract psychic qualities, the settings in which they "play out" these personality traits facilitate the mobilization of the relationship between and among the psychic forces. The sea, for example, is the setting of a large portion of *El mismo mar de todos los veranos* and *Varada tras el último naufragio*. It is the most significant of the countless universal symbols found in the tetralogy, equally in terms of its presence in the first and third novels, as well as of its absence in the second and the fourth, neither of which is gratuitous. As Cirlot tells us, "the two most essential aspects of the ocean are its ceaseless movement and the formlessness of its waters. It is a symbol, therefore, of dynamic forces and of transitional states between the stable (or solids) and the formless (air or gas)" (241). The ocean setting, accompanied by the recurring *leitmotif* of the ocean waters and its concomitants in the first and third novels, is consistent with the positive, active, transitive quality attributed to all uneven (odd) numbers. According to Cirlot, while the number one "is the active principle which, broken into fragments, gives rise to multiplicity," the number three "represents the solution of the conflict posed by dualism" (232).

El mismo mar... is an example of the former where a synthesis of a single female consciousness (mother) with the contents of its personal (daughter) and collective unconscious (the feminine principle in nature) unites all generations of females as one. Claremont de Castillejo explains it in the following way:

> We could say that every mother contains her daughter in herself and every daughter her mother, and every woman extends backwards into her mother and forwards into her daughter... The conscious experience of these ties produces the feeling that her life is spread out over generations... bringing with it a feeling of immortality. (58)

It is in this sense that the first novel of the tetralogy integrates an individual female psyche with its collective, universal counterpart. The third novel of the series, *Varada...*, resolves the problem of static dualism posed by the preceding second novel, by means of a mother-father-child archetypal triangle. In contrast to odd numbers, Cirlot affirms that even numbers express "the negative and passive principle" (231): "Two stands for echo, reflection, conflict and counterpoise or contraposition; or the momentary stillness of forces in equilibrium" (232), while four is "symbolic of the earth, of terrestrial space, of the human situation, of the external, natural limits of the 'minimum' awareness of totality, and, finally, of rational organization" (232). As we shall see subsequently, the closing novel of the tetralogy, *Para no volver*, elucidates Cirlot's description of the essential characteristics of the number four.

Throughout the author's seven-year interlude of reaching into the depths of her own personal psyche, creative energy involuntarily emerged from her collective unconscious in the form of archetypes. We recall that Jung understood archetypes to be the human aspect of universal symbols, stimulating and propelling the development of the Self. One of our primary purposes in undertaking the research and writing this book is to show that the structural-thematic unity of Tusquets' tetralogy is the artistic objectification of her own individuation process, some stages of which transpired prior to and early in her career as a writer of fiction, while others evolved synchronously with, or following, its novelistic formulation. It is impossible to determine with any certainty when each phase of the author's own individuation process took place since the unfolding of psychological development is neither linear nor chronological, stages of psychic maturation tend to overlap or become intertwined with other phases which often are re-elaborated upon and fine-tuned a countless number of times as new portions of the unconscious are brought to conscious awareness. The end result of Tusquets' psycho-artistic journey is a coherent novelistic tetralogy, a tetralogy which exists as a material objectification (matter) of the integrated psyche (spirit) of its creator. Ultimately, the formed contents—a circular "plot" structure framed within the four points or corners of the four texts—of the tetralogy and of the female psyche become indistinguishable the one from the other in their identically-shared *mandala* configuration. In their inseparable wholeness and oneness, psyche and tetralogy (what might appropriately be called a psycho-tetralogy) come to symbolize the concept of the *unus mundus* where spirit and matter, and time and space, are united as eternity and there exists no difference between psychic and physical facts.

5. *Mandala*: Symbol of the Self and Structure of the Tetralogy

> El término sánscrito *mandala* significa 'centro, círculo, anillo mágico'. Se refiere a una imagen simbólica basada en las figuras geométricas del círculo y del cuadrado que representan las relaciones existentes entre los distintos planos de la realidad.
> INFUSINO, *El extraordinario poder de los mandala* 5

According to Jung, *mandala* is the most genuinely perfect symbol of the Self, referring simultaneously to its wholeness (Self) as well as to the center of the total personality (self). The energy of the archetype of the self "is manifested in the almost irresistible compulsion to *become what one is*, just as every organism is driven to assume the form that is characteristic of its nature, no matter what the circumstances." Jung goes on to explain that the self—the innermost central point of the Self—is surrounded by a periphery containing everything belonging to the Self: the paired opposites that constitute the total personality. As already explained, this totality "comprises consciousness first of all, then the personal unconscious, and finally an indefinitely large segment of the collective unconscious whose archetypes are common to all mankind" (*The Archetypes...* 357).

Jung tells us that, as psychological phenomena, *mandala* configurations denote "circular images, which are drawn, painted, modeled, or danced" and appear spontaneously in dreams, states of conflict, and in cases of schizophrenia, and that they frequently contain "a quaternity or a multiple of four, in the form of a cross, a star, a square, an octagon" (*The Archetypes...* 387). The states of conflict to which he refers, and which are applicable to the plight of

Tusquets' fictional personæ as projections of her own psyche, are the result of a neurosis[19] and its treatment in adults who "are confronted with the problem of opposites in human nature and are consequently disoriented" (387). The depth psychologist explains that the circular image afforded by the *mandala* "compensates the disorder and confusion of the psychic state—namely, through the construction of a central point to which everything is related, or by a concentric arrangement of the disordered multiplicity and of contradictory and irreconcilable elements. This is evidently an *attempt at self-healing* on the part of Nature, which does not spring from conscious reflection but from an instinctive impulse" (388, Jung's italics).

We know that Jung considered the self to be an archetype of the universal collective unconscious and the fullest possible realization of the Self as an inherent goal toward which all individuals naturally strive unless impeded by a neurosis or complex. Through the process of individuation, the individual comes to recognize and appreciate his/her own uniqueness or individuality while, at the same time, harmonizing to the greatest extent possible the components inhabiting the distinct strata of the personality. The individual becomes undivided, un-fragmented—in a word, whole—by rejoining to consciousness those parts of the Self that have been repressed or split off from consciousness. Throughout his writings Jung has elaborated upon the various stages of the individuation process whose ultimate goal is the unification of the personality within which the self acts as its regulating principle.

The *mandala* has come to be identified in dreams, fantasies, and works of art, as a symbol of the Self during any one of the numerous stages of the inconclusive, lifelong individuation process, which is determined by a symbolic interpretation of the forms, numerical divisions, and colors that appear within the circumference. As affirmed by the Italian Jungian psychologist, Giampaolo

---

[19] According to Jung, the teleological purpose of a neurosis is an effort on the part of the psyche to cure itself of a conflict between consciousness and a portion of the unconscious. Goldbrunner explains that "a neurosis is not merely a danger signal, like pain; it is more than that: it is an attempt at self-help, a resolve to take a definite line and a definite direction. All psychic processes are directed towards a certain tendency but this has become jammed up, as in a dead end which blocks up consciousness. And raging against the symptom only makes the conflict worse." Goldbrunner goes on to say that "the way to a cure is obstructed by the attitude of the ego. Thus neurosis also can be defined as an inner schism, a dissension within. The treasure in the unconscious is waiting to be raised. The tangle of its contents must be taken up by consciousness, slowly unraveled and rejoined to consciousness again. This is the formal process of healing" (23).

Infusino, the shapes and colors appearing in a *mandala* express the deepest thoughts, feelings and intuitions of its creator. The choice is never fortuitous but, rather, always personal, providing a guide by which the individual may develop his or her own unique potentials, may achieve understanding of his or her particular problems, and may seek the most efficient solutions to them.[20]

It is the individuation process that which propels the archetype of the self to forge a meaningful relationship with the ego, and the ego to acquire a receptive attitude toward the self, although we may not be consciously aware that this is among the most fundamental changes taking place in the transition from the first to the second half of life. The alignment/alienation dynamics of the relationship are dramatized throughout Tusquets' tetralogy, manifesting itself as self-inflation and euphoria when the ego is closely identified with the self (as at the end of the first, third, and fourth novels), or as depression and estrangement when the relationship between ego and self is distant (as it is throughout the majority of the first, third, and fourth novels, as well as throughout all of the second novel). The activation of the symbiotic relationship between the narrator-protagonist and Clara in *El mismo mar...*, clearly promotes the ego-self identity with which the novel ends and which was conspicuously absent prior to the onset of the symbolic mother/daughter union. Throughout *El amor...* and all but the final scene of *Varada...*, when Elia is reunited with her son, we witness ego/self alienation as evidenced by the depressed, catatonic state of mind of the protagonist. In *Para no volver*, like in *El mismo mar...*, we see the ego and the self move closer together as the protagonist becomes increasingly aware and accepting of the contra-sexual shadow aspects of her Self. By means of these rhythmic patterns of estrangement and identification between the ego and the self that her protagonist(s) display, Tusquets captures the expanding, dialectical dynamics of the/her psyche, for which the *mandala*-like structure of the tetralogy exists as a symbol. Franz explains:

> The *mandala* serves a conservative purpose—namely, to restore a previously existing order. But it also serves the creative purpose of giving expression and form to something that does not yet exist, something new

---

[20] In the words of Infusino, "De hecho, las formas y los colores de los *mandala* expresan los pensamientos, las emociones y las intuiciones más profundas del autor. La elección no es nunca casual sino personal; indica la dirección a seguir para desarrollar las propias potencialidades, para comprender los propios problemas, para encontrar las soluciones más eficaces" (6).

and unique... The process is that of the ascending spiral, which grows upward while simultaneously returning again and again to the same point. (Cited in Fincher 148)

Joan Kellogg's development of the "Archetypal Stages of the Great Round of *Mandala*," consists of twelve prototypical *mandala* forms which capture the upward spiraling path toward psychic wholeness. While it cannot be emphasized enough that each and every *mandala* is unique to its individual creator, *mandala* therapists attest to certain patterns that the magic circles possess which reveal an underlying universal pattern of psychological development, or individuation. The propensity to create circular *mandalas*, often framed within a square or divided into four (or a multiple of four) sections, are examples of the universal recurring motifs characterizing visual renditions of the inner workings of the psyche. The unique detailing of the universal structure represents the concurrent individuality and universality of each of us.

The creation of a *mandala* represents not only an attempt to describe the archetype of the self, but equally to establish a communion between (wo)man and the divine essence (Infusino 10). In many oriental philosophies, the circle, or *mandala*, represents the path toward the ultimate state of divine illumination: perfect knowledge of one's Self (Infusino 12). In this quest for self-knowledge, the individual seeks to actualize his/her fullest potential, thereby activating the creative archetype housed within the collective unconscious. In opposition to the personal unconscious, the term used by Jung to refer to repressed experiences or memories from the personal life of an individual, the collective unconscious is inherited, transpersonal residue of the evolution of the human species. Consequently, it is shared by all human beings. The depth psychologist devoted large sections of his writings to demonstrating the likelihood of the existence of a superordinate archetype of the self around which all other aspects of the personality revolved and to which they all were subordinated. He found the clearest expression of its existence in *mandala* formations, "those spherical or circular patterns which are usually sub-divided into four parts and often exhibit a relationship to time." The relationship to time to which Jung is referring is not arbitrary; it is to be found, rather, in typical sequences, phases, or patterns denoting time. As we shall see, the temporal relationship between numbers and archetypal symbols plays a significant role in the structural unfolding of Tusquets' tetralogy. The circular, *mandala*-like configuration of the tetralogy is intimated by the identical age and circumstances of the narrators of the first and fourth novels. Just as any point on the circumference of a circle is simultaneously a beginning and an end, such is the case with *El mismo mar...* and *Para no volver*, insofar as the two novels are structurally interchangeable as closing the narrative circle by the joining of its incipience with its conclusion. These are, as will be elaborated upon in this study, one-and-the-same point. The relationship of the second and third novels to the fourth and first establishes a chronological pattern of development by virtue of the fact that, beginning with the second novel, in each successive novel the female protagonist is approximately ten years older than she was in the previous one. The Elia of *El amor...* is in her thirties while the Elia of *Varada...* is in her fourth decade of life. Elena in *Para no volver* is about to turn fifty, as is the anonymous narrator-protagonist of *El mismo mar...* Tusquets thus has established a rhythmic sense of development within a circular narrative structure. After the publication of her first three novels in three consecutive years (1978, 1979, 1980), the four-year hiatus between the completion of the trilogy in 1980 and the publication of the fourth novel, *Para no volver*, in 1985, attests to "the difficult step from three to four" due to "the inclusion (no longer avoidable) of the observer in his *wholeness* within the framework of his processes of understanding" (Franz, *Number and Time* 122, Franz' italics). The circularly formed content of Tusquets' novelistic tetralogy is framed by a heightened conscious understanding of her Self, which is the theoretical foundation of *Para no volver* and the *praxis* of *El mismo mar...* The circle is squared because the tetralogy symbolizes a great deal more than its mere circularly formed content. The tetralogy stands as a symbol of a heightened state of conscious awareness of the Self that is attained indiscriminately by novelist and (collective) protagonist alike. The central organizational force of the Self (symbolically depicted by the *mandala* configuration), and of the four-cornered narrative tetralogy (symbolically depicted by its squared framing of the *mandala*) within which the *mandala* is contained, are identical: the archetype of the self which is the force behind the evolution of the Self known as the individuation process. The archetype of the self synchronously constitutes the central point of the *mandala* (the psyche) and of the squared framing of the *mandala* (the narrative tetralogy) within which the psyche is contained. On a symbolic level, then, the squared circle symbolizes the psychological development of the Self, oriented by the centering and centralizing archetype of the self that is bisected by the four texts as a symbol of the conjunction of opposites toward which the self strives to overcome for the sake of the wholeness of the Self. According to Cirlot, "the cross stands for the world axis. Placed at the mystic Centre of the Cosmos, it becomes the bridge or ladder by means of which the soul may reach God" (65). The cross also expresses life's difficulties, with its "cross-roads of possibilities and impossibilities, of construction and destruction" (68). And, according to Susanne Fincher, "the cross is associated with the human challenge to attain consciousness through the attempt to know one's dark, hidden side" (121). Since all of these meanings of the cross lie at the core of Tusquets' tetralogy, we are compelled to visualize a bisected *mandala* whereby the circular structure (symbolizing the spiritual Self) of the tetralogy (symbolizing the literary materialization of the Self) would be internally divided according to the following structural principles: novels one and four (*El mismo mar...* and *Para no volver*, respectively) bisect the centralized self vertically. The 1978 novel constitutes the esthetic formulation of what is conceptualized in the closing pages of the 1985 novel. The fact that contemplation (the static quality of the number four and of all even numbers) and actualization (the dynamic quality of the number one and of all odd numbers) are synchronistic phenomena (both protagonists are approaching their fiftieth birthday) links the two novels vertically in the following manner:

> The upright position of the cross connects it with other symbols of the vertical, such as the tree, mountain, and ladder. These symbols suggest a connection between the earth and the sky, which is traditionally associated with the gods. The vertical connection is thought of as a pathway linking the spiritual world with the ordinary reality of earth. It is also a focal point, marking the place on earth where the superordinary exists side by side with the mundane. (Fincher 129)

Novels two (passive) and three (active), *El amor...* and *Varada...*, respectively, constitute the horizontal line of the axis, which we will define as the raw material used to tell the story off the transition from the first half of life to the second. Consistent with the static quality of all even numbers, the Elia of the second novel is immobilized by the binary oppositions of her personality as they are projected onto the characters of Clara and Ricardo. In contraposition to the psychologically stagnant Elia of the previous novel, the Elia appearing in the third novel undergoes a process of psychological flux, followed by the healthy union of ego and self with which the original (triangular) trilogy ends. When *Para no volver* appeared seven years after the publication of *El mismo mar...*, we are presented with the theoretical foundation of the pre-existing trilogy, that is, with the key to open the door to its objective meaning.

Hence, the cross is symbolic of the conjunction of opposites. According to Fincher, "the precise joining of the vertical and horizontal in the cross makes it an apt symbol for the wedding of the spiritual (vertical) with the material world of phenomena (horizontal)" (121). For Jung, the cross stands as a symbol for the balance of all opposites within the whole personality:

The cross, or whatever other heavy burden the hero carries, is *himself*, or rather *the* Self, his wholeness, which is both God and animal—not merely the empirical man, but the totality of his being, which is rooted in his animal nature and reached out beyond the merely human towards the divine. His wholeness implies tremendous tension of opposites paradoxically at one with themselves, as in the cross, their most perfect symbol. (*Symbols of Transformation* 303, Jung's italics)

The graphic depiction of the squaring of the circle, which in turn is bisected by the symbol of the cross, is a symbol of the synchronous four-part psycho-narrative development of the structure (the squaring of the circle, or Self) and theme (the reconciliation of opposites symbolized by the cross bisecting the central archetypal regulating principle of the personality, or the self) of individuation. Fincher admonishes those who create a *mandala* within which is contained a cross to view it as a evidence "that you are waging a hero's battle and carving chunks of consciousness out of that which has hitherto been dark and unknown... When a cross appears in your *mandala* you might want to consider the possibility that you are balancing, more or less successfully, the contradictions that are part of human nature" (122).

According to Marie-Louise von Franz, the quincunx (an arrangement of five objects in a square, with one at each corner and one in the middle) is of great significance in ancient Chinese number theory, "where five stands in the *center* of the first number series, 1, 2, 3, 4, 5, 6, 7, 8, 9 (before ten)" (Franz, *Number and Time* 123). Within this Chinese view, "the number five stands for the element of the earth carrying and centering all things at the center of the foundation of existence" (123). Nonetheless, the yellow color that is ascribed to the center of the earth characterizes it not as the soil of the earth but, rather, as the spiritual principle of *k'un*, "the expanding feminine, which brings the spirit into material and spatial manifestations. It stands at the center of quaternary *mandala* structures. The primal one made manifest, and its progressive ordering effect on the number hierarchy, is also recognizable in the number fifty as a symbol 'de la grande expansión'" (123). It would seem to be hardly coincidental that Tusquets' psycho-narrative journey begins and ends with the protagonist about to enter into her fiftieth year of life.

6. Squaring the Circle: Individuation as Thematic Structure

> The alchemist's statements about the *lapis*, considered psychologically, describe the archetype of the self. Its phenomenology is exemplified in *mandala* symbolism, which portrays the Self as a concentric structure, often in the form of the squaring of the circle. Co-ordinated with this are all kinds of secondary symbols, most of them expressing the nature of the opposites to be united. The structure is invariably felt as the representation of a central state or of a centre of personality essentially different from the ego. It is of a numinous nature, as is clearly indicated by the *mandalas* themselves and by the symbols used (sun, star, light, fire, flower, precious stone, etc.). All degrees of emotional evaluation are found, from abstract, colourless, indifferent drawings of circles to an extremely intense experience of illumination. These aspects all appear in alchemy, the only difference being that there they are projected into matter, whereas here they are understood as symbols. The *arcanum chymicum* has therefore changed into a psychic event without having lost any of its original numinosity.
> JUNG, *Mysterium*... 544

The title of the present study, *Squaring the Circle*, is borrowed from Jungian theory as a concept which the depth psychologist appropriated from his lifetime commitment to the study of alchemy and its parallelism to the psychological process by which an individual acquired increasing awareness of his or her specific individuality. He even referred to it as "the *archetype of wholeness*," because of which the "quaternity of the One" is the "schema for all images of God" (*The Archetypes*... 388, Jung's italics). In order to achieve individuality, one must first differentiate those psychic components emerging from ego-consciousness from those stemming from the realm of unconscious complexes with which the former are in oppositional conflict. One must come to an understanding and acceptance of the binary, paradoxical nature of all things—including the human psyche which is but a microcosm whose *modus operandi* replicates that of the universe—and strive to integrate as many of them as possible, the positive as well as the negative, into a conscious whole. It was Jung's contention that by becoming aware of unconscious identifications, one could withdraw projections, eliminate complexes, experience the archetype of the self, and strive toward the fullest expression and realization of the Self. This was, he believed, the goal and purpose of human life.

From the late 1920s until his death, Jung held firmly to the belief that the phases of alchemical practice[21] corresponded to distinct phases of the individuation process, in particular the notions of joint work, transformation, and a goal. Identical to the task of psychoanalysis,

> Alchemy is the art of transformation. The work of the alchemist is to bring about succeeding changes in the material he operates on, transforming it from a gross, unrefined state to a perfect and purified form. To turn base metals into gold is the simplest expression of this aim, and at the physical level this involves chemical operations performed with laboratory equipment. However, this is only one dimension of alchemy, since the 'base material' worked upon and the 'gold' produced may also be understood as man himself in his quest to perfect his own nature. Mainstream alchemy is a discipline involving physical, psychological and spiritual work, and if any one of these elements is taken out of context and said to represent the alchemical tradition, then the wholeness and true quality of alchemy is lost.
> For several reasons, it is not an easy tradition to understand. Firstly, the chief medium of alchemical expression is through the use of mythological symbols, which are the perfect means of conveying information that can be interpreted at both a material and a spiritual level, but which defy a single and precise definition. (Gilchrist 1)

Throughout his writings, Jung employed alchemy as a metaphor to describe the tension between opposites and their resolution by way of the transcendent function. As indicated by the sub-title of his last published work, *Mysterium Coniunctionis: An Inquiry into the Separation and Synthesis of Psychic Opposites in Alchemy,* he believed that, when held in a dialectical relationship (thesis/antithesis) of mutually permitting influences upon the one from the other, a third synthetic form partaking of aspects of the two opposing forces would emerge. According to Jung, this three-part dialectical process—differentiation of the opposites (the masculine *logos* principle of discrimination), holding them in opposition to one another until they are willing

---

[21] Jung contends that alchemical experiments "had the sole purpose... of stimulating the deepest levels of the psyche and of facilitating psychic projections in material things, or in other words, of experiencing material phenomena as symbols which point to a complete theory of the universe and the destiny of the soul" (Quoted in Cirlot, xxviii).

to be receptive to aspects of the other (the feminine *eros* principle of relatedness), and transcendental synthesis to a higher form partaking of the former two (the pneumatic or spiritual principle uniting the two opposites)—was the cornerstone of psychological growth.

Each of the four female psyches represents each of the four stages of the individuation/alchemical process, or *mysterium coniunctionis*. The first is the uroboric[22] oneness symbolically depicted as "the round 'container,' i.e., the maternal womb... also as the union of masculine and feminine opposites, the World Parents joined in perpetual cohabitation" (Neumann 13) of *El mismo mar...* as depicted by the as yet undifferentiated psyche of the narrator-protagonist who symbolically returns to the dark, humid maternal womb of her origin prior to the birth of her consciousness. The eerie sense of timelessness with which the novel opens suggests "the time of the beginning, before the coming of the opposites... when there was still no consciousness" (Neumann 12). Paradoxically, this begining-of-time *unus mundus* describes the manner by which *El mismo mar...* also ends, which is personified by the four-part alchemical union of the most (un)related of all opposites: masculine and feminine, personified by the protagonist, Julio (her husband), Clara (referred to by the narrator as the *princesa azteca* (Aztec princess = Julio's *anima*), and *el emperador* (the emperor = the protagonist's *animus*), with whom Clara has a sexual tryst in the closing pages of the novel as the protagonist is sexually reunited with her husband after the two women's twenty-eight day love affair. Interestingly enough, the union of sun *(sol)* and moon *(luna)*, as symbols of the masculine and feminine, respectively, was known to take place in Athens (and continues to be an Arabian custom to this day) on the day of the new moon, which took place on twenty-eighth day of the month (Jung, *Mysterium...* 129). Quite often, writes Jung, "the masculine-feminine opposition is personified as King and Queen (in the *Rosarium philosophorum* also as Emperor and Empress" *(Mysterium...* 4). The synchronous union of the royal and servile couples (Clara and her male partner, and the protagonist and her husband, respectively), attests both to the transconscious character of the pairs of opposites, as well as to the transformative nature of their union *(Mysterium...* 6). We will return to this subject shortly for the purpose of demonstrating graphically how the tetralogy has captured, and rendered visible, the transformation of the female psyche.

Following the embryonic state of ego-consciousness with which *El mismo mar...* opens is the narcissistic stage: "The second stage is that of the alimentary

---

[22] The Gnostic *uroboros* refers to a snake circling to bite its own tail (Fincher 118).

uroboros, a closed circuit whose 'own waste provides its own food'" (Neumann 34). In alchemical terminology, this second phase of the individuation/ alchemical evolution is referred to as the *unio mentalis*, or separation from the body, as exemplified by the erotic, hedonistic, self-gratifying orientation of the second novel. Here, the self-absorbed Elia projects the antagonistic binary division of her bisexual psyche into narcissistic feeling (portrayed by Clara's exclusively self-serving emotional neediness), and a narcissistic eroticism (the physical pleasure for which the insensitive Ricardo yearns at the expense of all feeling, be they his or anyone else's). Their incompatibility sets the stage for what follows in the third novel: the reunion of *unio mentalis* to a transfigured body as projected by Elia in the archetypal Pablo-Eva-Clara (father-mother-child) triangle. At the close of the novel, the projections are withdrawn as indicated by the transposition of their implications onto the actual Jorge-Elia-Daniel family unit, with psychic resolution and growth as the outcome. Finally, we witness in *Para no volver* the final stage of individuation whereby Elena's consciousness becomes receptive to the contra-sexual aspects of her psyche as inferred by her willingness to explore her creative potential (symbolic of the activation of her *animus* resources), the very creative energy that was behind the writing of the tetralogy whose reading we have just concluded. Hence, the end of the fourth is equivalent to the wholeness of the One. Franz elucidates what she calls "the powerful retrograde connection" that the four has to the primal one by reproducing a handicraft tile of the Tama Indian settlement which she had received as a gift (*Number and Time* 130). The tile depicts a modern Navajo Indian represented as four goddesses. In counting their heads, four units result. The series of goddesses actually begins, however, with the skirt of the fourth, so that one and four are identical while both framing and containing the other three figures. She explains that as a consequence of the difficult, often time-consuming passage from three to four, through which "our mental processes no longer revolve about intellectual theorizations, but partake of the creative adventure of 'realizations in the act of becoming'" (131).

The four phases of psychic transformation reveal an attempt to resolve an ambivalent, conflictive psyche that is torn between allegiances to matriarchal and patriarchal forms of consciousness. The four female protagonists—in actuality the four transformational stages of the individuation process of a single individual and of the universal female psyche—vacillate between an ego-consciousness that plays the *anima* in a compensatory role to a masculine mentality or, conversely, that pays homage to the *animus* in a female mentality. Consequently, she is caught in the tight grip of her contra-sexual (masculine) side, which realizes unconscious intentions at the expense of inhibiting her *eros*, that is, her feminine tendency to human connection and relatedness. In his insightful monograph entitled *Alchemy in a Modern Woman*, Robert Grinnell explains the manner by which *animus* possession in a woman manifests itself:

> She may become a good comrade to a man, but without access to his feelings. And, on the other hand, her *animus* has blocked the approaches to her own feelings. The consequences that can follow from this situation are unfortunate. She may become frigid as a defense against the masculine type of sexuality which corresponds to her masculine type of mind. If this defense is unsuccessful, she develops an aggressive, urgent, spasmodic type of sexuality with perverse undertones which is more like a man's than the receptive sexuality of a woman. Or, finally, she may develop a sort of optional homosexuality with herself in the masculine role. (7)

For those of us familiar with Tusquets' female protagonists, the situation described by Grinnell rings all too familiar. The masculine contexts and roles in which the author's female personæ systematically insert themselves, is meant to compensate for the lifelong absence of mother-daughter bonding. Whenever the situation will allow for it, the negative mother complex, which itself resonates with the characteristic separation and differentiation of the masculine principle of *logos*, is replaced by the *animus* complex, with which it shares a number of common denominators: a predominating contra-sexuality, a forcible intrusion of the unconscious, a predominance of the shadow, and a contra-sexual consciousness, the latter understood as the exclusion of the consciousness specific to a given sex and the predominance of the consciousness appropriate to the opposite sex (Grinnell 9).

The negative mother complex lying at the heart of the tetralogy, and its theme of female individuation, has mobilized a series of personality paradoxes that prove difficult to untangle. On the one had, there is a splinter personality that is resistant to anything maternal. In a supreme effort to not be anything like her mother, Tusquets' fictional projections of the effects of the negative mother complex reveal a personality that has become unlike anything associated with the feminine principle in general. Paradoxically, in an attempt to be nothing like her mother, the projected female psyche has not permitted herself to develop the very loving, nurturing aspects of femininity itself, which would have proven her to be so unlike her mother. Instead, the reckless forces of the negative mother complex have eclipsed her femininity almost entirely, and most noticeably her maternal instincts. Her *eros* (that is, her interpersonal connectedness through feeling) has been supplanted by an impersonal masculine obsession with sexuality devoid of feeling. As portrayed so vividly in *El amor...*, where the youngest of the four protagonists appears, Elia is, at one-and-the-same time, surrogate mother and dominant sexual partner to Clara, and dominant sexual partner and surrogate mother to Ricardo. Maternal nurturance and sexual dominance are dangerously confused in the thirty-year-old psyche; the incompatibility between Clara and Ricardo is symptomatic of Elia's inability to choose whether to live out a feminine consciousness supported by unconscious masculine attributes, or a masculine consciousness with compensatory unconscious feminine qualities. As suggested by the tragic conclusion of *El amor...*, resolution of this conflict is essential to curing the protagonist's frequent bouts of deep depression accompanied by suicidal thoughts. Nevertheless, the demands of her inner child, personified by Clara in the first three novels, render the task far more difficult than a mere matter of choice. This fearful, emotionally neglected inner child is yet another splinter personality challenging the stability of consciousness. While one unconscious portion of the female psyche strives to avoid anything associated with mothering, the unconscious child is clamoring for maternal love, care and acceptance. In a manner of speaking, the two feminine complexes cancel each other out, leaving the psyche caught in an intricate web of *animus* possession that has little or no access to the feminine qualities of sensitivity and human compassion.

Consistent with the goal of individuation, the collective female psyche must transform her physical bisexuality—in which *she* is *masculine-dominant*—which acts as a compensation for her masculine-possessed consciousness, into a psychic androgyny in which a dominant female consciousness is conjoined with a supporting compensatory masculine counterpart. This feat entails withdrawing the goddess-like qualities of the archetypal Great Mother (which are interfused with how her mother actually is and which are, to a great extent, responsible for the inferiority complex from which the protagonist suffers) and seeing and accepting her mother for the imperfect, emotionally-limited person that she is who, like herself, has inherited psychological baggage from her own mother. As she begins to view her mother as she truly is—as a person with good qualities accompanying other undesirable ones—she sets out to explore that same duality within herself. She is thereby enabled to assume a proper maternal role in the lives of her grown children and to commence the healing process of the emotional wounds of her own inner child who, as her fears and insecurities are allayed over time, becomes less and less of an intrusion on her adult consciousness. As these feminine qualities become further developed, her repressed femininity seeps into consciousness, loosening the tight grip of its *animus* possession. As the feminine lunar coldness and wetness (*eros*) interfuse with the masculine solar heat and dryness (*logos*), a warm, moist vapor comes to orient the psychic activity at the close of the third novel.

Jung's *logos-eros* dichotomy corresponds to the *sol-luna* symbolism of the alchemists. In an analogous relationship to the two alchemical figures, the two Jungian concepts symbolize an archetype of consciousness expressing the transformational function of the Self. *Sol* is the symbol of masculine consciousness while *luna* symbolizes feminine consciousness. Conversely, *luna* stands as a symbol of the unconscious in a masculine personality, with *sol* symbolic of the unconscious in a feminine personality. The conjunction of the two figures expresses the union of the conscious personality with its unconscious correlate. The union of man and woman is a symbol of the quintessential union of compensatory opposites. However, their matrimonial union, like the symbolic one with which *El mismo mar*... concludes in a state of *unus mundus*, is not a marriage of two, but a diagonally bisected interrelationship of four: masculine consciousness, feminine unconscious (*anima*), feminine consciousness, and masculine unconscious (*animus*). Four becomes the undifferentiated One—the *unus mundus* symbolized by the squaring of the circle—whereby all opposites are synthesized, transcend their differences and become undifferentiated and indistinguishably inseparable from any part of the whole.

"Squaring the circle," like the *lapis* or the *aurum philosophicum*, was one of the preoccupations of the alchemists. But whereas the *lapis* and the *aurum philosophicum* were symbols of the quest for the evolutionary goal of the spirit, "squaring the circle" was a concept related to the equating of the two great cosmic symbols of heaven (the circle) and earth (the square). In the case of Tusquets' novelistic tetralogy, we are using the phrase to refer to the Self (the symbol of which is the circle), as well as to the circular structure of her tetralogy insofar as the first and the fourth novels equally can be considered as beginning and end points of the circle, and the material expression or manifestation of both in the form of four novels (symbolized by the four corners making up the square) comprising an indivisible totality. In the physical and literary cosmos alike, we are confronted with a supreme union of opposites, with "the equation and canceling out of two components into a higher synthesis. The square was seen to correspond to the four Elements. The aim of 'squaring the circle,' then (which strictly ought to be called 'circling the square'), was to obtain unity in the material world (as well as in the spiritual life) over and above the differences and obstacles (the static order) of the number four and the four-cornered square" (Cirlot 307-08).

Even the most casual reader of Tusquets' fiction cannot help but recognize in all of her works the profusion not only of numerical, geometric, and color symbolism, but also of other great universal symbols such as that of the sea, the house, the sun, the moon, the boat or vessel, the bird, the butterfly, etc., as well as of mythological figures and innumerable archetypes of the universal collective unconscious. It should be evident by this point that not even the characters themselves are characters as we understand the term in reference to the traditional novel. They are most appropriately described as instruments or devices functioning as extended metaphors and/or symbols whereby they represent one thing in the guise of another and always connote more than what they actually are. Their thoughts, sentiments and moods intermingle in such a way that they imitate the structural dynamics of an individual psyche engaged in the arduous process of growth and change. They are concrete images of psychic abstractions, personifying a multitude of diametrically opposed pairs of psychological qualities in a state of unresolved conflict. For example, the relationship between the fifty-year-old narrator/protagonist of *El mismo mar...* and her adolescent student, interlocutor, and eventual companion, surrogate daughter, and lover, Clara, dramatizes the exhumation of repressed, unresolved conflicts that have evolved into neuroses. As an embodiment of significant portions of the protagonist's personal unconscious which are in conflict with her conscious life, Clara cannot be considered a literary character in her own rite. The presence of Clara in the novel, who is the exact same age that the protagonist was when Jorge committed suicide, throws the character back to that moment in time when her psychological maturation ceased in its development. The juxtaposition of the two females thus sets up a replay of that traumatic episode in her adolescent life when the implicit promise of eternal happiness was snatched away by Jorge's committing the ultimate selfish act, leaving her alone to pick up the pieces and somehow to find a way to go on with her life. In this reenactment, the roles are reversed; it is the narrator/protagonist who assumes the role of the one who loves and leaves Clara, thereby forcing herself to revisit and re-experience her own adolescent pain of love and loss where she has remained psychologically stuck throughout her adult life. Similarly, it affords her the opportunity to provide Clara (her young self) with the maternal nurturing of which she herself had been deprived as a child and to begin the healing process of those wounds resulting from years of emotional neediness, insecurity, and self-doubt. With her inner child satisfied, she is empowered to behave as a good parent to Clara by intuiting the appropriate time and way to push the young bird out of the nest. The juxtaposition of mid-life consciousness and adolescent unconsciousness signifies the confrontation of diametric opposites: maturity and youth; motherhood and childhood; experience and innocence; independence and dependence; heterosexuality and homosexuality; reality and fantasy, etc., which ultimately are transcended as echoed in the closing words of the novel: "Y Wendy creció" (229).

As we will discover in our analysis of the novels themselves, the particular configuration, ordering and repetition of these symbols within the tetralogy all herald transformation. On the level of artistic creation, the first novel is transformed into itself plus another, which in turn is transformed into a novelistic trilogy with the appearance of the third, which subsequently is transformed into a tetralogy of oneness and wholeness emerging from the fourth novel for which the first novel paradoxically serves as an overture *and* culmination. Each novel carries remnants of all of the others in their shared, collective theme of psychic transformation. As Jung graphically depicts and elaborates upon quite extensively, a quaternity series (such as the novelistic one under analysis here) could be expressed in the form of an equation in which **A** stands for the initial state, and **BCD** for intermediate states. For our purposes, **A** = *El mismo mar*..., **B** = *El amor*..., **C** = *Varada*..., and **D** = *Para no volver*. The formations that split off from them are denoted in each case by the lower case letters **abcd**. With respect to the construction of the formula, we are concerned with the continual process of transformation of one and the same substance: a/the female Self in this particular case. The transformation turns rightwards with the sun, symbolizing the process of becoming conscious as indicated by the splitting (discrimination of **ABCD** each time into four qualitatively discrete units):

$$\begin{array}{ccccccc}
 & & b^3 & & & d & \\
c^3 & & a^3 & = A = & a & & c \\
 & & d^3 & & & b & \\
 & & \parallel & & & \parallel & \\
 & & D & & & B & \\
 & & \parallel & & & \parallel & \\
 & & d^2 & & & b^1 & \\
a^2 & & c^2 & = C = & c^1 & & a^1 \\
 & & b^2 & & & d^1 & \\
\end{array}$$

The formula reproduces the essential features of the symbolic process of transformation. In accordance with the Jungian principle of synchronicity, which will be discussed in the next section, it simultaneously shows the relationship of the four novels to each other and within the tetralogy *and* the rotation of the *mandala*, that is the antithetical play of complementary (or compensatory) processes, then the apocatastasis, i.e., the restoration of an original state of wholeness. We are reminded that the alchemists expressed this through the symbol of the *uroboros*. Finally, the formula repeats the ancient alchemical tetramer, which is implicit in the fourfold structure of unity:

$$A = a \begin{matrix} d \\ \\ b \end{matrix} c$$

The formula can only hint at the higher plane that is reached through the process of transformation and integration. The "sublimation," or process of qualitative change, consists in an unfolding of totality into four parts four times. This signifies that it has become conscious. When psychic contents are split up into four aspects, it means that they have been subjected to discrimination by the four orienting functions of consciousness: thought, feeling, intuition and sensation. Therefore, the process described by the formula and depicted in the diagram above implies that the originally unconscious totality has become a conscious one (Jung, *Aion, passim* 257-59) Specifically, it has become a novelistic tetralogy whose structure is that of a *mandala* (as symbol of the psyche whose self is driving the successive stages of development of the tetralogy) *and* indistinguishably of an *unus mundus* (as symbol of the literary cosmos for which individuation/creationism serves as the unifying theme).

7. Synchronicity: Psyche and Tetralogy as *Unus Mundus*

Viewing the world as a circle had some very practical applications as our ancestors took to the high ground for a clear view. They saw that the horizon line appears to be a circle. Human beings, in an effort to move safely about in large land areas, devised ways to orient themselves within this vast circle. In developing schemes for finding their bearings, it would have been natural to begin with the space they knew best: that occupied by their own body. Let us

consider the body, with its arrangement of limbs and organs, as a focal point for organizing the space within the circle of the horizon.
The bilateral arrangement of the body creates a right and left side. With arms outstretched in opposite directions away from the body, one might imagine lines extending beyond the outstretched arms to the horizon. This establishes two opposite directions in the circle. The placement of the eyes in front of the head naturally suggests the line of sight as another direction, and implies its opposite as a continuation of this line extending behind. Thus we can imagine the classic *mandala* pattern consisting of the horizon line (circle) and four lines converging at the body in the center.
FINCHER, *Creating Manalas* 7

According to Jung, the symbolic structure of the *mandala* constitutes our psychic equivalent of the *unus mundus*. The Latin term *unus mundus*, refers to the unity of all existence; specifically, to the unity of psyche and matter. Jung writes that the idea of an *unus mundus* is founded on the assumption that "the multiplicity of the empirical world rests on an underlying unity, and that not two or more fundamentally different worlds exist side by side or are mingled with one another. Rather, everything divided and different belongs to one and the same world." The justification for this assumption is that, "until now, no one has been able to discover a world in which the known laws of nature are invalid" (*Mysterium... passim*, 767-70). The synchronous evolution of individuation, Jung's term for the natural human tendency to evolve toward the goal of psychic wholeness unless such development is obstructed by a neurosis, and of the creative process that characterize the coming-into-being of Tusquets' novelistic tetralogy, lends further credence to the existence of an *unus mundus*, as well as to the unity of psyche (wholeness of the Self) and matter (in the objectified form of the completed esthetic object).

Just as the physical universe is an objectification of its Creator, Tusquets' fictional universe exists as an objectified form of the psyche of its demiurge. Throughout the seven-year (as opposed to seven-day) act of creation of her fictional universe, she has psychologically integrated into her conscious life personal as well as universal contents of her unconscious. Her seven-year act of creation was a process of self-discovery—a mirrored reflection of the coming into being of her Self synchronously as unique individual and universal woman—consisting of an unconscious animation of the creative universal archetype, and in a personal development and shaping of this image until her work reached completion. Those who claim to know God can only know Him through his work of creation. Similarly, those of us wishing to know Esther Tusquets need only read *El mismo mar...*, *El amor...*, *Varada...* and *Para no volver* and discover its meaningful configuration as a literary *unus mundus*.

This is meant to imply that it is the art that explains the artist and not the life experiences of the artist which explain his/her art. While no one would dispute the fact that the artist's temperament and personal experiences do influence and are traceable in his/her creative works, they cannot account for the work of art itself. To put it another way, those claiming to know of God know of Him through the universe that He created, and not vice versa.

The autobiographical magnitude and scope of Tusquets' tetralogy is described accurately by the title of James Goodwin's book entitled *Autobiography: The Self Made Text*. Goodwin argues that "genre, like other forms of culture, is subject to social, and ultimately historical, permutation and recombination. Thus, as the terms self, life, and writing shift and develop in meaning, the genre autobiography enlarges its boundaries and characteristics" (16). Since autobiography is such a heterogeneous genre, Goodwin proposes that "a more inclusive ground for understanding the genre is to consider the components to the combinative word *auto/bio/graphy*. The combining stem *auto* means self, self-acting, or self-caused. *Bio* derives from the root meaning in Greek: 'mode of living' or, simply, 'life.' *Graphy* is another combining form; in English this is derived from Greek, with the root meaning 'to write.' By definition then, autobiography brings into direct association self, life, and writing, with each component in dynamic, reflexive relationship to the other two" (3). Goodwin reminds us that although "one long tradition within the genre is historical in function," the fact is that the root definition "does not require that *personal history* provide the shaping form for the interrelationship between self, life, and writing" (3, Goodwin's italics). As is the case with the New Novels, Tusquets' "autobiographical" novelistic tetralogy is, to say the least, innovative: it vacillates between fictional autobiography and autobiographical fiction, between discursive subjectivity and narrative objectivity, identified with both while never completely identifying itself with the one or the other. The author's life experiences are not the goal of the literary enterprise; rather, they are some among the many ingredients with which Tusquets transforms her unique Self engaged in a never-ending process of becoming into a creative writing project. The finished (circular) product is a fictional rendition of the real-life, lifelong process of becoming one's true Self via the creative process.

Whether of conscious design, of unconscious inspiration, or a combination of the two, the end of Tusquets' literary quest constitutes an *unus mundus*—wholeness of being of the female Self and the ontological wholeness of the work of art. "Wholeness" possesses a multitude of meanings: in sound health; uninjured; intact; entirety; totality; a thing complete in itself; a complete organization of integrated parts; a unity; a system. All of these definitions are applicable to the synchronously evolving process(es) of psychic and artistic integration which constitutes the theme of Esther Tusquets' four novels. The two developmental processes ultimately become indistinguishable from each other when each one realizes its autonomous wholeness and the two merge into a single act of psycho-literary completion. Esther Tusquets' novelistic tetralogy forms a cosmogony, a self-contained created world, which is the result of the heightened consciousness of selfhood that is acquired indiscriminately by author, narrators, and female protagonists, throughout the process of creation of the four novels.

Esther Tusquets' four novels form a squared circle because they constitute an exclusive four-cornered, circularly structured, fictional universe. Like both the psyche of its creator and the physical universe that we inhabit, the tetralogy is an *unus mundus*—the unity of all existence—comprised of the synthesized integration of dichotomously opposed elements. It was created following the same principles by which the *Book of Genesis* tells us that God created His work of art:

> In the beginning God created the heaven and the earth. Now the earth was unformed and void, and darkness was upon the face of the deep; and the spirit of God hovered over the face of the waters. And God said: 'Let there be light.' And there was light. And God saw the light, that it was good; and God divided the light from the darkness. And God called the light Day, and the darkness He called Night. And there was evening and there was morning, one day.

Of particular relevance to Tusquets' tetralogy is that the concept of "one day" is not considered to be the sum total of "day" and "night," but instead is derived from the co-presence of "morning" and "evening," both of which are integrated blends of the extreme contrasts of "day" and "night." "Morning" and "evening," occur at identically distinct hours of the day (i.e., 7:00 am versus 7:00 pm, for example), and also share an identically distinct appearance just before the sun emerges on the horizon (in the east) and just after it sinks into the horizon (in the west). In this sense, "morning" and "evening" transcend the mutual exclusivity suggested by "day" and "night."

The creative development of Tusquets' tetralogy evolves in a manner similar to the creation of the universe according to the *Old Testament*: the differentiation of polar opposites followed by their convergence and transcendence to a higher synthetic form. We'll use the first novel to illustrate the *modus operandi* applicable to each of the four novels—and to the intertextual dynamics of the tetralogy as a whole—although it should be remembered that each novel depicts a different phase of the individuation process. It also should be mentioned that the chronology of the publication of the four novels does not correspond with the age chronology of the four female protagonists. As we already know, the anonymous protagonist in the first novel is fifty-years-old as is Elena in the fourth novel, while the Elia appearing in the second and third novels is thirty-something in the former and forty-something in the latter.

The theme of female psychological development in *El mismo mar...* is at once highly individualized and generically universal. This is explained by the fact that it structurally begins and ends the tetralogy, a dual role shared by the fourth novel, *Para no volver*. The anonymous narrator-protagonist appears in the opening pages of the novel in a state of undifferentiated oneness as her physical wandering through the home of her now distant childhood awaken repressed contents of her personal unconscious. As the novel progresses, her psyche becomes increasingly differentiated as more and more contents of her personal unconscious are exhumed and filtered through consciousness (mother versus daughter; wife versus lover; heterosexuality versus homosexuality; fantasy versus reality). In particular, her physical maturity as a middle-aged woman is contrasted to her emotional immaturity. In the final tale told to Clara, her seventeen-year-old interlocutor and lover, we learn that her one and only true love, Jorge, had committed suicide when she was but seventeen years old. As a result of her repression of this traumatic event, coupled with a series of unresolved mother/ daughter issues between herself and her mother, and between herself and her daughter, Guiomar, (the latter obviously resulting from the former) and, at best, an ambivalent relationship with her emotionally distant father, she had remained stuck in adolescence throughout her adult life. Her erotic/maternal relationship with Clara enables her to merge and transcend all of these diametric opposites at war within her psyche, culminating in her becoming a significant link (as is each and every woman) on an uninterrupted chain of universal female presence and continuity. The four generations represented by Guiomar, her mother (the protagonist), her grandmother (the protagonist's mother), and her great-grandmother (the protagonist's grandmother) are modified at the end of the novel to include Clara upon the death of the protagonist's grandmother. We do not deem it to be a mere coincidence that Clara assumes greater significance in the protagonist's life at that time; it is as though Clara were replacing the grandmother as a symbol of the birth of a new generation to replace a disappearing one. As will be discussed at the appropriate time, Clara comes to symbolize the reawakening of the seventeen-year-old adolescent who had died spiritually and emotionally within the narrator/protagonist as a result of Jorge's abandonment of her through the taking of his own life. During their month-long lesbian affair, Clara replaces Guiomar in the role of the protagonist's daughter, thereby affording the middle-aged woman an opportunity to experience a type of mother/daughter bonding and sharing unknown to her either as a mother or as a daughter. Her final reconciliation with her husband and abandonment of Clara so that the young adult may move on with her life in a manner that will afford her continued psychological growth and well-being, comes to symbolize the rebirth of the fifty-year-old woman of whom Clara became an integrated part. The protagonist's conscious confrontation with her previously repressed personal unconscious led her to access some of the most important universal archetypes of the female unconscious according to Jung and his theory of individuation: the mother archetype, the shadow archetype, the *animus* archetype (the *anima* archetype in males), and the archetype of the self.

Since the number four symbolically connotes totality or wholeness within the physical (the four corners of the earth, the four directions in space, the four seasons, the four elements, etc.) and psychological (the four functions of consciousness, identified by Jung as thinking, feeling, sensation, and intuition) realms, the narrator/protagonist symbolically becomes an integral part not only of all female generations within her own personal family, but also with all of womankind. She simultaneously has discovered her own individuality and universality. She becomes a whole woman unto herself and within the universe, having physically and psychologically transcended the previously antagonistic conflict of opposites presented in *El mismo mar...* and elaborated upon more extensively throughout the remainder of the tetralogy.

The particular pattern of structural development encompassed by the four novels indicates that it serves as an object onto which unconscious individual and collective contents of its creator's psyche are projected. As those projections come to be recognized as such by the fictional female protagonists, who themselves are projections of the author, they are withdrawn and incorporated into her individual and the universal female consciousness, widening the horizon of both. Thus there exists a fluid reciprocity between the psyche of Esther Tusquets and her tetralogy; the former constitutes the structured contents of the latter while the latter serves as a playing field onto which unconscious projections emanating from the former are unleashed. After completing the fourth novel, *Para no volver*, at the close of which all opposites have been united, we are left at the threshold of the dawn of creation of the first and, simultaneously, of the whole: *El mismo mar de todos los veranos*. Ultimately, a fully integrated cosmic order—a miscrocosmic *unus mundus*—is perceived by means of the self-contained circularity of both the work of art and the psyche of its demiurge, and the symbolic relevance of the same. As Erich Neumann eloquently explains,

Circle, sphere and round are all aspects of the Self-contained, which is without beginning and end; in its pre-worldy perfection it is prior to any process, eternal, for in its roundness there is no before and no after, no time; and there is no above and no below, no space. All this can only come with the coming of light, of consciousness, which is not yet present; now all is under sway of the unmanifest godhead, whose symbol is therefore the circle. (8)

The round is the egg, the philosophical World Egg, the nucleus of the beginning, and the germ from which, as humanity teaches us everywhere, the world arises. It is also the perfect state in which the opposites are united—the perfect beginning because the opposites have not yet flown apart and the world has not yet begun, the perfect end because in it the opposites have come together again in a synthesis and the world is once more at rest. (8)

It is the synchronicity of Esther Tusquets' psychic and literary creation of an *unus mundus*—for which the novelistic tetralogy is a symbol—that constitutes the subject matter of the present study.

II. Analysis

1. *El mismo mar de todos los veranos*: One as the Beginning and the End

> There was a time when to be a woman was to be directly in the image of the Divine. There was a time when God was a Woman and Her spaciousness filled the vision and touched the hearts of every man, woman, and child who worshipped Her. She was called Goddess, Lady, Mother of All. Her manifestations were many: Huntress and Mistress of Animals, Lady of the Plants, Queen of Heaven and Earth, Creator, Sustainer, and Destroyer. It was She who created life and nourished it and She who deprived it and took it away. All things were subject to the Great Mother who was the origin and resource of every living thing and of the inanimate world as well.
> CARLSON, *In Her Image: The Unhealed Daughter's Search for Her Mother* 74-75

THE PLOT OF *EL MISMO MAR de todos los veranos* cloaks a symbolic journey undertaken by a middle-aged woman toward psychic wholeness, or center of the personality, referred to in Jungian psychoanalytic theory as "individuation." As explained in the theoretical introduction, the symbol of the circle as described by Jung "is the premonition of the centre of personality, a kind of central point within the psyche, to which everything is related, by which everything is arranged, and which is itself a source of energy" (*Arquetypos...* 357). Marie-Louise von Franz reminds us that "one primordial image in particular has survived in scientific tradition for a greater length of time than most, one that has appeared as a visual image of God, of existence, of the cosmos, of space-time, and of the particle: the image of a circle or of the 'sphere whose center is everywhere and whose circumference is nowhere.' Over the centuries this image has undergone many transformations, until finally it was understood more and more as the image of the endopsychic reality in the human being" (*Projection...* 57).

This first novel of the tetralogy is circular in structure insofar as its narrative is enclosed within J. M. Barrie's twice-quoted "...Y Wendy creció" (5, 229), which serves as both the preface to and closing words of Tusquets' own fiction. The immortal phrase from *Peter Pan* likewise summarizes the ending point of the preceding fourth novel, *Para no volver*, in relation to which *El mismo mar...* arguably could be considered a continuation. Within the context of *El mismo mar...*, Barrie's memorable quote is intended to signify the protagonist's eventual loss of innocence and rite of passage into the world of knowledge and responsibility. Like Wendy, Tusquets' quincuagenerian has relinquished her fantasy world of make-believe where men are heroic princes and women are helpless beauties who wait to be swept off their feet by a knight in shining armor and carried off to a faraway castle where they will live happily ever after. The narrator's marital reconciliation with Julio becomes equivalent to Wendy's transformation from the little girl who participated in Peter Pan's flying fantasies to the near obliteration of his memory:

> For a little longer, she tried for his sake not to have growing pains; and she felt she was untrue to him when she got a prize for general knowledge. But the years came and went without bringing the careless boy, and when they met again Wendy was a married woman, and Peter was no more to her that a little dust in the box in which she had kept her toys. Wendy was grown up. (Barrie 162)

When asked by her daughter why she no longer could fly, Wendy replied: "Because I am grown up, dearest. When people grow up they forget the way... because they are no longer gay and innocent and heartless. It is only the gay and innocent and heartless who can fly" (164). As will become clear throughout our analysis of the symbolic meaning of the relationship between the middle-aged woman and her adolescent lover, Clara, the abandonment of the young girl by the elder woman is analogous to Wendy's relinquishment of flying.

On a more subtle social level, Barrie's phrase might be interpreted as an effort to rebuke the subservient, complacent role traditionally assigned to women, in particular to Spanish women during the Franco years when an autocratic theocracy constituted the formative building blocks of the female personality, including the author's, who in turn has projected them onto her fictional protagonists'. As Linda Gould Levine points out, *Peter Pan*, in the company of Homer and Shakespeare, are the favorite readings of the adolescent Clara. The critic comments that "despite the fact that this preference once again points to the importance and weight of a male literary tradition indicative of Tusquets' own reading patterns, Clara is not trapped in by her readings or fused with them. Neither Ophelia crazed nor Desdemona killed, she instead emerges as a strange combination of Penelope—weaving, yes, her own tale—and Wendy, intent on leaving behind a Never-Never Land of fixed roles and dreams" ("Reading..." 206). Since it is our contention that Clara incarnates an undiscovered part of the middle-aged female Self who is the autobiographical narrator of the work, we maintain that the phrase anticipates and reverberates female development as its central theme, made possible by Clara and all that she symbolizes for the protagonist. When all is said and done in the novel, each woman completes the other and makes it possible for her to cross the bridge leading to the next stage of life. Both women become One Woman and All Women.

The anonymous protagonist of Tusquets' first novel—a highly unique individual and at the same time the universal female archetype—is spurred into introspection and retrospective self-analysis by a profound sense of solitude, physical as well as emotional, as she confronts her disappointment and disillusionment with the most significant people in her life: her husband, mother, daughter and, perhaps most significantly in terms of her thwarted psychological development, her fiancé, Jorge, who had committed suicide when she was but seventeen years old. Equally disturbing is her sense of disconnectedness from the physical world, coupled with an acute awareness of her own inner fragmentation. She feels lost, abandoned, scattered, useless, unable to find a center of gravity within herself from which to derive inner strength and peace as she confronts the difficulties inherent in leaving behind one stage of life and entering into another that is frightfully unknown. Hence, of personal as well as universal implications is the character's passage from the first half of life—dominated by the acquiescence and adaptation of the ego to the external demands imposed by cultural and social norms—to the second half of life during which, according to Jung, the individual typically abandons concern with the outer world and turns inward to attend to the messages emanating from the unconscious.

For women, passage from the second quarter of life to the third corresponds to the onset of menopause, which typically takes place between the ages of forty-five and fifty. This is precisely the age of our autobiographical narrator and protagonist. Therefore, it is reasonable to assume that, along with her other psychological problems, she is preoccupied with the prospect of losing her female reproductive function and perhaps even is suffering from the physical discomforts often associated with menopause. As Geraldine Cleary Nichols justifiably affirms, the twenty-eight day reproductive cycle associated with catamenia—which she either is in the process, or on the verge, of losing—endows the numerous textual references to numbers hovering around twenty-eight with special significance: "28 pages of introduction, 27 of conclusion" ("The Prison House..." 367), not to mention the brevity of the protagonist's affair with Clara, "veinticinco días, veintiséis, veintisiete a lo sumo" (226). No longer capable of physical fertility, reproduction and birth, it would then appear as though the twenty-eight day temporal enclosure of *El mismo mar...*, should stand as a symbol of creative fertility, reproduction and birth. As we hope to demonstrate throughout our analysis of the first published novel of the tetralogy, the very existence of Esther Tusquets' novelistic *corpus* (the artistic production of each individual novel as well as of the integrative wholeness of the tetralogy) to a great extent is attributable to the incorporation of the *animus* function into female consciousness in the previous fourth novel, *Para no volver*. Recalling that the natural function of the *animus* in a female (and of the *anima* in a male) is to occupy a mediating role between individual consciousness and the collective unconscious, it should come as no surprise that the fourth novel opens the innermost door of the female psyche, wherein dwell the universal archetypes populating the first novel and the projection-making psyche that it engulfs.

In a 229-page novel containing a 28-page introduction and a 27-page conclusion, the main body occupies just under 180 pages (the number of degrees of a triangle and one half of the number of degrees of a circle), also a highly significant number for Jung, who compares the four stages of human life to the 180-degree movement of the sun: "The one hundred and eighty degrees of the arc of life are divisible into four parts. The first quarter, lying to the east, is childhood" (*Aspects of the Masculine* 36). Using the metaphor of the sun's daily journey, Jung describes the initiation, or passage, from youth to mid-life as the ascent from bright consciousness to the descent into the dark unconscious, not for the purpose of substituting one for the other, but rather, for the purpose of integrating the two so that a higher form of consciousness may be achieved. It is, therefore, highly symbolic that *El mismo mar...* begin with just such a descent from the sunny realm of bright consciousness to the dark, profound depths of the unconscious. Entrance into the middle stage of life thus corresponds to the beginning of "life's (the sun's) decline," (*Aspects of the Masculine* 32), during which "an inexorable inner process enforces the contradiction of life. For a young person it is almost a sin, or at least a danger, to be too preoccupied with himself; but for the ageing person it is a duty and a necessity to devote serious attention to himself. After having lavished its light upon the world, the sun withdraws its rays in order to illuminate itself" (*Aspects of the Masculine* 33). The deeper one explores and brings to conscious light contents of the personal and collective unconscious—particularly by means of the withdrawal of projections—the higher will be the resulting state of consciousness and the more one will experience the integrative wholeness of the uniquely individual Self that one truly is. Returning to Jung's metaphor of the sun, from the darkest night the sun rises anew each day seemingly more radiant and full than ever before. Such are the lavish rewards of the arduous task of individuation.

The opening sentence of the novel, "Cruzo la puerta de hierro y cristal, pesada, chirriante, y me sumerjo en una atmósfera contradictoriamente más pura—menos luz, menos ruidos, menos sol" (7), suggests a symbolic passage from one realm of existence into another, as well as the initial stages in the search for the lost Mother and, ultimately, the completion of the female Self. The reader is not told this explicitly; (s)he intuits, senses, feels in an unmistakable way that this narrating consciousness is passing to a lesser known region of being: from the conscious world to inner solitude ("Cruzo la puerta"); from light to darkness ("menos luz," "menos sol"); from height to depth ("me sumerjo"). From the very first sentence of the novel, the author establishes a meaningful connection between "descending" and the sea, both of which, united by the concept of profundity, symbolize the unconscious. Like the feminine archetype of the Great Mother who is both the giver and taker of life, the sea likewise symbolizes the birth/death dualism since it is both the origin of life and the place where all life returns to die.

As we read on, the woman's return to the abandoned residence of her childhood in "mi ciudad sin primavera" assumes the qualities of a symbolic return to the maternal womb: "como si... me hubiera refugiado en el frescor de piedra de una iglesia muy vieja, donde huele remotamente a humedad y a frío, el frío de un invierno no ahuyentado todavía aquí por el bochorno del verano... Me gusta la penumbra y el silencio" (7). The tranquil darkness, accompanied by the musty, damp, humid feel and smell of the timeless space in which she has taken refuge, intimate a symbolic return to the pre-nascent, pre-conscious state of existence. This middle-aged woman physically has abandoned the suffocating summer heat of her "ciudad sin primavera" (Barcelona) and has entered into a cold, dark, wet, dreary winter-like space. Symbolically, she (her psyche) has embarked upon a circular regression from the autumn (not coincidentally the only one of the four seasons not mentioned in the first sentence of the novel) of her life to its embryonic, vernal incipience, where she seeks to establish the mother-daughter connection that never took place in her early years of development. In her illuminating article, "A Case of Pre-Œipal and Narrative Fixation: *El mismo mar de todos los veranos*," Mirella Servodidio picks up the theme of discovery of the matrilineal roots originally introduced by Elizabeth Ordóñez, and takes it one step further in postulating that "the originating difficulties of this relationship are grounded in a pre-

Œdipal phase bereft of the symbiotic bonding and the unclouded specularity that psychoanalytical theoreticians view as the determinants of female identity" (158).

Considered not only from the matrilineal perspective, but likewise from a universally feminine need to bring an unbalanced culture back to its harmonious origins, the feminine collective unconscious of the narrator-protagonist serves as a conduit by means of which the long lost feminine universal principle is exhumed so that it might assume its rightful complementary role with and within masculine-orientated patriarchal society. *El mismo mar...* may best be understood as a Jungian overture both anticipating and enclosing the four stages of the individuation process to be elaborated upon throughout the remainder of the tetralogy: 1) the detachment of the protagonist from her persona in an attempt to harmonize her inner and outer life, 2) the confrontation of the ego with its shadow, that dark, painful threshold that must be crossed as she ventures deeper and deeper toward the collective unconscious, 3) the dissolution of the character's persona and of her personal unconscious, which gives way to the ultimate crossing of the threshold between consciousness and the collective unconscious in the form of the contra-sexual archetype (here the *animus*),[1] leading ultimately to 4) the protagonist's experiencing of the images of the collective unconscious, primarily and most significantly in the form of the Great Mother, the latter being a symbol of the former by virtue of encompassing an experience that is shared by all living things.

When we say that *El mismo mar...* begins where *Para no volver* left off, we primarily are referring to the "threshold" that Elena customarily crosses from the psychiatrist's outer waiting room to the inner sanctuary where psychoanalytic treatment takes place. As we know, however, Elena opts not to take those steps following her psychological epiphany during the party honoring her husband's return from the United States; hence, the sanctuary turns out to be not the psychoanalyst's office but, rather, the middle-aged woman's return to her childhood residence—the opening of the opening novel of the tetralogy. We wish to postulate the theory that this return to the origins of her personhood following Elena's discovery and acceptance of her *animus*

---

[1] Jung claims that "the natural function of the *animus* (as well as of the *anima*) is to remain in (their) place between individual consciousness and the collective unconscious; exactly as the persona as a sort of stratum between ego consciousness and the objects of the external world. The *animus* and the *anima* should function as a bridge, or a door, leading to the images of the collective unconscious, as the persona should be a sort of bridge into the world" (*The Essential Jung* 415).

in the previous fourth novel, symbolizes the crossing of the threshold from consciousness to the images of the unconscious, for which the *animus* may be understood as the key that unlocks the door. In this sense, *Para no volver* is proleptic in relation to *El mismo mar*... Furthermore, immediately upon entering the house, a bronze statue of Mercury—the ultimate symbol of the *animus*—beckons the narrator/protagonist to proceed with her descent into darkness: "Está sentado en un reposo sin desmayos, una mano extendida en gesto amistoso, baja y extendida con la palma hacia arriba, en un gesto tranquilizador, como el que utilizamos ante un perro desconocido que no puede estar seguro de nuestras intenciones, un gesto de aproximación que preludia casi la caricia" (7-8). Among the richest of all symbols along with the ocean, both of which are central symbols of the first novel, Mercurius shares many of the same characteristics as the sea. Just as the ocean is the "mediator" between heaven and earth, Mercury's "Greek name of Hermes signifies 'interpreter' or 'mediator'" (Cirlot 198). And because of his fecundatory capabilities, he again is likened to the great bodies of water: "He epitomizes the power of the spoken word—the emblem of the word—and for the Gnostics he was the *logos spermatikos* scattered about the universe, an idea which was taken up by the alchemists who equated Mercury with related concepts of fluency and transmutation.[2] At the same time he was seen as god of roads (that is, of potentialities)" (Cirlot 198). Like the sea, Mercury shares a close affinity with the sun by virtue of being the planet closest to it.[3] As a metal, Mercury "symbolizes the unconscious because of its fluid and dynamic character; it is essentially *duplex* for, in one way, it is an inferior being, a devil or monster, but

---

[2] Of the ocean, Cirlot affirms that, apart from its grandeur, its two most essential traits are "its ceaseless movement" (fluency) and the "formlessness of its waters" (transmutation), in that water readily lends itself to being converted into different substances or conditions since it has no form of its own" (230).

[3] We recall that Tusquets was born on August 30, under the sign of Virgo, which is ruled by Mercury and is said to be the sign under which the deities were born: "Virgo is the sign of the virgin (its name is Latin for virgin): it is a mutable, feminine, earth symbol and is ruled by Mercury. In Greek mythology, Astræa, the goddess of innocence and justice, was transformed into this constellation. It could also represent fertility goddesses such as Demeter, and it was said that deities were born under this sign. It is a sign of discrimination, for the virgin considers no man good enough for her. Because Virgo is governed by Mercury, it can symbolize the hermaphrodite. Traditionally introverted, those born under the sixth sign of the zodiac (between August 24 and September 23) are considered analytical, precise, orderly and moderate but can also be overcritical, pedantic and nervous" (Gibson 72).

in another sense it is the 'philosophers' child" (Cirlot 198, Cirlot's italics).[4] As in the case of all liquids due to their unlimited capacity for transformation, Mercurius "came to be symbolic of the essential aim of the alchemist to transmute matter (and spirit) from the inferior to the superior, from the transitory to the stable" (Cirlot 198).

Mercury greets the protagonist/narrator as a projection of the *animus* component of her compensatory shadow; that is, as "the sum of all the qualities conforming to our sex that were neglected or rejected while the ego was being built up" (Jacobi, *The Way...* 38) during the first half of life. As we recall, Jung and his associates understood projection as "an unconscious, that is, unperceived and unintentional, transfer of subjective psychic elements onto an outer object" (Franz, *Projection...* 3). As a projection of the unconscious *animus* aspect of the shadow, the bronze statue represents that which gives every appearance of being contradictory, but is in fact compensatory, to the character's ego. In a compensatory relationship to an apathetic, unmotivated, insecure woman whose sense of self-worth is nil and who has spent the first half of her life waiting for someone—anyone—to fulfill her and make her happy, the rich, multiple positive and negative aspects of Mercury symbolize all of the character's unawakened (the lifeless quality of a statue) potentialities. In other words, Mercury symbolizes all that the character is not in her conscious life, but has the capability of being if the path toward individuation remains unobstructed. Jung sums up the complexity of Mercury in the following way: (1) Mercurius consists of all conceivable opposites. He is thus quite obviously a duality, but is named a unity in spite of the fact that his innumerable inner contradictions can dramatically fly apart into an equal number of disparate and apparently independent figures. (2) He is both material and spiritual. (3) He is the process by which the lower and material is transformed into the higher and spiritual, and vice versa. (4) He is the devil, a redeeming psychopomp, an evasive trickster, and God's reflection in physical nature. (5) He is also the reflection of a mystical experience of the artifex that coincides with the *opus alchymicum*. (6) As such, he represents on the one hand the Self and on the other the individuation process and, because of the limitless number of his names, also the collective unconscious" (*Aspects of the Masculine* 160).

---

[4] Like Mercury, the ocean symbolizes germinant (positive) as well as destructive (negative) potentialities: "The ocean, then, denotes an ambivalent situation." And while it is the source of all life, "the power of salt water to destroy the higher forms of land-life means that it is also a symbol of sterility, so confirming the ambivalent nature of the ocean—its contradictory dynamism" (Cirlot 230).

Mercury thus is a psychic projection of the protagonist's undiscoverred inner man. As a symbol, he embodies all of the masculine traits which indeed could have pulled her out of the psychological stagnation that qualified the first half of her life. However, because these masculine traits would have been in such severe conflict with the demands of her family and social class, consciousness did not permit them to surface and wreak inevitable havoc upon her life. While deeming the confrontation between the ego and *anima* in a man, or *animus* in a woman, as the most important stage in that it is the one from which the greatest psychic benefits may be reaped in and along the journey toward individuation, Jung admonishes man and woman alike about the ensuing difficulties. Referring specifically to the female ego that seeks to come to terms with its *animus*, Jung forewarns that "the conscious attention a woman has to give to her *animus* problem takes much time and involves a lot of suffering." But if she somehow can turn the stranglehold that the unconscious *animus* forces have on her into the invaluable conscious tools for living that they have the potential of becoming, she will possess for life an "inner companion who endows her with the masculine qualities of initiative, courage, objectivity, and spiritual wisdom" (*Man and His Symbols* 194).

Therefore, as a symbol of androgyny and, for a woman, of the complex *animus* portion of the her shadow, Mercurius appears in the opening sentences of the novel is a projection "partly of repressed, partly of unlived psychic features which, for moral, social, educational, or other reasons, were from the outset excluded from consciousness and from active participation in life and were therefore repressed or split off" (Jacobi, *The Way*... 38). His alluring, beckoning posture, combined with his known attributes as a symbol, exhibit the four stages of the development of the *animus* as described by Jung. In the first stage of the female ego's readiness to wrestle with the reality of her sexually binary nature, the *animus* appears "as a personification of mere physical power—for instance, as an athletic champion or 'muscle man'" (*Man and His Symbols* 194). The first thing that the protagonist/narrator does when she reaches the statue is to confirm its physical masculinity: "Le miro curiosa—realmente curiosa—entre las piernas, y compruebo con un suspiro de alivio—realmente todavía hoy con un suspiro de alivio—que todo sigue en orden y que el sexo campea desnudo entre las largas piernas" (8). In the following phase, the *animus* "possesses initiative and the capacity for planned action" (*Man and His Symbols* 194) which is suggested by the extended hand with which the statue summons the visitor to continue with the initiative to venture into the realm of her unconscious that she has taken by willfully abandoning the outside world and entering the house where he awaited her. Recalling that Mercury, among his countless attributes is, first and foremost, "the emblem of the word" (Cirlot 198), in the third stage of the *animus* making its appearance and seeking incorporation into female consciousness, "the *animus* becomes the 'word,' often appearing as a professor or clergyman" (*Man and His Symbols* 194). This juncture attests to the previously discussed parallel between the role of the fictional character with regard to the plot of *El mismo mar...* and the mechanics of creation of the same by its author. Just as the beginning of the third stage of life is identified with the transitional period from the first half of life to the second—during which the psyche not only becomes aware of the contents of the unconscious but must find a way to synthesize its contents into consciousness in a meaningful, productive way—the third stage of development of the contra-sexual male archetype establishes the two-tier metaphoric and symbolic structure of *El mismo mar...* alluded to earlier. In the same way that the plot is a metaphor via symbolic representation of the confrontation between, and integration of, the conscious with the unconscious within the psyche of the fictional middle-aged character, the symbolically rendered individuation process undergone by the fictional narrator/protagonist is but a metaphor for literary creationism: the artistic struggle to integrate indivisibly form and content into a meaningful, coherent artistic whole through the medium of the written word. This metaphoric bifurcation is reinforced later on in the novel when the protagonist/narrator discloses the fact that she is a professor of literature, a word of authority (fictional character) on the published words of literary artists (like her creator, Esther Tusquets). And finally, as Jung tells us, in the fourth stage of the manifestation of the *animus* within the female psyche, it "is the incarnation of *meaning*. On this highest level he becomes (like the *anima*) a mediator of the religious experience whereby life acquires new meaning. He gives the woman spiritual firmness, an invisible inner support that compensates for her outer softness. The *animus* in his most developed form sometimes connects the woman's mind with the spiritual evolution of her age, and can thereby make her even more receptive than a man to new creative ideas" (*Man and His Symbols* 194-95, Jung's italics). For the fictional narrator/protagonist of *El mismo mar...*, the projection of Mercurius within a context symbolizing the unconscious (the house) anticipates the achievement of the long-awaited psychological growth and maturity echoed by the closing words of the novel: "...Y Wendy creció" (229). For our author born under the zodiacal sign of Virgo which is governed by Mercury, it signifies the capacity to create *El mismo mar de todos los veranos*. Like Mercury, this sixth sign of the zodiac "is symbolic of hermaphroditism, or that state which is characterized by dual—positive and negative—forces... In mythology and in religions generally, this symbol is always associated with the birth of a god or a demigod, as the supreme expression of the dynamic consciousness" (Cirlot 341).

In *El mismo mar...*, wholeness is shown to be the result of the integration and transcendence of opposing, yet complementary principles, for which the bronze statue of Mercurius functions as a symbolic projection emanating from the unconscious psyche of the autobiographical narrator. Recalling that the contra-sexual archetype opens the door to the images of the collective unconscious, Tusquets has set the stage for the deeper descent into the female unconscious which will be dramatized by the middle-aged woman and the adolescent Clara in the form of the symbolic realization of the mother/daughter (Great Mother/maiden) reconnection. It is to this end that the author appropriates the Demeter/Kore[5] myth that is personified by the protagonist and Clara, respectively. Ordóñez draws our attention to the paradoxical nature of the protagonist's mother who, while initially appearing "an inhabitant of a green world of matriarchal erotic freedom, an adherent of a playful phallic cult" ("A Quest..." 39), subsequently is revealed to be a paradox: "Her matrilineal aspects are immediately counterpoised to her cold, forbidding, and distant patriarchal counteraspects" (39), whereby the autobiographical narrator-protagonist disdainfully refers to her mother as "la diosa de la luz, Atenea tonante" (26), culminating in her being thought to incarnate "la diosa que aniquila a su paso los cultos de Démeter, que ignora para siempre y desde siempre los secretos festejos dionisíacos" (34). We concur with Ordóñez that the protagonist's mother "parallels the collective evolution in western culture as she annihilates the cult of Demeter of the old matriarchy, is unaware of Dionysian religion and the agon between the Demetrian matriarchal principle and the male-phallic principle, and comes to personify the final triumph of the Apollonian age when the divinity of the mother gives way to that of the father, and the presiding goddess becomes Athens" ("A Quest..." 40).

Throughout the course of the novel, the protagonist will lure her student and young lover, Clara, into a relationship designed to heal the emotional scars of childhood on a personal level, while at the same time redressing the disequilibrium of the phallocentric, patriarchal universe from which the feminine principle has been ostracized. Their reenactment of the Demeter/Kore myth announces the universal feminine orientation of *El mismo mar...*, as it is one of the relatively few myths that elucidates the complex nature of the feminine principle to almost the complete exclusion of the masculine: "Demeter-Kore exists on the plane of feminine experience, which is alien to man and shuts him out. In fact, the psychology of the Demeter cult bears all the features of a matriarchal order of society, where the man is an indispensable but

---

[5] Kore is also known as Persephone in Greek and Roman mythology.

on the whole disturbing factor" (Jung, *Archetypes*... 203). The myth of Demeter, goddess of harvest and fertility, and Kore, daughter of Demeter and Zeus, goddess of fertility and queen of the underworld, celebrates not only the feminine principle of *eros* as the inseparable bond between mother and daughter, but also the intimate connection that exists between the feminine principle and the cosmos. After being abducted by Pluto, god of the underworld, and held captive in Hades, Demeter makes an emotional supplication to Zeus to return their daughter to her. He agrees, but with one stipulation: Kore must not have eaten anything while in the underworld. Because she has eaten a few pomegranate seeds, her return to the upper regions of the earth is limited to eight months out of the year. As an expression of revenge and sadness over the mother/daughter separation during one third of every year, Demeter forsakes the earth, thereby bringing about the cold barrenness of winter. Upon her daughter's yearly return to her, Demeter and the cosmic order are reborn with the advent of spring.

The Demeter/Kore myth is celebrated in the Eleusinian Mysteries as the uniting of the female generations whereby the mother experiences rejuvenation in the personality of the daughter and the daughter in the personality of the mother. As we will see, the profound physical and emotional love shared by the aging protagonist and the adolescent Clara, depicts an image of totality resulting from the union of opposites (maturity/youth; experience/innocence; realism/idealism, etc.); their relationship is symbiotic insofar as each half of the whole discloses and completes the other half, both of which await crossing the threshold of the next stage of life. The myth also has the effect of taking the individual out of isolation and of manifesting the rightful place of the feminine within the cosmic order, connecting woman equally to death (winter) and to rebirth (spring). Jung explains the spatial and temporal expansion of the Demeter/Kore myth in the following manner:

> Demeter and Kore, mother and daughter, extend the feminine consciousness both upwards and downwards. They add an 'older and younger,' 'stronger and weaker,' dimension to it and widen out the narrowly limited conscious mind bound in space and time, giving it intimations of a greater and more comprehensive personality which has a share in the eternal course of things. (*Archetypes* 188)

Symbolizing not only the psychic, but also the physical foundation of human existence as well, the mother archetype constitutes the principle structural and thematic image of Tusquets' first published novel. In the chronologically first and fourth novels, identical incipient/ending points of the symbolic circle, the awakening of the collective unconscious takes distinct, although mutually-dependent forms. The end of *Para no volver*—the recognition, acceptance and integration of the *animus* (as Father Spirit, personified by the psychoanalyst and symbolizing the masculine principle of *logos*) archetype into female consciousness—makes possible the creation of the tetralogy that we have just, and/or are about to, read. The dawn of creation of the fictional cosmos, *El mismo mar de todos los veranos*, dramatizes the procreative power of the masculine "fertilization" (symbolized by the newly-activated *animus* at the close of the previous fourth novel) of the receptive female reproductive capability (as Great Mother, symbolizing the feminine principle of *eros*). As indistinguishable beginning and ending points of a circle, the two novels herald the symbolic marriage of principles which oppose one another while being at the same time the *conditio sine qua non* of all existence: the father, who symbolizes the active, creating principle, and the mother who symbolizes the receptive, nourishing one.

In *The Great Mother*, Erich Neumann identifies two bivalent characters of the Great Mother as goddess: the elementary character and the transformational character, both of which possess a benevolent and a terrible form (24-25). The positive elementary mother functions as a protective "container" that shields the child from potential danger. She has symbolic connections with the cave, house, temple, cradle, etc., and her relationship to her child is defined by connectedness (Carlson 94). For women who did not experience enough of this maternal connection, such as Tusquets' female protagonists, "subsequent experiences of this with other women as lovers, friends, mentors, therapists, or even women in dreams can be extremely healing and come with the fullness of the archetype" (Carlson 95). As we will explain shortly, this is the perspective from which we are meant to interpret the increased consciousness and overall positive psychological growth that takes place in the middle-aged protagonist of *El mismo mar...* as a result of her twenty-eight day relationship with Clara.

Conversely, the negative elementary mother is the devouring mother in the form of extreme possessiveness where the maternal "container" is constrictive and impedes the child's freedom to grow and discover his/her own individuality. Symbols connected with the negative aspect of the elementary mother "include the underworld, devouring animals, the coffin or grave as 'container' and the image of the vagina dentate" (Carlson 97). The human form of this goddess is experienced as "the binding mother who cannot allow her daughter to be different from herself, or support her desires for autonomy" (Carlson 97). The protagonist of *El mismo mar...* recalls on a number of occasions how disturbing it was to her mother that the two of them did not resemble each other in the least. Believing her mother to be a gorgeous goddess, the physiognomical dissimilarity produced an inferiority complex of such proportions that the autobiographical narrator came to refer to herself as the ugly duckling. Feeling abandoned and ignored not only by her husband, but by her mother, "la diosa" (22), and her daughter, a university professor living in the United States to whom she refers as "la doctora" (22), the "huerfanita envejecida" (16) admits that she wishes that her own daughter, Guiomar, looked and behaved more like her instead of like her mother: "y ya no hay niños, sólo esta Guiomar, tan distinta, tan lejana, tan legítima nieta de la elegante dama anglosajona, de la diosa viajera, que no ha interrumpido naturalmente su viaje" (34). It is also noteworthy to mention the sense of alienation that she feels with respect to these three most important people in her life: "para ninguna de las dos existo de verdad, al igual que tampoco he podido existir nunca para Julio" (29).

In her positive transformational aspect, "the Great Mother promotes development, emphasizes independence, and stimulates transformation in Her child and the universe that She governs. In this dimension, process and change are all and supplant the emphasis on bonding and sameness that is held by the elementary Mother" (Carlson 98). The negative transformational aspects, on the other hand, also promote growth and independence, but bring them about by negative means: "rejection, deprivation, attack, or abandonment. Such experiences can also challenge their recipients and stimulate new development, in addition to the hurt and damage they may inflict" (Carlson 100). We witness in the fifty-year-old protagonist of *El mismo mar...* an evolution from manifesting negative aspects of the elementary Great Mother with her own daughter, Guiomar, to demonstrating positive aspects of the transformational Great Mother in her handling of the relationship with Clara, who provides her with a second chance at motherhood.

Traces of the positive and negative aspects of both the elementary and transformational manifestations of the Great Mother can be found in our own human mothers. However, unlike the archetypal Great Mother who "carries in Her fullness the quaternity of Her aspects," the human mother generally carries parts of some of them, a factor which contributes to the distorted image, either positive or negative, that we have of this imperfect mortal, and the often unreasonable expectations that we place on her as a result. The child tends to confuse contents of the universal archetypal with his or her temporally and circumstantially bound mother who is incapable of performing the balancing act that appears so naturally in the archetype. When these expectations are not met by our mothers, the inner child feels hurt, rejected, disappointed and disconnected from his/her source of life, all of which may produce an angry, resentful, bitter inner child who unconsciously interferes with the adult individual's ability to forge healthy relationships. In the words of Dr. Kathie Carlson,

> The emotional thrust of the unhealed child is emotionally attuned to this need to balance, for usually what the unhealed child in us is searching most for is the mother we *didn't* have. Our task *vis-à-vis* this is twofold. On the one hand, we need to take the unhealed child's needs for compensatory experiences very seriously and recognize them as the basis of a spiritual quest for the wholeness of the Mother and the wholeness of ourselves. But we need also to bring to this the adult apprehension that the fullness of the Mother is beyond the capacity for one human being to manifest. Thus we must gently wean our inner children away from their fixations on our personal mothers and the demand that our mothers provide for all of our needs, and teach that wounded part of us to seek its healing in relationship with other women and in inner experience as well as with the personal mother. On the other hand, we must also help our wounded selves make sense of what we have already experienced and to penetrate it to the depths of its meaning where it too can be acknowledged as part of the Mother's truth and a contribution to our growth. (102-03)

Woman's handling of such obvious dichotomies points us in the direction of understanding perhaps the most daunting of all tasks entailed in the individuation process: the coming to terms with the paradoxical nature of the elements making up any totality, especially that of the human psyche. If the narrator and Clara make up two halves of an indivisible whole, that is, complete each other, then in each female psyche resides a countless number of sets of paired opposites. Similarly, in order to reap the benefits of psychological growth, a certain amount of pain and suffering must be endured. Each and every rite of passage through which we cross represents further progression along the individuation continuum. Each step along the way signals a new beginning, a re-awakening or re-birth of the Self, that must be preceded by a sacrifice of ego-consciousness. A symbolic death, with its concomitant suffering, is the price to be paid for greater self-knowledge (gleaned from the personal unconscious) and for assuming one's place in the cosmic order (derived from the collective unconscious). In symbolic terms, however, "death means not something final but rather a transitional stage, a transformation. This attitude to death has deep roots in the human psyche; that is why there are so many death and resurrection mysteries in mythology and religion, which all signify metamorphosis" (Birkhäuser-Oeri 38). Of the perilous voyage toward the collective unconscious, M. Esther Harding, writes the following:

In these depths are the dark, sinister, feminine beginnings, in a region ruled over, not by the bright *Logos* of intellect, but by the dark *Eros* of feeling. The *Eros* is a spiritual or psychological principle, or in the older term, it is a divinity... Submission to either principle in fact, implies that one is redeemed from a personal ego orientation and from the desire for personal power and gives one allegiance to that which is beyond the personal. (33-34)

Movement along the individuation continuum necessarily implies participation in a symbolic rite of initiation in which the demands of the ego are forsaken in the name of submission to the instinctual powers of the universal archetypes dwelling in the collective unconscious. Like the difficult labor that often precedes childbirth, psychological growth (rebirth) requires a period of intense suffering: "To find the limits or boundaries of one's own nature, and to come to know the impersonal principles which really rule in the depths of the psyche, necessitates exploring one's own capacities to their uttermost" (Harding 209-10). In the case of the protagonist, she must abandon her personally satisfying relationship with Clara and confront her marital difficulties with greater self-awareness, maturity and fortitude. Where the complementary younger half of the Self is concerned, individuation demands that she accept the relinquishment of the maternal nurturance and security with which the symbolic "Earth Mother" has provided her for nearly a month, and assume her rightful role in society as a mature, independent young adult. Specifically, Clara's bereavement of adolescent desire and passage into adulthood, symbolizes the liberation of the narrator/protagonist from the psychological stagnation brought about by her inability to suffer the loss of adolescent desire as a result of Jorge's suicide years earlier when she was exactly Clara's age. Freed from the grips of immature yearning, the middle-aged woman is prepared for passage from the first half of life to the second.

The sacrifice of the young maiden by the "Earth Mother" thus symbolizes the abandonment of childhood innocence, and acceptance of the need to move forward into the next phase of life. The dramatization of this rite of passage is enacted by the sexual awakening of the young, innocent girl as she is stimulated to the heights of erotic pleasure by the older, experienced mother figure:

> La tumbo de espaldas, la fuerzo a no moverse, la sujeto contra el suelo con mis dos manos, y mi boca empieza un recorrido lentísimo por la garganta fina, palpitante, donde agonizan los gemidos, la garganta de alguien que se está ahogando y que no quiere gritar—silencio, Clara, quieta, todavía es de

noche, tenemos todo el tiempo—, un recorrido lentísimo por los hombros redondos que no logran de cualquier modo contener el temblor, por los huesos que se le marcan delicados en el escote, por los pechos chiquitos, por los pezones pálidos, de pezón a pezón mi boca mordisqueante, hasta que crecen hacia mí erizados y locos... y mi mano va abriendo suavemente el estrecho camino entre su carne y mi carne, entre nuestros dos vientres confundidos, hasta llegar al húmedo pozo entre las piernas... y crece el vaivén de nuestros cuerpos enlazados y el roce de mi mano entre sus muslos, y el gemido de Clara es de pronto como el aullido de una loba blanca degollada o violada con las primeras luces del alba—pero no hay temblores locos esta vez, no hay gemidos entrecortados, por que el placer brota, seguro y sin histerias, de lo más hondo de nosotras y asciende lento en un oleaje magnífico de olas espumosas y largas—, y después Clara yace a mi lado, desmadejada como un muñeco de estopa, jadeante todavía, pero relajada al fin, recuperada finalmente su sombra o liberada para siempre de la caterva de los niños perdidos. (154-55)

The orgasm to which Clara is brought by her maternal lover, and from which she subsequently experiences release, hearkens the painfully pleasurable (or pleasurably painful) transition from virginity (innocence) to its loss (experience). We may now begin to appreciate how the theme of the search for identity is rooted in a female individual's search for a personal totality—symbolized by the interlocked, indistinguishable union of the two female bodies—, whose point of origin is the search for the lost mother and reconnection with her. Perhaps this explains why some sculptures of Demeter and Kore depict mother and daughter as mature, full-bodied women, virtually indistinguishable the one from the other except for the different symbols they carry in their hands (Carlson 94). *El mismo mar...* dramatizes this search for the female Self both as procreator in the literal physiological sense, and as literary demiurge in the metaphoric sense, to which the abundance of mother archetypes permeating the fiction unmistakably draws our attention. As Jung tells us, "the mother archetype appears under almost an infinite variety of aspects" (*Aspects of the Feminine* 109), nearly all of which make their appearance in *El mismo mar...*:

> First in importance are the personal mother and grandmother, stepmother and mother-in-law; then any woman with whom a relationship exists—for example, a nurse or governess or perhaps a remote ancestress. Then there are what might be termed mothers in a figurative sense. To this category belongs the goddess, and especially the Mother of God, the Virgin, and

Sophia. Mythology offers many variations of the mother archetype, as for instance the mother who reappears as the maiden in the myth of Demeter and Kore... Many things arousing devotion or feelings of awe, as for instance the Church, university, city or country, heaven, earth, the woods, the sea or any still waters, matter even, the underworld and the moon, can be mother-symbols... It can be attached to a rock, a cave, a tree, a spring a deep well, or to various vessels such as the baptismal font, or to vessel-shaped flowers like the rose or the lotus. Because of the protection it implies, the magic circle or *mandala* can be a form of mother archetype. (109-10)

In conjunction with the protagonist's obsession with her aloof, emotionally unapproachable, goddess-like mother, "la insolencia sin límites de la diosa rubia y riente" (11), her intimate mother-daughter relationship with Clara seems both to anticipate and be born out of the death of her grandmother. Shortly after the commencement of her affair with Clara, the narrator-protagonist loses the woman with whom she has most identified physically and emotionally throughout her life: her maternal grandmother. The three surviving matrilineal generations attend the funeral. It is highly symbolic that the protagonist appears with her mother standing to one side of her and her daughter to the other: "Asciendo por la colina entre mi madre y Guiomar" (140), as though to infer that she has become an integral link in the uninterrupted chain of female generations. Yet another relevant mother symbol is her childhood governess—not coincidentally named Sofía—with whom her father was having an affair of which her mother eventually learned, and for which the protagonist's surrogate mother was dismissed from the household. The narrator vividly recalls her father's cowardly betrayal of his mistress within the context of not wanting to commit the same act of treason—the abandonment of a lover and presumably one's own happiness—against Clara and herself: "No quiero correr el riesgo extremo de tener que destruirla finalmente como destruyó cobardemente mi padre aquella mañana con su silencio la mirada de Sofía, traicionándola a ella y perdiéndose a sí mismo para siempre" (172). Inasmuch as this childhood memory foreshadows the protagonist's abandonment of Clara at the end of the novel, at a symbolic level it is a necessary step in the dialectical individuation process; it is a symbolic death (antithesis) followed by rebirth (synthesis and transcendence). In the final pages of the novel, the narrator/protagonist is indistinguishably engulfed in present and past, adulthood and adolescence, motherhood and childhood, thereby underscoring the repetitive (circular), chronologically sequential chain of female generations. The narrator/protagonist and Clara are joined, separated, then re-integrated in a symbolic act of union and death (the narrator's/protagonist's termination of their sexual interlude), followed by a rebirth as she emerges at the close of the novel a "new," more fully integrated person as symbolized by the protagonist-Julio-Clara-emperor symbolic "marriage" (226), or *coniunctio* of opposites.

The initial environmental setting of the novel forms a generic coherence with the later presentation of Clara as a mermaid[6] or siren[7] "belonging to" the narrator-protagonist ("mi sirena"—pp. 66-7). Symbolizing the undifferentiated unconscious—the physical union of the middle-aged woman and the naïve adolescent who is but a part of her Self, symbolizes the fluid reciprocity that is achieved between consciousness and the unconscious within the female psyche. As Clara's body metaphorically is equated with a sea-cave, entrance into the cave, located at the mysterious (symbolized by the color blue) depths of the sea, signifies a symbolic return to the womb: "No siento ya dolor, ni oigo ningún ruido, porque he llegado al fondo mismo de los mares, y todo es aquí silencio, y todo es azul, y me adentro despacio, apartando las algas con cuidado, por la húmeda boca de la gruta" (139). In this embryonic state, she is a circle that occupies the center of the maternal womb, which in turn is the center of the female body, which is a microcosm of the macrocosmic Mother Earth from where all life begins, is nurtured and is sustained, and is perpetuated by the reproductive function of all subsequent female generations. Thus, she has returned to the beginning of her life, to the origin of her existence, from which she ultimately will re-discover the oneness and wholeness of her psychic being through sexual union with Clara, symbol of the Kore archetype. She will, in short, re-experience the integrated whole female self as a symbolic re-birth in the middle of her life. Hence, her personal, microcosmic quest for psychic wholeness assumes universal, macrocosmic proportions: one summer-like day in the month of May in the autumn of her life, the narrator/protagonist retreats to a winter-like space (symbolic of death) in order to recapture the springtime origin of her life (symbolic of a quest for rebirth).

---

[6] Clare Gibson defines the mermaid in the following manner: "A fantastic creature, half woman, half fish, the mermaid is the divinity of the sea symbolizing the unconscious (especially the feminine) aspect of the male psyche" (133).

[7] Of the siren, Gibson has the following to say: "The siren can assume two forms: a bird-woman (as in Greek mythology) or a fish-woman, sometimes with two tails. Both forms entice male passers-by to their deaths by singing songs of irresistible sweetness, as told in the story of the Lorelei of the Rhine. They symbolize the dangerous worldly temptation along the spiritual path of life" (136).

The protagonist's goal to be born again into another—into her true, unique Self[8]—is consistent with the intended purpose of rites of initiation. In philosophical terms, "initiation is equivalent to a basic change in existential condition; the novice emerges from his ordeal endowed with a totally different being from that which he possessed before his initiation; he has become *another*" (Beane 164, Beane's italics). Although the initiatory ordeals through which a youth must journey on his/her way toward becoming a responsible, respected adult member of the tribe or community tend to entail often brutal physical suffering, and therefore are quite different from the process of individuation viewed as an initiation or transition "ordeal" *of the psyche* from conflictive incompatibility between the conscious and the unconscious to a state of synergetic, integrated coexistence, they share some surprising similarities. First and foremost is the fact that both are symbolic representations of a rebirth. From the very beginnings of human culture, the initiation of adolescents includes a series of rites through which "the novice is first transformed into an embryo and then is reborn... The return to the womb is signified either by the neophyte's seclusion in a hut, or by his being symbolically swallowed up by a monster, or by his entering a sacred spot identified with the uterus of Mother Earth." This *regressus ad uterum* takes place in order that "the beneficiary shall be born into a new mode of being or be regenerated. From the structural point of view, the return to the womb corresponds to the reversion of the Universe to the 'chaotic' or embryonic state. The prenatal darkness corresponds to the Night before Creation and to the darkness of the initiation hut" (Beane 174-75). It is therefore not surprising that in a novel infused with color imagery and symbolism on practically every page,[9] the only reference to color that we

---

[8] Catherine Bellver refers to the protagonist's odyssey toward rebirth as a "quest myth": "The narrator in Esther Tusquets' first novel, *El mismo mar de todos los veranos*, seeks to be reborn through a lesbian relationship, which serves as a kind of quest myth. Having been abandoned by Jorge as was Ariadne by Theseus on the island of Naxos, Elia, now at once Theseus and Ariadne, seeks a new guide to accompany her through the intricate labyrinth of her memories as she journeys back to her childhood in search of freedom and her own genuine personality" ("The Language..." 14).

[9] Although just about every known color is referred to at least once in the novel, the reader cannot help but notice the repetitive predominance of the colors blue, yellow or gold, red, green (each of which appears at least fifty times in the first novel alone), pink, white, and black (frequently, but much less than the previous ones), all of which are rich in symbolism associated with individuation. In *mandalas*, these colors often appear in specific combinations (such as black and white to reveal an emphasis on thought to the exclusion of feeling, gold and silver as emblems of the *sol/luna* dichotomy, while in

encounter at the beginning of *El mismo mar...* is the black primordial darkness of the beginning of Creation. In *mandalas*, the color black often suggests "a dark, velvety matrix for new life, the boundless creativity of the unconscious, or the allure of the unknown" (Fincher 40). The blackness with which the novel opens also identifies it as both the beginning and the end point(s) of the magic circle insofar as "all life begins and ends in darkness" (Fincher 40).

As we read the opening lines of Tusquets' first novel, not only do we embark in the literal sense upon the artistic process of the author's literary creation, but also symbolically upon the protagonist's journey of self-creation into a purposeful, coherent psychic whole: the process of artistic individuation with respect to the author and of psychological individuation in the case of the protagonist onto whom the former is being projected. Dr. Joseph Henderson, a psychiatrist and Jungian psychoanalyst, affirms that despite the philosophical versus scientific orientation to the human psyche that oriented Jung's and Freud's approaches to the psychoanalytic process—and ultimately forged an irreparable wedge between them—the two psychiatrists shared an essential fundamental conviction: both physicians espoused the esthetic quality of psychological growth:

> One of the happy products of their association, also fostered by their contemporary culture, was the emergence of something that was neither scientific nor philosophic. It was esthetic. In different ways they both affirmed that their work was concerned with human development as a process of creative discovery. They both show that the interpretation of dreams or fantasies may awaken in the analyst an esthetic response, to the

---

psychology, the colors blue, yellow, red, and green represent the four functions of consciousness: thinking, intuition, emotion and sensation). Since it is these four colors that command the greatest attention in the first novel, it is worthwhile to quote the Jungian psychoanalyst, Dr. Jolan Jacobi, with regard to their general symbolism in the field of psychology: "The correspondence of the colours to the respective functions varies with different cultures and groups and even among individuals; as a general rule, however,... blue, the colour of the rarefied atmosphere, stands for thinking; yellow, the colour of the far-seeing sun, which appears bringing light out of an inscrutable darkness only to disappear again into the darkness, for intuition, the function which grasps as in a flash of illumination the origins and tendencies of happenings; red, the colour of the pulsing blood and of fire, for the surging and tearing emotions; while green, the colour of earthly, tangible, immediately perceptible growing things, represents the function of sensation" (Quoted in Cirlot 50-1).

nature of certain patterns or images that promote the kind of apperception evoked by artists in the greatest literature, painting, and music. (8)

The common denominator of estheticism allows for the harmonious thematic co-existence of literary creativity and individuation throughout Tusquets' tetralogy. In her first novel, the two processes temporally run parallel to each other; the author fuses form and content in her novel synchronously with, and in direct proportion to, her protagonist's integration of conscious and unconscious material in her psyche. The symbolic quality of the text effectuates a convergence of the physical, atmospheric reality of the outer world and the inner world of the protagonist's psychodynamics of change. Rollo May refers to symbolism as a "bridging act" that closes the gap between the outer world and inner meaning (21). By employing a symbolism that so powerfully communicates the most vital truths about the human condition in general, and of the feminine experience in particular where the power of creativity is concerned, Tusquets conjoins the tangible reality of the literary work in its process of becoming with the numinous process of female individuation.

Although we speak of form and content as though they were two distinct entities in the make-up of a literary work of art, and the conscious and the unconscious as though they were two unrelated, diametrically opposed realms of the human mind, it is merely for the sake of convenience that we do so. In fact, there exists an analogous relationship between form and content in literary art, and the conscious and unconscious in the human mind insofar as form and content, like the conscious and the unconscious, comprise two sides of an indivisible coin. A work of art is not form plus content; it is formed content. Similarly, the psyche is not composed of two distinct realms known as the conscious and the unconscious. As Meredith Anne Skura correctly asserts, to make such a distinction is "misleading," and is "the product of a falsely neat dichotomy between our rational, acceptable thinking (supposedly all conscious) and our irrational, primitive, and repressed thinking (supposedly all unconscious)" (2). Just as we must speak of the literary work of art as formed content, we must speak of the make-up of the psyche as a "whole range of what has been called 'modes of consciousness,' or modes of representation" (Skura 3). As the form of a literary work of art is an inseparable, indistinguishable part of the content, our conscious acts, perceptions, beliefs, etc. contain spillovers from the unconsciousness. Just because we are not aware of the extent to which irrational thinking and repressed emotions influence our conscious life does not mean that it is not so. We need only to stop and think about how often we are aware of overreacting to a situation without knowing why, or how often the behavior of another stirs something deep within us whose origin we cannot identify.

As discussed in the introduction, both literary creation and psychoanalysis are integrative processes that involve a harnessing of raw, unbridled material into a series of compatible, complementary relationships from which coherence—a sense of the meaningfulness of the whole—may be derived. The author is motivated to write by a theme or idea about which (s)he feels a strong desire to express himself/herself and to which (s)he will strive to give coherent artistic form. The analysand typically is driven into analysis (also a need for self-expression) by a problem whose symptoms are too acute to be ignored, the origin and nature of which (s)he understands little or nothing. Subordinated to the theme or problem, the writer like the analysand will create a text for an intended recipient. The written text of the literary artist presumably will be received, internalized, processed and evaluated by a trained, critically-thinking reader, while the verbal text mounted by the analysand will be received, internalized, processed and evaluated by a trained, critically-thinking psychoanalyst. Naturally, literary critic and psychoanalyst alike bring their own psyches and life experiences to the task at hand, both of which play no small role in the interpreting of the text placed before them.

If we consider the relationship between the literary work of art and the critical reader, and that of the analysand's discourse and the psychoanalyst, not only do we discover that the relationships are analogous, but also that the *real* intended recipient of the literary or psychic text is not *another*, but the *Self.* The critic, like the psychoanalyst, mirrors the Self for the Self. In other words, the critical reader performs exactly the same function for the literary artist as the psychoanalyst does for the client: that of pointing out "textual" attributes or flaws, consistencies or inconsistencies, coherencies or incoherencies, both in the way that the artistic or psychic process functions and in the degree to which all of the component parts ultimately "hang together." Therefore, while both literary and psychoanalytic discourses appear to be created for the benefit of another, they actually are vehicles for communicating with another in order to learn more about the Self.

Writer and analysand must confront many of the same difficulties and dilemmas when they embark upon the process of textual creation. First and foremost, they must grapple with the limitations imposed by language (that is, after all, precisely the reason for the need for symbols). They also must address the issue of their own linguistic competence, that is, the extent to which they are skilled and articulate enough to maximize written and verbal expression, respectively. As they develop their discourses, they must constantly ask themselves if all of the necessary elements are present and organized in such a way that the recipient will receive a text that is coherent enough for the/an intended/correct meaning to be derived. And if the text is misunderstood and, therefore, misinterpreted, how is the writer or analysand to know if the problem lies with inadequate communication on his/her part, or with defective interpretative skills on the part of the critic or analyst, or with some combination of the two, or with none of the above?

Since the goal of the artistic creativity and psychoanalysis is a refracted glimpse of one's Self, a great deal is at stake in the relationship between literary writer/critical reader on the one hand, and between analysand/psychoanalyst on the other. The relationship is successful if the writer or analysand can make himself/herself understood, valued and respected for his/her uniqueness by the recipient of the text, for such comprehension and appreciation validates not only the individualized coherent wholeness of the created text, but also his/her worth as an artist and/or human being. It also connects him/her to the human race and to the cosmos for it implies that there are universal laws and principles shared by all of humanity that make communication between and among people possible. It confers a meaningful place in the world, a sense of belonging to the cosmic order of things.

All of the similarities in the nature of the psychoanalytic and creative processes make possible the co-presence of a psychopathic and a creationistic form/content indivisibility in *El mismo mar*... Both types of novel demand a highly trained, qualified reader who possesses the cultural and intellectual sophistication that is required to "decode" the hidden "true" meaning of the text. The difficulty is due primarily to the fact that both types of novel operate on at least two levels of meaning, one literal and the other(s) metaphoric. In the case of *El mismo mar*..., the critic must grapple with three layers of meaning: 1) the literal, which metaphorically shrouds the 2) psychopathic, which metaphorically conceals 3) the creationistic. To complicate matters even further, the metaphoric levels of meaning—what we might term the secondary and tertiary plots—are developed as rich tapestries into which are woven a vast wealth of symbols, myths, fairy tales and archetypes, all of which require interpretation both individually and in terms of their interconnectedness within the totality of the work.

Although ironic, it is well within the extremist, paradoxical nature of baroque esthetics that the authentic purport of a baroque novel be unrelated to the plot to which it is subordinated. One of the essential characteristics of the psychopathic novel is that "aunque las peripecias se revisten de tangibilidad, las apariencias engañan: lo que ocurre no es lo que pasa. Su significado ha sido codificado por la mente y se transmite mediante una imagen que, para ser entendida, requiere una interpretación, pues su sentido es indirecto" (Gil

Casado 203). Similarly, a literary work of art whose thematic is the creative mechanics of its own ontological being is governed by false appearances; what appears to be of primary importance in fact is of secondary importance, and vice versa. In a creationistic and psychopathic novel alike, the deception is most clearly visible with the author's handling of the plot—which more often than not has to do with the frustration or disillusionment of love—in that what originally captured the reader's interest becomes more and more trivialized as the novel develops. This is because it is not an end unto itself; it is a mere pretext for something abstract and transcendental. It is a means to a much more ambitious end whose very existence at best is obscure and whose meaning the highly-educated, trained critic must decipher: "La función del asunto sentimental es mantener la atención del lector y servir de pantalla para proyectar el asunto verdadero, o sea la captación del proceso creador en sus múltiples planos, el teórico, el imaginativo, el estilístico, el del autor, el del lector, el del crítico, etc" (Gil Casado 108).

In the case of *El mismo mar...*, the superficial plot is incongruous with the dense, hermetic, periphrastic discourse by means of which it is narrated. As in the quintessential neo-baroque example of Luis Martín-Santos' *Tiempo de silencio*, this is a signal that the mode of expression (form) is more important than what is being expressed (content) at the same time as it is an integral part of the very content which it supercedes. Plot and style, content and form, indeed are out of synchronization if the reader mistakingly confers upon Pedro's professional demise in *Tiempo de silencio*, or upon the protagonist's lesbian affair with Clara in *El mismo mar...*, a first-order meaning when it is, in fact, a smoke screen for the communication of something more far-reaching. While in the former the plot camouflages Martín-Santos' demythification of the rhetoric of national grandeur during the first two decades of the Franco regime,[10] in Tusquets' novel the plot is but a vehicle upon which she mounts her own idiosyncratic periphrastic style,[11] one that reproduces with remarkable exactitude the dialectics of elaboration (thesis and antithesis) and integration (synthesis) that characterize the dynamic processes of individuation and literary creation alike.

---

[10] I refer the reader to my book, *La novela desmitificadora...*

[11] Servodidio accurately characterizes Tusquets' narrative style as being replete with "syntactic complications, verbal complexity... digressions, disjunctions, parenthetical insertions and interpolations, and by the persistent use of locutions like 'acaso' 'tal vez' 'quizá' which introduce exhaustive explorations of all the permutations of the narrator's tortured thought processes" ("A Case..." 172).

The characters who act out the plot perform the same function as the plot itself: they anchor the reader to the text by keeping him/her engrossed in a story about seemingly real people involved in seemingly plausible situations. In her first novel, as the author creates this false sense of security for the reader, plot and characters perform the more important function of dramatically projecting the psyche of an oligophrenic protagonist (narrator) striving toward psychic wholeness, and of a potential novelist (Tusquets) grappling with self and artistic expression through the medium of the written word for the first time. At the secondary (psychopathic) level of meaning, events and characters project a myriad of psychological dysfunctions, complexes, conflicts, fears, insecurities, stages of personality development, repressed instincts, the *animus*, the shadow, etc., of the narrator/protagonist, while at the third (creationistic) level of meaning, the projections are associated with distinct phases of the creative process in which Esther Tusquets is engaged.

Hence, the reader is the recipient of a text that is psychopathic and at the same time is about the process of writing a psychopathic novel. *El mismo mar...* is at once the projection of an oligophrenic, dysfunctional psyche (that of the narrator/protagonist) and of a creative one (that of the author). Both psyches must recognize, accept, integrate and implement their *animus* function in order to successfully complete their missions: individuation for the fictional character and artistic creativity for the author. For the former, this requires the symbolic act of forsaking Clara and returning to her married life. For the latter, it necessitates the writing of a coherent work of art, for the completion of *El mismo mar de todos los veranos* epitomizes the integration of the Feminine and the Masculine insofar as the theme of female individuation is rendered visible by means of the masculine function of artistic creativity. The character's psyche *is* the novel that we hold in our hands; the interpretation of the one invariably implies the interpretation of the other, for they are two sides of an indivisible textual whole authored by a single artistic imagination. It would be erroneous, therefore, to suggest that the psychopathic and creationistic processes exclusively run parallel, for in actuality they do and they do not in that they also are intricately braided together into an elaborate design of difference and complementation, duality and indistinction, and, ultimately, femininity and masculinity, which are the product of one creative/integrative endeavor on the part of Esther Tusquets.

El mismo mar... is a/the blueprint of *a* personal (that of the fictional narrator/protagonist) and of *the* collective (universal) female psyche. The countless textual mentions of wells, caves, grottos, the undersea world, and the like, all symbolize plummeting the depths of the psyche—from consciousness to the repressed contents of the sub-conscious and the personal unconscious, ultimately to uncover what lies at the most remote layers of the feminine unconscious. Esther Tusquets is the mediator between the uniqueness of the psyche of her fictional narrator/protagonist and of the universal female archetypes buried deep in the recesses of the collective unconscious of all women, making possible a deep bond of identification between and among us irrespective of age, social class, religious, national or ethnic differences, etc. She is (not) her fictional narrator/protagonist. Despite numerous autobiographical similarities between author and narrator/protagonist (both are approximately the same age, belong to the Catalonian bourgeoisie, are an only child and are similar in physical appearance), the very theme of the novel—individuation—precludes the possibility of two distinct individuals being one-and-the-same individual. Furthermore, there exists a time warp between the fairly advanced stage of individuation at which Esther Tusquets would have had to have been in order to have been able to write *El mismo mar...*, and the preparatory phase of individuation in which we meet the narrator/protagonist at the beginning of the novel. Since the novel is a fictionalization of the process of tapping into the unconscious, awakening all that has been forgotten and repressed, and projecting it onto objects and persons outside the self, confronting it (often painfully), accepting it as part of who one is, and allowing it to rise and merge with consciousness, then the author would have had to have been conscious of this process prior to her writing of the novel. In order to fictionalize unconscious psychic material or energy, it must already reside in the conscious mind of the writer. What this implies, of course, is that Esther Tusquets consciously is presenting at least some material of which she is conscious as unconscious material for her fictional character. Despite the fact that the novel gives every appearance—albeit false—of being a vehicle of self-discovery for the author, it is so only for the narrator/protagonist. It would appear then, that individuation is a process with which Esther Tusquets is all too familiar.

As the reader turns the pages of *El mismo mar...*, it becomes increasingly more obvious that the narrator/protagonist has remained psychologically stuck in shattered childhood hopes, fantasies and illusions throughout her adult life. The cause for this abrupt halt in her psychological maturation is disclosed in the final tale that she webs for Clara near the end of the novel, seemingly a fairy tale in its beginning and middle, but tragic in its end unlike that of "Peter Pan," "Hansel and Gretel," "Rapunzel," "Beauty and the Beast", "Snow White," "Cinderella," and "Sleeping Beauty" to which she makes countless references throughout her narrative. In other words, she never underwent the challenging ordeal of initiation—passage from adolescence to adulthood—at the proper time. The adolescent teenager was cast into an emotional "death" where she has remained motionless, asleep, never having awakened into a mature, fully-functioning adult. Consequently, the pronounced disjunction between her mature, aging body facing the onset of menopause, and the frightened, insecure, immature child housed within it, have precipitated a mid-life crisis that is far too painful to be ignored. The causes of the personal psychic injuries that have splintered from her ego-consciousness and been buried in the unconscious along with its collective content, suddenly have been awakened and stirred up. The narrator/protagonist now must "get to the bottom" of what has stunted her emotional development and annihilate it by incorporating it into consciousness.

Characteristic of the archaic mentality that bore the rites of initiation is "the belief that a state cannot be changed without first being *annihilated*"(Beane 165, Beanes's italics). In the particular instance of the puberty initiation, this means "without the child's dying to childhood. It is impossible to exaggerate the importance of this obsession with beginnings, which, in sum, is the obsession with the absolute beginning, the cosmogony" (Beane 165). In this way, the symbolic act of crossing the threshold of her childhood home, of "mi vieja casa, mi única casa, la antigua casa de mis padres" (18) and penetrating its forboding, secluded obscurity means delving into the deepest, darkest realms of the female psyche: "Mystics have always traditionally considered the feminine aspect of the universe as a chest, a house or a wall, as well as an enclosed garden," while in architectural symbolism "the house carries not only an overall symbolism but also particular associations with the human body and human thought (or life, in other words), as has been confirmed empirically by psychoanalysts" who have found that "in dreams, we employ the image of the house as a representation of the different layers of the psyche" (Cirlot 146). Interestingly enough, "the outside of the house signifies the outward appearance of Man: his personality or his mask" (Cirlot 146). In this sense we may justifiably say that by entering the house and leaving the outside world behind, the protagonist/narrator symbolically has shed her persona and left it behind as well. This implies that *El mismo mar...*, consistent with the hermetic, intellectual "New Novel," is an internalized novel. Therefore, events, secondary characters, objects, etc. must be read and interpreted accordingly as graphic symbolic projections emanating from the collective unconscious of (wo)mankind. For example, repeated textual references to the labyrinth in which the minotaur roamed are significant on the tripartite cosmic, social, and psychological levels of the novel. On the cosmic plane, it communicates the mutual dependence of the masculine and feminine principles, since it was Ariadne's thread which enabled Theseus to overcome the minotaur and find his way out of the labyrinth. From the social perspective, the labyrinth housing the monstrous half-man, half-bull, functions as a symbol of a culture governed by oppression; specifically, the subservient role of Spanish women during the Francoist years of Church-State indivisibility and, more generally, western civilization's oppression of women and the feminine principle. From the human psychological point of view, the labyrinth is equated with the *mandala* in the sense that "the maze represents the confusion and contradiction of the unconscious mind. Arriving at its center or emerging into the light of day signifies personal individuation and the discovery of the Self, while wandering blindly in the labyrinth of the psyche signifies a loss of direction" (Gibson 147). The half-human, half-beast inhabiting the maze refers to the dual or binary nature of man in the form of human consciousness and its shadow. In *El mismo mar...*, the narrator and Clara each represent one half of the eventual "Beauty and the Beast" union. As their relationship develops, the two halves overlap—"¿Cuál de las dos es la Bella? ¿Y en qué rincón nos espera la Bestia?" (84)—and ultimately merge to form an indivisible One—"ahora sé que las dos somos la Bella y las dos somos igualmente la Bestia" (183).

Even descriptions of the external world must be recognized and understood as projected psychographics of the unconscious and not taken literally since "in the unconscious the inner world and the outer world are not differentiated. Only that which has become a content of consciousness is described as an inner or outer phenomenon, that is, either as an introspectively perceived condition, like the welling up of an emotion, or as an outer event or object" (Franz, *Projection...* 19). The novel is populated with references to various species of birds as metaphors either for the protagonist or Clara, most notably the duck (referring to her "ugly duckling" syndrome) in the case of the former, and the swan, swallow, nightingale and peacock attributable to the latter, as well as to the union that is forged between the two females. These are not randomly selected birds, however, all of them are endowed with a symbolism that reverberates the novel's theme of individuation. In the case of the swan, for example, its extraordinary beauty (Clara) is juxtaposed to the awkward, homely, insecure ugly duckling (the protagonist), thereby underscoring the all-encompassing theme of the union of complementary opposites. Furthermore, "because it has a rounded body and a long neck, swans can represent both masculinity and femininity, as well as water and fire and, by uniting these qualities, symbolize perfection" (Gibson 113). Not only does the swan give the appearance of being androgynous, but likewise suggests the co-existence of consciousness with its shadow insofar as its white plumage conceals black flesh. Furthermore, the belief that the swan sings only when about to die underscores the binary nature of the individuation process. In the case of the swallow, since it is a migratory bird, "the swallow's return in spring signifies hope, fertility and the renewal of life. Because it was once believed to hibernate (variously in mud, caves or water), it can symbolize resurrection" (Gibson 114), both of which prefigure the life-death-rebirth of the protagonist. Where the peacock is concerned, it might be said to set the stage for the royal/common marriage *coniunctio* with which the novel reaches its climax, since "its stateliness has often led it to be associated with royalty, and some cultures, such as the ancient Babylonians and Persians (who thought that two peacocks guarded the Tree of Life, signifying man's duality), seated their royalty on peacock thrones" (Gibson 112). In a similar fashion, the author repeatedly evokes the stages of development of the butterfly, thereby underscoring the psychological transformation that is taking place as the two women's relationship intensifies:

> Nuestras dos vidas enlazadas, espía Clara el lento crecer de este capullo, ya casi terminando, que me envuelve, un capullo tan tenue, tan frágil, pero tan prodigiosamente resistente, que nada podrá arrastrarme ya a las ciénagas de un pasado que se desvanece día a día, nada podrá hacerme ya retroceder, cuando se haya tejido el último hilo de seda y el capullo quede cerrado sin fisuras sobre mí, y tal vez entonces pueda al fin Clara descansar... dormir hasta el día... en que se abrirán por sí solas todas las cárceles antiguas y volveré a nacer transformada en mariposa. (199)

It goes without saying that the butterfly is a symbol *par excellence* of transformation and rebirth due to its process of evolution—seemingly from death to the creation of magnificent life—from egg to caterpillar to chrysalis and then emerges from an inert cocoon into the most splendid of insects. Interestingly enough, "in Ancient Greece, Psyche was represented as a butterfly because both shared the same name, and in dream analysis, the butterfly denotes new beginnings" (Gibson 115).

The interior feminine space where the two females practice their cult to Demeter—"los secretos ritos subterráneos donde juega Deméter" (81)— is projected as being surrounded by the sea, "rodeada por las olas" (18), making it a dynamic intermediary between microcosm and macrocosm—between the protagonist/narrator who views herself as an island surrounded by the sea (microcosm) and the ocean encompassing the earth (macrocosm). The island, like the earth, "is the opponent of the ocean and symbolic of the metaphysical point of irradiating force" (Cirlot 230). The ocean also is a symbol of "transitional states between the stable (or solids) and the formless (air or gasses)" and "for the sum of all the possibilities of one plane of existence" (Cirlot 230). In relation to the sun, its appearance and disappearance back into the ocean "confirm that the 'Lower Waters' signify the abyss out of which forms arise to unfold their potentialities within existence. Thus, the ocean is equated also with the collective unconscious, out of which arises the sun of the spirit" (Cirlot 230). Each and every one of these symbolic meanings of the sea or ocean is highly relevant to the decoding of the symbolic meaning of *El mismo mar de todos los veranos*.

The sea or ocean also suggests a return to the mother so that child and childhood may confront the death that is required prior to the birth of a new state of being. The psycho-graphic image of the house surrounded by the sea symbolically depicts the unconscious self surrounding the centripetal female force of the center of the personality. Jung tells us that "in dreams and fantasies the sea or a large expanse of water signifies the unconscious" and that "the maternal significance of the water is one of the clearest interpretations of symbols in the whole field of mythology, so that even the ancient Greeks could say that 'the sea is the symbol of generation.' From water comes life" (*Symbols of Transformation* 218). Paradoxically, just as all of life springs forth from water, it also is to water that man returns at the time of death: "Those black waters of death are the water of life, for death with its cold embrace is the maternal womb, just as the sea devours the sun but brings it forth again" (218). The sea also is a symbol of transition from one state of being to another and of mediation between opposites: "The symbolic significance of the sea corresponds to that of the 'Lower Ocean'—the waters in flux, the transitional and mediating agent between the non-formal (air and gasses) and the formal (earth and solids) and, by analogy, between life and death. The waters of the oceans are thus seen not only as the source of life but also as its goal. To return to the sea is 'to return to the mother,'that is, to die" (Cirlot 268).

Each of the three levels of meaning within the novel (the simplistic plot, the psychic and the creationistic) mutually enhances and completes the other two. But because of their intertwined, overlapping complexity, a fourth dimension—interpretation—is required if their fullest range of relevance to the human condition is to be achieved. Within this context, the present study stands as a symbol for the missing fourth element in the total enterprise of literary production with specific regard to *El mismo mar de todos los veranos*: the reader reception/critical evaluation of the text. In relation to the tetralogy, this study may be said to occupy a unifying centric position within the textual quaternity. This *quinta essentia* is by no means "additively joined onto the first four as a fifth element, but represents the most refined, spiritually imaginable unity of the four elements" (Franz, *Number and Time* 120-21). It is what allows four successively created texts to be considered not just diachronically, but synchronistically as well, as an *unus mundus* whose total meaning is far greater than the sum of its individual parts. From a critical perspective, we are not merely concerned with Esther Tusquets' four novels as a series of successive acts of creation, but equally with the eternal presence of the single creative act. In number symbolism, this means that the tetralogy as matter (form) would be represented as 1+1+1+1 = 4, but as spirit (content) would be represented as 1+2+3+4 = 10. As Cirlot tells us, ten is "symbolic, in decimal systems, of the return to unity" while "in the *Tetractys* (whose triangle of points—four, three, two, one—adds up to ten) it is related to four." For this reason, among others, the number ten has come to be viewed as symbolic of "spiritual achievement" (223).

If an inordinate amount of attention has been given to the symbolic importance of numbers, an equal amount of attention must be paid to the innumerable allusions to fairy tales and myths in *El mismo mar...* The shared common denominator of numbers, myths, and fairy tales is that they are the key to unlocking the door of the collective unconscious behind which lives the rich, mysterious world of universal archetypes. The unraveling of the symbolic meaning behind numbers, myths and fairy tales has proven to me to reveal the most complete and coherent meaning of Tusquets' first novel both in terms of breadth and of depth. Furthermore, it has what led us to conclude that the tetralogy needed to be analyzed from the point of view of Jungian depth psychology.

El mismo mar de todos los veranos is, at one and the same time, a fairy tale on the psychic plane and a myth on the creationistic plane. These two planes are meaningfully connected by a simplistic plot whose principles of order, structure and dynamic development are expressed symbolically by numbers. The number symbolism employed by Tusquets is, in fact, the most significant instrument of novelistic coherence since fairly tales and myths, individuation and creation, psyche and matter, are governed by identical numerical patterns of meaning. Number, according to Jung, "may well be the most primitive element of order in the human mind... thus we define number psychologically as an archetype of order which has become conscious" (*Symbols of Transformation* 870). Since numbers establish patterns of regularity and order, it is no wonder that Jung deems them to be the most logical tools our mind can employ for expression and understanding of order. And it is the ordering of events in fairy tales and myths that reveal their hidden meaning.

The symbolic significance of numbers is part and parcel of the elucidation of universal *truths* inculcated in fairy tales and myths. We emphasize the word "truths" because all fairy tales and myths, and, yes, even some novels, paradoxically are fictions that reveal the deepest, most eternal truths about the human condition. Marie-Louise von Franz defines fairy tales as "the purest and simplest expression of collective psychic processes" (*Introduction* 1). She elaborates further:

After working for many years in this field, I have come to the conclusion that all fairy tales endeavour to describe one and the same psychic fact, but a fact so complex and far-reaching and so difficult for us to realize in all its different aspects that hundreds of tales and thousands of repetitions with a musician's variations are needed until this unknown fact is delivered into consciousness; and even then the theme is not exhausted. This unknown fact is what Jung calls the Self, which is the psychic totality of an individual and also, paradoxically, the regulating center of the collective unconscious. Every individual and every nation has its own modes of experiencing this psychic reality. (*Introduction* 1-2)

Myth, which also affords us access to the deepest inner workings of the psyche, "narrates a sacred history; it relates an event that took place in primordial Time, the fabled time of the 'beginnings'. . . . Myth, then, is always an account of a 'creation'; it relates how something was produced, began to *be*. Myth tells only of that which *really* happened, which manifested itself completely" (Beane 3-4, Beane's italics). What is most essential to the understanding of myth is that it is regarded as a "sacred story" and, therefore, as a "true history, because it always deals with *realities*" (Beane 4, Beane's italics).

El mismo mar de todos los veranos is a fairy tale that tells the story of how its narrator/protagonist came to discover her Self both as an individual and as part of a feminine collectivity. The novel also encompasses a cosmogonic myth of which its material existence as a novel created by the demiurge, Esther Tusquets, offers tangible proof. The innumerable numerological references permeating the text create a single principle of structure and order to these two layers of meaning, leading us to the realization that the integrated psyche (the Self) is but a microcosm of the universe (God). In this sense, to truly know oneself (one's Self) is to know the universe (God). And, yes, in all likelihood, Esther Tusquets created her protagonist in her own image. After all, in what other image could she have created her?

Consistent with the thematic structure of all fairy tales, *El mismo mar...* narrates a rite of passage from one stage of life to another that is achieved by means of the dynamic, transformative nature of the individuation process. Rejection, abandonment, orphanhood, or some combination of the three, generally propels the individuation process into motion as the protagonist confronts the seemingly unsurmountable task of "starting over." Forced to overcome the cruel, dark realities of life (projections of the shadow) as a demonstration of one's worth, a higher level of Selfhood invariably is synonymous with the "happily ever after" ending shared by the overwhelming majority of these tales. The resulting new Self is achieved by virtue of the fact that individuation always involves a portion of the contents of the unconscious rising to consciousness and being integrated into its repertoire.

In contrast, however, to the vast majority of fairy tales which convey a story either about lost innocence (Hansel and Gretel, Peter Pan), or else about the passage from youth to adulthood, typically culminating in the marriage ceremony by means of which the main characters assume their rightful place within the social order (Cinderella, Sleeping Beauty, Rapunzel, Beauty and the Beast, Snow White, etc.), *El mismo mar...* depicts the rite of passage not from the first to the second stage of life as do all of the former, but from the second quarter or phase of life (adulthood) to the third —middle age— which, as previously discussed, corresponds to the passage from the first half of life to the second. Although the reader is presented with a union of beings, what we have before us in *El mismo mar...* is not the romantic prelude culminating in a social ceremony uniting a man and a woman in holy matrimony but, rather, the psychological overture to the joining together of the oppositional parts of the Self into what Jung has defined as the "marriage quaternio" (*Aion* 242). As we recall, in addition to circular or spherical forms, any quaternity structure, be it geometric or else four objects or persons related to one another by some special meaning or by some meaningful arrangement, is an archetype of wholeness and, therefore, a symbol of the Self. Jung qualifies the quaternity as "a system of co-ordinates that is used almost instinctively for dividing up and arranging a chaotic multiplicity, as when we divide up the visible surface of the earth, the course of the year, or a collection of individuals into groups, the phases of the moon, the temperaments, elements, alchemical colours, and so on" (*Aion* 242). He refers to it as a marriage because "the arrangement took a form that derives from the primitive cross-cousin marriage" (242).

Those fairy tales whose theme is the female search for the Self via the individuation process invariably reveal either an explicit or an implicit quaternity ending. The former holds true in the cases of Cinderella, Sleeping Beauty, and Rapunzel, where the prince and princess are joined by and united with the elderly parents of one of them (usually a royal couple) at the end of the tale. The foursome symbolizes the union of all conceivable human opposites: male/female; father/mother; husband/wife; king/queen; prince/princess; mother/daughter; queen/princess; father/son; king/prince; mother/son; father/daughter; young/old; experience/inexperience; royal/common; etc. At the same time, the two pairs of successive generations symbolize the uninterrupted continuation of the family line warranted by the marital union of the younger generation.

There is an implicit quaternity ending to both "Beauty and the Beast" and "Snow White and the Seven Dwarfs" since in both cases the maiden is to marry a prince, which is to imply that a king and a queen await them at the palace although the royal couple does not physically make an appearance in the tale. These two stories, however, reveal more far-reaching implications than the mere "marriage quaternio." "Beauty and the Beast," and its countless literary derivatives, is the most clear-cut example of the harmonious quaternity union between man, his *anima*, woman, and her *animus*. In this well-known tale, it is the maturity, wisdom and insightfulness of Beauty (*animus*) which compel her to look beyond the terrifying external appearance of the Beast while, conversely, it is the Beast's willingness to externalize his emotions (*anima*), which enable the two of them to discover and express their mutual love and devotion. Even before the spell is broken and the Beast is transformed back into a prince, each of them is able to see the shadow of the Self reflected lovingly in the eyes of the other, making possible the ultimate link between *eros* and *logos*. As will soon be discussed, "Beauty and the Beast" not only is one of the most frequently alluded to fairy tales in *El mismo mar...*, but it also is one of the most obvious structural models for the optimistic ending of the novel.[12]

The most likely explanation for Tusquets's numerous references to "Snow White and the Seven Dwarfs" is the reciprocal relationship between the female psyche (microcosm) and nature (macrocosm) that the tale reveals. As a personified symbol of pure, true love, even nature mourns when Snow White is cast into a fatal sleep after eating the poisoned apple: "The dwarfs are not

---

[12] The majority of critics have interpreted the ending of the novel as a failure on the part of the protagonist to break away from social norms and expectations which continuing in her relationship with Clara would have implied. Ordóñez's interpretation of the novel's ending is typical: "Though Clara weaves a silken pupa around the protagonist, promising chrysalis and the emergence of a truly different future, the paths of the two women ultimately bifurcate: the quest of the older woman becomes truncated by her accomodation to the patriarchal backlash (her abrupt return to Julio, a deadening marriage, bourgeois enclosure). Significantly, she comes to view herself as a manipulated mannequin and a butterfly immobilized and crucified by sexual brutality (thus violently ending her brief flight out from the pupa). The future of the younger woman, however, becomes pregnant with possibility, in spite of her lover's abandonment. The younger companion becomes her own hero as the mature female becomes antihero" ("A Quest..." 44). Needless to say, this interpretation is derived from a strictly literal reading of the text with no consideration given to the symbolic meaning of forsaking Clara and resuming marital relations with her husband within the context of the individuation process that we have been describing throughout this study.

alone in mourning Snow White; the animals too come and lament her death: first an owl, then a raven, finally a dove. That could mean that the whole of nature suffers when genuine emotion dies" (Birkhäuser-Oeri 38). When the kiss of the prince awakens Snow White, nature simultaneously is revived.

The evil with which each fairy tale hero or heroine much wrestle is but a personified symbol of the dark side of the Self known as the shadow. The shadow must be acknowledged and conquered (assimilated into ego consciousness) before transcendence from one stage of life to another is possible. For example, had the wicked queen not disguised herself as an old beggar woman and visited Snow White at the dwarf's cottage, Snow White probably would have continued caring for the seven dwarfs indefinitely. In all likelihood, the prince never would have discovered her, which is to imply that she would have remained "stuck" where she was. Death in this sense should be viewed as a catalyst for rebirth.

Returning to Tusquets's protagonist, the dynamic structure of her psyche as it is projected onto nature, objects, and a number of significant people in her life, is wholly consistent with the psychological evolution undergone by the young maidens who dramatize the female individuation process in the aforementioned fairy tales. Unlike Snow White, Cinderella, Rapunzel, etc. who, at the appropriate age, confront and overcome their evil shadow (symbolized by the wicked queen, the wicked step-mother and the wicked witch, respectively), and subsequently experience wholeness as a result of merging their entire femininity with a positive *animus* (symbolized by marriage to a prince), she has been stuck in her undifferentiated oneness for nearly thirty years. She is trapped between shattered idealism and a negative *animus*, which conditions her outlook on everything. Consequently, she is bitter, sarcastic, judgmental, highly critical of herself and others, skeptical, cynical, and unable to share intimacy with anyone. The development of the novel is synonymous with her delving deeper and deeper into the recesses of her unconscious and unleashing the archetypes harbored there, thereby bringing about differentiation and the ensuing confrontation between the contradictory aspects of her Self (ego versus shadow, femininity versus *animus*, etc.). In accordance with the internal dynamics of fairy tales, undifferentiated oneness (Snow White) will split into differentiated opposites (the pure innocence of Snow White versus the narcissistic queen), the hostile intensity of which will be mitigated by a third element (the seven dwarfs collectively), creating a triad which will progressively strive toward quaternity wholeness (enter the prince). As we recall, Franz contends that the difficult step from three to four is "based on the inclusion (no longer avoidable) of the observer in his *wholeness* within the framework of his process of understanding" (*Number and Time* 122, Franz's italics). At the end of "Snow White and the Seven Dwarfs," (wo)man and nature, the whole universe, is restored to the state of undivided, undifferentiated wholeness with which the tale began in the character of Snow White, but at a higher, more transcendental level. So it would not appear to be mere coincidence that Snow White + the wicked queen + the seven dwarfs + the prince add up to ten individuals since, "according to some theories, ten symbolizes the totality of the universe—both metaphysical and material—since it raises all things to unity. From ancient oriental thought through the Pythagorean school and right up to St. Jerome, it was known as the number for perfection" (Cirlot 223),

El mismo mar de todos los veranos captures the dynamics of these four progressive, transformative and ultimately transcendent stages of female individuation, culminating at the close of the novel with a "marriage quaternio" of the psyche. The one, undifferentiated narrator/protagonist undergoes a process of psychic differentiation that replicates the descriptive cosmic differentiation with which the novel opens. After the narrator/protagonist crosses the otherworldy threshold of the unconscious upon entering her childhood residence, the first object that she comes upon is in fact a projection of the differentiated components of her potential oneness, or Self: the bronze statue of Mercurius. While seemingly nothing more than an interesting decorative item at the plot level, the bronze statue of Mercury is no less than a symbolic projection of the structural thematics of the novel that we are about to read. The statue symbolizes and prefigures the thematic psychic quest for a fully integrated, indivisible wholeness of being. Following the predictable dynamics of individuation during the second half of life, the process is structured along the principles of an ambivalent and somewhat hostile confrontation of conflictive, yet complementary and mutually dependent, conscious and unconscious elements within the psyche. After a period of psychological turmoil, each aspect of the psyche ultimately will acquiesce to its rival, making it possible for the conscious willfully to embraces the positive as well as the negative aspects of the Self that it previously had suppressed or repressed, or simply not even known were there. In terms of literary creationism, consciousness will give coherent *form* to the *contents* of the unconscious. The harmonious convergence of form and content will yield a fully integrated, coherent whole Self on the psychic plane (belonging to the fictional character) and a fully integrated, coherent work of literary art on the literary plane (belonging to the author).

2. *El amor es un juego solitario*: The Oscillating Duality of Binary Oppositions

The recurrence in 1979 of the lush, sinuous, sensual prose that had set Esther Tusquets apart from other contemporary Spanish woman novelists just one year earlier, in conjunction with the apparent reemergence of the two female characters that we met in the previous novel, leaves little doubt that *El amor es un juego solitario* is a sequel to *El mismo mar de todos los veranos*. The first-person narrator/protagonist of the incipient novel, about whose name the author only would divulge the melodic beauty with which Clara would pronounce its two syllables, "las dos sílabas de mi nombre, tan sonoras y hermosas cuando las repite Clara hasta el infinito" (*El mismo mar*... 203), is referred to as Elia by a third-person omniscient narrator in the second. The anonymous protagonist and Elia display a similar, if not identical, psychological make-up: an inferiority complex originating in childhood; low self-esteem; emotional dysfunction resulting from having been deprived of a loving, nurturing mother-daughter relationship; an absent father; marital disenchantment; and maternal unfulfill-ment, all of which is constellated around a present that is devoid of meaning, purpose and personal reward, and is tainted with painful childhood memories of social exclusion and ridicule.

Elia has been involved for an undisclosed length of time in a lesbian relationship with a much younger girl. Like the adolescent in the first novel, Elia's lover also is named Clara, which initially suggests that the homosexual relationship that is terminated at the close of *El mismo mar*... has been resumed by the same two women in *El amor*.... Elia's involvement with Clara is somewhat cold and dispassionate, again verifying narrative continuity, at least at the plot level, between the two texts since it was the middle-aged protagonist who broke off the affair in the first novel. Clara, on the other hand, is hopelessly in love with, and emotionally dependent upon, her sexual partner and surrogate mother: "Clara ama a Elia de un modo tan desesperado, tan exclusivo, tan doloroso y total, que ni fijarse puede en nadie más" (31). Both of the Claras share a seemingly identical physiognomy which accentuates their large eyes and skinny, shapeless figure. While driving to her grandmother's beachfront home in *El mismo mar*..., the first-person narrator describes Clara as a "gata flaca y esquiva que se agazapa al otro lado del asiento" (76). Elia's description of Clara similarly places emphasis on the adolescent girl's lost, homely quality: "esta niña flaca de ojos grandes que la acompaña y la sigue hace semanas, desde hace quizá meses, a todas partes, que le hace favores y recados" (31). Although neither of the two texts specifies exactly how old Clara is, in each of the novels she is in her first year of college, making her somewhere between sixteen and eighteen years of age.

It is not long before the author skillfully undermines sequential consistency between the 1978 and 1979 novels. The sexual neophyte, Ricardo, whom Clara brings to Elia for initiation into the art of erotic lovemaking, is half of Elia's age: "Ricardo es apenas un muchacho y Elia le dobla casi la edad" (22). Since we know that he and Clara are first-year college classmates and, hence, the same age, it logically follows that Elia would be in her early thirties. It is not until the reader has completed more than half of the novel that her age is revealed as being "treinta años" (92). This poses a disturbing problem with regard to Clara, for if the Clara of the first novel is the same age as the Clara appearing in the narrative that follows, but her lesbian lover is twenty-some years younger in the second novel than she is in the first, then the two Claras cannot be the same person. We learn that, in fact, she is not: Elia's lover is Catalonian whereas the narrator's interlocutor in the previous novel is Colombian. Or, if they are meant to be taken as the same character, the age discrepancies dictate that Elia and the autobiographical narrator in *El mismo mar...* cannot be the same individual. But, if this is the case, it is impossible to explain the temporal consistency between the latter protagonist's memory of her cat, "una gata que se llamaba Muslina y que vivió y murió hace ya muchos años" (198), and Elia who carries a cat named "Muslina en brazos" (17).

The effect created by these numerous vestiges of continuity/discontinuity, similarity/difference, progression/regression, movement/stasis, development/ repetition, order/chaos, is a fluctuating tension between the two texts. Paradoxically, the very differences that repel them magnetically draw them together, but without meaningful integration. Like a pendulum, the reader's focus swings back and forth from the one to the other in a attempt to discern a relational meaning that, while at times established, at others is obfuscated; while repeatedly clarified, is just as frequently obscured; while undeniably existing, has its existence undermined as often as it is confirmed. This paradoxical relationship shared by the first two texts comprising the tetralogy is consistent with the qualitative symbolism of the number two (the Other) in relation to one (the One), of which Cirlot writes:

> Two stands for echo, reflection, conflict and counterpoise or contraposition; or the momentary stillness of forces in equilibrium; it also corresponds to the passage of time—the line which goes from behind forward; it is expressed geometrically by two points, two lines or an angle. It also is symbolic of the first nucleus of matter, of nature in opposition to the

creator, of the moon as opposed to the sun. In all esoteric thought, two is regarded as ominous; it connotes shadow and the bisexuality of all things, or dualism (represented by the basic myths of the Gemini) in the sense of the connecting-link between the immortal and the mortal, or of the unvarying and the varying. (221-22)

As is the case with all instances of two, or the One and the Other, the sequential juxtaposition of the two texts creates an inevitable "dualistic structure of threshold phenomena" (Franz, *Number and Time* 167). At the content level, the co-presence of the two novels portrays unconscious psychic matter at the threshold of consciousness, eager to break through but unable to disrupt the oscillating dynamic polarity that manifests itself as a systolic-diastolic rhythm (Franz, *Number and Time* 96-97) within which it is entrapped. In the absence of a third mediating, synthetic element, transcendent passage is not possible. Hence, while mirroring, reverberating, and enlightening numerous (unvarying) aspects of *El mismo mar...*, thereby substantiating essences and relationships and systolically thrusting meaning onward, at diastolic intervals the second novel reaches an irresolute, immobilizing impasse with other (varying) contradictory, mutually-exclusive ones in its predecessor. The ensuing result is an expression of "the negative and passive principle" (Cirlot 221) that is associated with all even numbers. At the level of structure, the two novels as the One and the Other cast the reader into the uncomfortable space between the second (the sum of the One and the Other) that exists, and the positive, dynamic third that is needed in order to break the monotonous rhythmic pattern between the first and the second. As each of the first two novels throws positive-negative, mobile-stationary relief onto the other, their relationship becomes increasingly strained by virtue of the fact that no release—no third element—is available to it until 1980, one year after the publication of *El amor...* and two years after the publication of *El mismo mar...*, when *Varada tras el último naufragio* appeared. One (*El mismo mar...*) plus two (*El mismo mar... + El amor...*) equals three (*El mismo mar... + El amor... = Varada...*), and so it is that in three years Tusquets produced a trilogy, a triadic structure that symbolizes the synthesis and transcendence—the whole being greater than the sum of its parts—characteristic of all dialectically dynamic processes. Architectonically, the author's novelistic production evolved from a systyle to a diastyle—from two to three—symbolizing a dynamic growth and expansion of consciousness as unconscious material crosses its threshold and becomes structurally integrated. Reflecting upon the organizational process of her first three novels, the author herself identified not only the contrapuntal thesis/antithesis relationship between *El mismo mar...* and

El amor..., but also the need to write a third "mediating" novel even before she had completed the second: When we spoke about the relationship among her first three novels, Tusquets had the following to say: "Cuando terminé *El mismo mar*... tenía una segunda parte que se parecía a lo que sería *El amor es un juego solitario*. Y luego escribí esta novela como un relato de tipo corto. Cuando estaba terminando *El amor*..., como me pareció muy duro, más cínico, más desagradable, creí que no acababa de dar mi imagen del mundo y que requería una tercera novela" (Dolgin, "Conversación..." 399). Although Tusquets never states whether or not she consciously intended for *Varada tras el último naufragio* to be an integration of the previous two novels, after its publication she did regard her third novel as a successful synthesis of the first two: "Creí que *Varada*... englobaba mejor el sentido de los otros libros porque si la leías, no tenías que ver ni *El mismo mar*... ni *El amor*.... Por eso en Italia insistí en que no publicaran *El amor*... y publicaran *Varada*..., porque me parecía que era una novela que resumía las otras" (Dolgin, "Conversación..." 400-01).

Returning to the novel presently under analysis, the intrinsic dynamics of *El amor es un juego solitario* constitute a fictional creation by Esther and enactment by Elia of this One-and-the-Other polarity in which it is extrinsically engaged with its narrative predecessor. The oscillating duality is analogous to "the polaristic structure of the psyche, which it shares with all natural processes," the latter being "phenomena of energy, constantly arising out of... 'states' of polar tension" (Jung, *Mysterium*... xvi). This factor permits the psyche of our author synchronously to develop multiple thematic processes—erotic, creative, and psychological—by means of the psychodynamic interplay between her own conscious and unconscious levels. Elia is, in fact, a projection of the latter. Her role as a fictional character, in other words, is purely psychic; she is an objective embodiment of the psychic processes of her creator. The complexity of the autobiographical/fictional tension does not end here. Through the fictional manifestation of author/character neuroses, personal as well as archetypal contents of the unconscious that are as yet incompatible with conscious life emerge, providing a causal relationship between the internal psychic dysfunction shared by creator and creation, and its externalized physical symptoms that are exhibited in the case of the former by the creative process and, in the latter, by erotic fantasizing. To complicate the structural thematics of the novel even further, the interaction between two of the universal archetypes inhabiting Elia's unconscious, the inner child and the *animus*, are personified respectively by the secondary characters, Clara and Ricardo. The sum total, then, of Clara and Ricardo equals portions of the unconscious psyche of Esther Tusquets as subject (the One) projected onto a fictional object: Elia (the Other). The form/content complexity of *El amor...* thus is to be understood in the following way: a form/content esthetics of eroticism is crafted by Esther Tusquets in the narrative body of the novel, within which it is projected psychophysically onto Elia. Just as Elia is a function of Tusquets' psyche, Clara and Ricardo dramatize a bi-polar psychophysical relationship that is an unconscious projection of Elia's psyche and of Tusquets', twice removed. In this manner the novel is able to operate on multiple erotic, literary, and psychological structural-thematic planes simultaneously. The perplexing title of the novel, *El amor es un juego solitario*, that is at once a complete sentence made up of discordant fragments of meaning (love /game, love/solitary, game/solitary),[13] echoes the polarized, yet complementary, nature of divisiveness-within-wholeness that constitutes the common denominator shared by eroticism (mind/body), creationism (form/content) and individuation (conscious/unconscious). The ludic precepts of the New Novel constitute a formal game that is played out on an erotic game board (content) whose seemingly autonomous players (Elia, Clara, and Ricardo) are but distinct manifestations of a single, solitary psyche that is at once individual (belonging to the creative psyche of the author) and universal (archetypal).

While distinct from one another in substance, the trifurcated themes are intertwined structurally by virtue of sharing an identical rhythmic accumulation and expenditure of psychic energy. All three levels are psychophysical, for on each of the three levels, substance and structure must be negotiated: eroticism entails the physical expression of what is stimulated in the imagination, and their mutual enhancement; creativity requires that both a meaningful and an artistic process of integration be achieved between an imaginatively conceived

---

[13] Mirella Servodidio observes that "unlike the other two novels of Tusquets' trilogy, *El amor es un juego solitario* offers the reader a title with a fully articulated sentence. Yet despite its grammatical orthodoxy, the title is ridden by contradictions that defy the experiential and poetic conventions associated with love. The sign love, sacramentalized and mythified by cultural convention, celebrates the union of two subjects rather than the rivalry and contrivance of games aimed at producing 'winners' and 'losers.' The disruption of meaning is exacerbated by the use of 'solitario' as a predicate adjective which further undermines the semantic correlation of subject and predicate and subverts a basic principle of game theory, namely that the different categories of play presuppose company rather than solitude. The copulative verb ('ser') thus joins the clashing codes of subject and predicate in an 'unnatural act' which... requires the reader's interpretation. Read referentially, the title is perplexing. Read figuratively, however, it provides a rhetorical codification of deviance by employing language to mean something other that what it says" ("Perverse Pairings..." 238).

content that must be formally expressed by the medium of language; and psychological growth— individuation— demands an awareness, acceptance, and structural integration by consciousness of the unconscious components of the psyche. All three processes are intensely difficult—often painful—to achieve by virtue of the interfacial tension that naturally exists between bi-polar elements. As previously mentioned, bi-polarities operate on the principle of paradox: dependency and rejection. Whereas their co-presence stimulates a mutual attraction, constantly reminding each that it is incomplete because it does not possess what the other has, at the same time each pushes the other away as a result of seemingly irreconcilable differences. As Mirella Servodidio correctly asserts, Elia is a walking paradox made up of binary oppositions:

> Elia's adult life is characterized by an uneasy truce with social conventions punctuated by transgressions which mirror the unorthodoxy of her childhood. The absence of her husband and children from the space of the novel magnifies Elia's disconnection from her surrounding milieu and its received values as well as her marked narcissism. Financially privileged and emotionally deprived, world-wise yet child-like in her vulnerability, alternately apathetic and frenetically active, Elia is both a "part of" and "apart from" the social world in which she moves. ("Perverse Pairings..." 239)

The nature of paradox likewise characterizes the Clara/Ricardo dichotomy, which acts as a projection of Elia's psychic bisexuality that has yet to achieve peace with itself. The inherent bisexuality of the human psyche perhaps offers the clearest example of how the conscious mind is so quick to dismiss the notion of the dichotomous structure of the psyche by casting incompatibilities or contradictions deep into the recesses of the unconscious. This factor, in conjunction with the social and religious stigma attached to any sexual concept or practice that departs from consecrated male-female heterosexuality, explains why the contra-sexual *anima* in the male psyche and the contra-sexual *animus* in the female psyche are, according to Jung, the most challenging of the universal archetypes confronted by consciousness along the individuation continuum. Jung explains that "since conscious thinking strives for clarity and demands unequivocal decisions, it has constantly to free itself from counter-arguments and contrary tendencies, with the result that especially incompatible contents either remain totally unconscious or are habitually and assiduously overlooked" (*Mysterium*... xvii).

This factor might well explain the abundance of critical studies dealing with one of Tusquets' novels independently from the other three, in contrast to the scant number that even modestly confront their complex interrelationship. In those rare instances when critics have entertained the possibility of an interrelationship among the texts, be it of the trilogy or of the tetralogy, they invariably have come up empty-handed except where the most obvious similarities—the repetitive names of characters, the depiction of the upper stratum of the Catalonian bourgeoisie to which the four protagonists belong, the similar psychological problems that all four share, the role that eroticism plays in all of the texts, the common concern with challenging the male canon, etc.—are concerned.[14] That a relationship does exist between and among the four novels and/or any numerical combination of them, is indisputable. Discerning the nature of that relationship is another matter, for rather than being related by the conventional modes of character or plot, their substantive and

---

[14] Linda Gould Levine, for example, views the trilogy as providing the reader "with a fascinating study of the dynamics of women reading, rereading, misreading and rewriting the male literary canon." While acknowledging the countless ways in which the three texts deviate from each other, she is equally swift in pointing out some common threads: "In each text of the trilogy, the scenario is somewhat different, but certain patterns emerge. First, each one deals with the upper-class Catalan society of the seventies, a social setting which enables Tusquets to focus of her characters' emotional insufficiencies rather than on their economic dependencies. Secondly, in each novel, many of the names of the characters are the same and certain structures of 'three' emerge. There are three main characters: Elia, Clara and Jorge, subsequently joined by three other players: Ricardo, Pablo and Eva, cast into three different sexual patterns: heterosexual, lesbian and bisexual, and defined against the backdrop of three literary models: traditional myths, fairy tales and revisions of the two" ("Reading, Rereading..." 203). Likewise, Catherine Bellver sees an erotic unity in the novels comprising the trilogy, in each of which Tusquets' "three protagonists, all of whom share common features including identical names, seek in their erotic experiences a self-defense, an escape from frustration, and an avenue of self-discovery. Love for them is a dream from which they are forced to awake because, in one way or another, each has been abandoned by the man she loves. Each of Tusquets' three Elias, as young girls, fell under the spell created by fable and fairy tale which projects an image of men as prince charmings who choose, woo, and carry off their loving and passive maidens to their castles where they live happily ever after. Tusquets' contemporary middle-aged 'Sleeping Beauties' awake to the devastating realization that their prince has left them and that their complete dependence on men for psychological sustenance has left their lives painfully empty. Each protagonist sets out alone to reassemble the broken pieces of her life and to reindentify the fundamental components of her existence. Along this psychological journey towards self-realization, she attempts to fill with sexual experiences, primarily of a homosexual nature, the emptiness resulting from her loss of illusion" ("The Language of Eroticism..." 13).

structural affinity is of a numinous quality; it is rhythmic, arithmetic and geometric, symbolizing the production and expenditure of psychic energy that it is meant to reproduce. This rhythmic ebb and flow of psychic energy pulsating throughout the tetralogy is both propelled by and reflective of Tusquets' inimitable baroque, periphrastic narrative style. To put it another way, *what* is written in the tetralogy and *how* the tetralogy is written virtually are identical.

The oscillating polarity generated by the juxtaposition of *El mismo mar...* and *El amor...* assumes a rhythmic psycho-narrative pattern whereby the latter anticipates the former and the former comes to be seen as a natural development of the latter. The paradoxical nature of their relationship has its explanation in the fact that "paradox is the natural medium for expressing transconscious facts" (Jung, *Mysterium...* 82). From the perspective of the thematic structure of the individuation process, the act of reading *El amor...* as a "sequel" to *El mismo mar...*, that is, along a chronological temporal continuum, only reveals, paradoxically, that the relationship of the former to the latter is proleptic in one sense and endoscopic in yet another. *El amor...* not only follows *El mismo mar...*, it also anticipates it and at the same time is housed within it.

Developmentally, Elia is in the initial throws of the individuation process, and it is in this sense that the 1979 novels precedes the 1978 one. As previously discussed, individuation typically is set into motion either as the result of a neurosis that is unleashed during psychotherapy, or a traumatic event happening in daily life that forces an individual to turn inward, or through an inner compulsion to discover the truth about oneself (Goldbrunner 119). As Jung discovered throughout his decades of work with hundred of clients, in the absence of the first two causes, the third almost inevitably occurred at the onset of mid-life. Although Elia has not reached the threshold of the second half of her life, we remember that her anonymous predecessor in *El mismo mar...* had. It also would serve us well to recall that the age of the author at the time she published her first two novels (forty-two and forty-three, respectively) not only corresponds to a period of intense psychoanalysis but, not accidentally, we do not believe, is the age at which she separated from her marital partner, Esteban. Nor should it go unnoticed that the age of the author bisects the age of her two protagonists (fifty and thirty-something, respectively). During our interview, Tusquets offered an enlightening theory regarding the unconscious motives that might well have driven her toward marital separation at age forty-two, and its possible relationship to her fifty-year-old protagonist: "Las cuatro novelas son un caso de mujer, de la cual la pareja se desinteresa, porque encuentra a una chica joven. Eso sí es un tema central de mis novelas, y es algo que no he vivido nunca. A lo mejor me separé yo a los cuarenta y dos para evitar que me dejara a los cincuenta, no lo sé" (Dolgin, "Conversación..." 401). The end result in terms of her artistic production is the following: from the vantage point of a woman in her early forties, Tusquets projects in her first novel a psychological evolution that has its origins in the second, continues in the third in which the protagonist's age is the average of the ages of the first two and likewise equals that of the author, and culminates in the fourth in which the protagonist's age not only is identical to that of the author when she published it, but also matches the age of the original fifty-year old projection in *El mismo mar*.... Once again, the interpenetration of autobiographical and fictional factors offers further evidence that the first and fourth novels indiscriminately are beginnings and ends of an archetypal circle of the Self, whose internal meandering design, consistent with the individuation process, is spiral, and whose creative and structural centrifugal force is the psyche of Esther Tusquets whose self (as archetype) occupies its center.

The trifurcated development of the erotic, creative and psychic dimensions of the novel are propelled into motion by its three word opening sentence: "una oscura llamada." Not only do the first three words of *El amor es un juego solitario*, serve as a prelude to a provocative description of the springtime mating habits of jungle primates, it is revealed twenty lines later that it is, in fact, an excerpt from a children's *novela de aventuras* that many years earlier Elia remembers having been caught in the act of reading by one of her upper-middle-class childhood peers. Tusquets has interpolated into her own "adult" novel, of which Elia is the protagonist, a portion of a novel written for children of which Elia, an adult in Tusquets' fiction, was a reader during her childhood. It goes without saying that Esther Tusquets must also have been at one time a reader of the same novel in order to have been able to incorporate a portion of it into her present fiction. Or has she authored this ostensible meta-fiction as well? Probably, since its narrative style is indistinguishable from her own self-proclaimed fiction. But a far more pertinent question to pose is its appropriateness to a children's *novela de aventuras* and, analogously, the relevance of meshing an excerpt from children's literature—be it Tusquets' meta-fiction or someone else's—within a dense, hermetic New Novel like *El amor*....

It is not long before the answers are disclosed. At the plot level, the sensorially depicted jungle scene that so visually, auditorily, and olfactorily captures the male simian in pursuit of the scent emitted by his chosen female in heat, sets the stage and tone for the forthcoming erotic adventures shared among Elia, Ricardo, and Clara. Although reproduction and the perpetuation of the species is the end result of animal mating, it is a "natural" consequence, not an artifically imposed one. Within the socio-religious context of Francoist

Spain during the 1950s, "en esta religión monolítica de la España de los años cincuenta en la que todo está medido y cuantificado" (9) when the young Elia's—not to mention Esther's, who was Clara's and Ricardo's age at the time—gender was being molded, "mating" was regulated in a most "unnatural" way by the Catholic Church. Elia (Esther) and her entire generation were brought up to believe that the one and only acceptable form of female sex was reproductive, performed strictly within the confines of the institution of marriage. Not so for males, however, as evidenced by the "natural" reaction of the boys who "escuchan el párrafo sobre la selva en primavera y los simios en celo" (9), in contrast to the socially conditioned, "unnatural" one of girls who "simulan escandalizarse y fingen no atender" (9), as one of the boys reads to the group the very passage for which they had ridiculed Elia. Although both sexes are even more intensely interested in the passage than was Elia, they hypocritically treat her "como a una extraña al grupo, como a alguien que no podrá ser nunca incondicionalmente aceptado y que deberá moverse siempre en la periferia de este cerrado mundo veraniego" (8-9). While the boys feel free to reveal their fascination, the nice, respectable girls from society's most influential families have been taught to hide their interest and to feign embarrassment.

The Spanish children's reactions to Elia's possession and the boy's reading of this (meta)-fictional prelude to Elia's narrative present, at once establishes a lengthy set of binary oppositions to be wrestled with throughout the remainder of the novel: masculine/feminine; conscious/unconscious; Apollonian/Dionysian; nature/culture; jungle/city; reality/myth; prey/predator; passive/aggressive, just to name a handful of them. In a context of solitude and boredom, "un marasmo de aburrimiento" (12), Elia's detailed recollection of the (meta)-fictional passage signals stirrings within her unconscious of "un rumor subterráneo que no logra siquiera aflorar y hacerse oír entre el ajetreo de la vida consciente" (13). The return to Elia's narrative present—springtime in Barcelona—corresponds to her return to consciousness, at which time she identifies the source of "the dark call" that had awakened her unbridled unconscious: "Y lo cierto es que las primeras llamadas fueron tan débiles que apenas si pudo percibirlas: sólo una remota ansiedad al oír cierto nombre, pronunciado desde hacía mucho y muy a menudo—pero siempre con total indiferencia, o con un asomo de burla y de desprecio—por Clara" (12). Clara's repeated, but seemingly innocuous, mention of Ricardo's name to Elia on the literal level of meaning of the text, sets into motion a confrontation between the aforementioned binary oppositions. At the plot level, Elia will attempt to transpose the dark, primordial, mysteriously harmonious balance of forces between male and female simians engaged in springtime jungle mating into her culturally refined, feminine bedroom where she spends endless hours "en la cama, desnuda, en una alcoba blanca y rosa, viendo cómo se deslizan sobre su cuerpo las rayas paralelas de la luz que se filtran por las rendijas de la persiana" (18).

At the most obvious plot level of the novel, it would appear as though the illicit Elia-Ricardo-Clara erotic triangle has as its objective the sexual gratification of the three participants. As the ostensibly erotic novel that *El amor*... appears to be, this would have to be the case in accordance with the definition of eroticism as the human imitation of nature (Paz 185-86), socialized sexuality devoid of the reproductive motivation sanctioned by the Catholic Church as the only acceptable form of sexual activity. The self-conscious literariness of the opening pages has been engineered to undermine the social reality propagated by Spain's mid-century religious monolith, in which human behavior was weighed, measured and qualified. Under the established order, sex as a pleasure-seeking, self-mirroring activity was deemed sinful. From a posture of mockery and rebellion, the novelist rejects the prevailing social norms in favor of an erotic anarchy that imposes no rules on either sex. Hence, the behavior of the predatory male ape and his chosen female in heat is transposed from the jungle of the meta-fictional scene to Elia's airy, feminine room, where it is re-enacted as a drama of liberation from the socio-religious mandates of the Franco era.

Deceptive appearances being what they are, namely the founding principle of the New Novel, erotic escapism turns out *not* to be the motivational thrust of the text. Sensual pleasure of and for its own sake, devoid of any secondary motive (as eroticism must necessarily be), is not the driving force of the triangular relationship, or even of any of the possible paired combinations (Elia and Clara; Elia and Ricardo; Clara and Ricardo). The three characters in fact are drawn together into a loveless, time-bound, non-transcendent relationship, by deeply rooted emotional drives and voids that are unrelated either to the attainment of sexual pleasure for the self or the offer of love to another. Psychophysical eroticism and emotional loving are nothing more than false pretenses at the form and content levels, respectively. This narrative game of deceptive false appearances creates a disturbing form/content discordance since the sensual play of the three characters is not an end unto itself as the erotic esthetics stylizing the narrative unfolding would lead us to believe. Nor is the novel about love as its title would suggest. It is about the loveless quality of life for these three individuals who, in Elia's mind, typify the human race: "No hay amor en el mundo para nadie, piensa Elia la amarga" (29). As the reader delves deeper and deeper into Tusquets' narrative quagmire, it becomes readily apparent that the common bond drawing Elia, Clara, and Ricardo together is an inability to truly love another human being as a result of not knowing what it is to be loved by another, not even by the very parents who gave life to them:

> If the three principals are thus marked by personal histories that veer from the social norm, their mutual relationship radically undermines our presuppositions regarding love. In this three-way affair, the unorthodox couplings of youth and age, beauty and ugliness, privilege and privation, homosexuality and heterosexuality, break out of all boundaries, classes and exclusions. Poetic conventions of love and platonic archetypes of beauty are mocked and thwarted by the glaring inadequacies of the young lovers. (Servodidio, "Perverse Pairings..." 241)

This unlikely trio, in fact, have more in common than they or the reader might think: a common quest to fill the immense void left by a loveless existence. Tusquets employs an esthetics of eroticism to tell the story of three individuals who use sex as a vehicle to explore the possibility of finding the love of which they have been deprived since childhood. In the case of the attractive, intelligent, economically and materially privileged Elia, depression and boredom, accompanied by feelings of helplessness and uselessness, compel her to fill the void of her existence any way she can. The naïve Clara clings to Elia in the absence of meaningful bonding with her own mother. Her emotional dependence on her surrogate mother is so extreme that she has relinquished her own selfhood—or any possibility of acquiring it—in favor of attending to the needs of others even at the expense of her own emotional well-being. This is evidenced by the role that Clara assumes as go-between, "a servir de mensajera y hasta tal vez de cómplice" (32) for the sexual neophyte, Ricardo, and Elia, his chosen mentor, "su iniciadora... para entregarse a su cuidado, a fin de que ella, por gracia y merced de las ninfas, acoja a este aprendiz ferviente, dócil y sumiso y sea su mæstra" (14). Given Clara's emotional insecurity and over-dependency, it is not in her best interest voluntarily to "share" Elia with anyone, regardless of how remote the possibility of creating competition for herself may seem. Operating under the illusion that her relationship with Elia will be everlasting, while a sexual encounter between Elia and Ricardo will be a transitory form of entertainment for all three, she places Elia's needs and well-being before her own, "en un afán supremo o en un intento desesperado por atenuar durante unos días el aburrimiento omnipresente, el hastío letal, la ansiedad destructiva de Elia, un intento por alejar este tedio que lo devora todo" (33). As for Ricardo, he seeks sexual initiation and practice with an experienced partner like Elia as compensation for his sense of worthlessness. Fatherless since the age of two and having been raised as an only child by a cold, distant, bitter mother, Ricardo seeks from his sexual encounter with Elia a way to inflate a weak ego and to redirect the love and validation for which he has yearned since childhood from his mother. In the words of Mirella Servodidio, the adolescent boy's "complicated attachment to his mother, vexed by the death of his father fifteen years prior, grounds Ricardo neurotically in a pre-Œdipal sphere from which he is banished by an undemonstrative 'madre de cera' (107). Maternal inaccessibility creates an unbridgeable gulf which feeds the boy's sense of deprivation and powerlessness while stimulating his desire" ("Perverse Pairings..." 240).

Hence, the story of Elia, Clara, and Ricardo is anything but erotic; only the style in which it is narrated is. The seeming incompatibility between the form and content of *El amor...* acts as a signal pointing to other not-so-obvious textual readings. Consistent with the tenets of the Spanish New Novel, the erotically depicted adventures shared by the three characters act as mere devices to keep the reader interested in turning the pages, while disguising deeper, more significant levels of meaning in the text. As the characters use sex to get other personal needs met, Tusquets employs an esthetics of eroticism to elaborate more subtle psychological and creationistic themes. For example, there exists an analogous relationship between heterodox sexuality as a vehicle of liberation against the stagnant role of women in mid-century Spanish society, and the post-1967 New Novel, which emerged as a reaction against the ineffectual, static view of reality that was portrayed in the preceding "objectivistic" novels of socio-critical realism. In contrast to social realism, which seeks to redress the dehumanization of modern man, the New Novel strives to create innovative expression and artistic design for its own artistic sake. Similar to the solipsistic quality of the New Novel, love, according to Tusquets, is a self-conscious artifice:

> Creo que el amor es una historia que te montas tú. Es un cuento que te inventas a ti misma. El otro se está contando otro cuento él mismo. Aunque el otro te quiera y lleves una vida muy feliz, es un montaje. Es un montaje muy artificioso el amor... el amor como lo entiendo yo en mis libros. Naturalmente el amor de un chico y una chica que se enamoran a los dieci-siete años es diferente. Pero el amor éste que yo describo, volcánico y pasional, que se desencadena en un instante, y que lo pone todo patas arriba, es bastante un juego solitario. (Dolgin, "Conversación..." 399)

The view of love that is presented in *El amor...* curiously resembles the founding principles and *praxis* of the New Novel. A reverberation of the author's view of love, Elia refers to her summer "affair" with Ricardo (begun in May and pre-determined to conclude in September) as a literary artifice: "Esta aventura artificiosa y bella, tan literaria, tendrá que seguir siendo artificiosa y bella hasta su final, un final previsto con cuatro meses de antelación" (77). The notions of game-playing, coupled with its objective of deceit, are the cornerstones of both the Tusquetsian view of love and of the poetics of the "playful" quality of the New Novel. *El amor es un juego solitario* is permeated with references to its own artistic exhibitionism and literariness. This formalistic concern is of a ludic nature and is propelled by the author's propensity to display her technical craft. As a result, reader expectation continually is undermined because of the peculiar traits of the narrative game. For example, two references to a situation, thought, or expression, may complement one another in the form of a simile or parallelism, or they may contradict each other. The contradiction may be opposed to the complementation, the parallelism may contradict the parallelism, or the contradiction may be parallel to the contradiction. In other words, the game is a process of combining and recombining in a similar, and at the same time different, way the components of the presented fictional world. The effect of Tusquets' particular erotic esthetics, and of the New Novel in general, is one of sabotaging the perception of a stable, fixed reality. As a means of counteracting the prevailing rigid norms of mid-century Spain and, consequently, produce an unsettling effect on the reader, the sexual scenes in *El amor...* are performed in a context that is "metasexual." "Metasexuality" is a term coined by the American erotic writer, Marco Vassi, to refer to sexuality that dispenses with "categories such as heterosexuality, homosexuality, bisexuality and perversions, replacing them with sexual modes: theatrical, masturbatory, romantic, therapeutic, and procreative" (191). In his book chapter entitled "The Metasexual Manifesto," Vassi attempts to establish a distinction between sex and metasex: "Sex is biological, metasex is psychophysical. Sex, the biological eroticum, is for procreation and for no other reason; metasex, the psychophysical eroticum, is for any other reason whatsoever. Metasexually, there is no real difference between what two men do in bed, from what three women might do in bed, nor from what a man and a woman do in bed" (188). Erotic description such as that which one encounters with regularity in the majority of Tusquets' fictional narratives is, in a certain sense, a type of foreplay by means of which the author stimulates characters and readers alike into an emotional receptiveness toward the ultimate climactic euphoria: the moment of heightened consciousness that occurs during sex" (Perkins 128).

The metasexual acts performed by the three characters are motivated by narcissistic need and desire on a personal level, and by socio-religious defiance on another. Metasexualty assumes the proportions of a Dionysian revenge against an austere society whose members are incapable of loving because they themselves have been the victims of early childhood love deprivation that is now irreversible: "la humanidad entera reducida a una caterva, a una manada de niñitos perdidos que no han sabido crecer, que llaman a mamá con múltiples nombres diferentes, que no saben amar porque no fueron amados, y que engendran a su vez nuevas generaciones de niños sin amor, en un círculo cerrado e interminable" (84). Elia, whose unconscious contains the inner child and *anima* archetypes portrayed by Clara and Ricardo, both of whom are in pursuit of the Lost Mother, is in search of the mother she never had. This factor ties *El amor*... to its narrative antecedent insofar as both female protagonists are suffering from the same emotional void whose origin is identical. Tusquets effectively juxtaposes the cold Apollonian severity of the Spanish character, which she deems responsible seemingly for all of her characters' maladjustments, with Dionysian recklessness and frivolity. Her intention seems to be that of neutralizing an excessively controlled society that has lost contact with its feminine *eros* principle. The flexible, permutable nature of metasexuality is designed to correct a personal psychic imbalance brought about by an excessively masculine, *logos*-dominant society. Bettina L. Knapp theorizes about the social conditions under which the Dionysian myth returns to life: "When man fears woman or those values she represents for him, in the objective world of reality (a projection of an inner condition caused in part by an unintegrated *anima*),... the overtly subordinated female will be transformed into a disruptive and chaotic force, thus bringing an end to the smooth-running rationally oriented society in power" (6-7). Explicit descriptions of the character' multifarious metasexual adventures allows the reader to experience the heightened pleasure of his/her erotic fantasies as they are reflected in the mating patterns of primates; that is, in nature, where there are no social taboos. The literary (non)-51*ménage-à-trois* undermines sanctioned beliefs and codes of behavior that buttress male hegemony while suppressing the female Dionysian principle, which "has always been equated with the dark elemental forces of nature, with what is ecstatic, uninhibited, fruitful in its way" (Knapp 7). In this manner, Tusquets achieves the effect of disarming the reader, of having the reader cast aside all pre-existing value judgments and any tendency toward moral censorship. Once (s)he becomes non-discriminatorily receptive, the novel naturalizes sexual forbiddances regarding incest (in addition to being a sexual partner to Clara, Elia at times is a mother figure to her as well, by virtue of the way that she bathes and rocks her to sleep like a child), homosexuality, bisexuality, sodomy, the female as predator and aggressor, the female as a recipient of sexual gratification, and age differences among partners.

As the author demonstrates by the parallels between the predatory behavior of the male ape and Ricardo, female dependency and submissiveness are relegations that begin in nature and are appropriated by society. Elia's unorthodox sexual relationship with Ricardo and Clara alike, is construed as a rebellion against the traditional role of wife, mother, and passive sexual partner. Not only has she sought equality by abandoning her family—a world in which she is conscious of her growing hatred of a husband and children who wander in and out of the house oblivious to her needs, wants or emotional state—but she also has discovered that she is able to equalize the duration and quality of sexual pleasure for both herself and Ricardo only because her age and experience grant her the upper hand. Elia recognizes that she is incapable of postponing the moment of sexual climax with mature, experienced men because, all things being equal, they dominate. With Ricardo, however, she possesses the leverage and consequently establishes the rules of the game.

From a Jungian perspective, Tusquets' second novel offers two allegorical readings. The first is related specifically to the fictional Elia and involves the character's newly-discovered awareness of her shadow, also known as the unconscious. According to this reading, Elia is her Self (the totality of her psyche which includes her conscious as well as unconscious) while Clara and Ricardo act as projections of two of Elia's unconscious archetypes, the inner female child in the case of the former and an underdeveloped, self-destructive *animus* in the case of the latter. Clara and Ricardo are, in other words, personified aspects of Elia's unconscious whose interaction with her consciousness dramatizes the confrontation and attempted interaction of the two great hemispheres of the psyche. Elia's physical bisexuality thus would act as a metaphor for her dawning awareness of the inherent binary quality of all things, including the conscious/unconscious duality of the psychic make-up. At yet a deeper allegorical level of meaning, each of the three characters may be interpreted as the embodiment of a universal archetype: Elia (*él y ella*), the bisexual self; Clara, the feminine contra-sexual counterpart of the masculine self (of Elia); and Ricardo, the masculine contra-sexual counterpart of the feminine self (of Elia). This is not to suggest that Tusquets created these characters with the conscious intention of establishing multiple levels of reading, or of endowing them with universal significance. It is meant to imply simply that the forms of these universal archetypes have become manifest in these characters.

The color symbolism of these opening pages adumbrates a pattern of unconscious manifestations of Elia's personality moving toward conscious awareness. Like the moon symbolizing femininity and the female principle governing the universe, Elia's bedroom is a spacious, airy white, accessorized in pink with "paredes tapizadas en rosa, cubierto el suelo por moqueta rosa" (16), and infiltrated by beams of radiant yellow sunlight shining through the window blinds, "las rayas paralelas de la luz siguiendo a lo largo del día su inexorable recorrido por el techo y por las paredes, a ratos por su cuerpo" (16-17). In addition to light symbolism representing human consciousness in creation stories, beginning with God's creation of the universe, art/mandala therapist Susanne Fincher reminds us of the scientific discovery several hundred years ago that "white light expands into the full spectrum of colors when it passes through a prism," from which she concludes that "white can be said to represent unity from which multiplicity (colors) flows" (41). While typifying the feminine ideal of virginity and purity, the color white "is also the color of semen, the essence of creativity, and of milk, the sustainer of new life" (42). Ultimately, says Fincher, "white in *mandalas* may suggest heightened spirituality, clarity, and readiness for change." It also may symbolize "an opening to transpersonal dimensions of the psyche" (45). Pink, a blend of white and red, traditionally has stood "as a symbol of female sensuality, emotions, and youth" (Fincher 64). Because it is the color in which newborn baby and young girls commonly are dressed, the appearance of pink in *mandalas* typically refers to "the young feminine: the inner child for women, the *anima* for men" (65). The yellow beams of sunlight that penetrate the white and pink bedroom symbolize "the active fructifying principle in nature associated with the masculine... For women, the color yellow may be an attribute of the *animus*" (Fincher 55). A profusion of yellow "can speak of a polarization of light and dark aspects of the psyche," causing one to experience extreme mood swings such as energy and lethargy, activity and passivity, elation and despair (Fincher 55).

The two-tier archetypal reading of *El amor...* described above would cast Elia in the role of the archetype of the (2)self as the central regulating principle of the (1)Self, or bisexual psychic totality, of which she is an embodiment at the plot level of the story. Clara and Ricardo are subsidiaries of Elia insofar as they represent aspects of Elia's unconscious while Elia as (1)Self and (2)self is self-sufficient. As an archetype, Clara would be viewed as a projection of Elia's unconscious inner female child (symbolized by the color pink) while Ricardo acts as a projection of the protagonist's unconscious *animus* (symbolized by the color yellow). Their meeting ground—Elia's highly symbolic white bedroom—suggests the confrontation of these two key components of Elia's shadow which first will attempt to negotiate a peaceful coexistence within Elia's psyche, followed by integration with her consciousness. The imitation of nature in which her imagination and body will be engaged metaphorically will represent the mental harnessing and organizing of creative energy needed to produce a coherent esthetic object. On yet another metaphoric plane, Elia's erotic adventures will force a confrontation between her conscious ego and shadow, the latter comprised of her unconscious inner child (personified by Clara) and the dark, hidden recesses of her *animus* (personified by Ricardo). Elia's alternating interactions with Clara and Ricardo reveal increasingly profound layers of Elia's psyche. Little by little the sources of her psychological dysfunction emerge and we come to understand how and why Clara and Ricardo coexist within Elia but cannot transcend their differences and be integrated as a greater whole. The inner female child/*animus* incompatibility is dramatized when, after Elia and Ricardo reach such an elevated state of physical pleasure, they sink into a lifeless complacency where they remain stuck. To remedy the situation, Ricardo suggests that they make it a threesome, referring to the inclusion of Clara as "casi una necesidad estilística" (97). Clara acquiesces, only for the plan to backfire miserably when the young girl's jealousy of Elia's relationship with Ricardo makes her participation impossible. Her ensuing hysteria signals the negative mother complex from which the composite female protagonist of the tetralogy suffers, causing her to be *animus*-possessed and, therefore, out of touch with her maternal instincts. Put simply, the insensitive *animus* frightens the little girl away: "Clara llora y grita y se debate, agita enloquecida la cabeza de un lado a otro de la almohada, rehuyendo el contacto de sus labios, Clara se revuelve, y le golpea, y le rechaza, mientras él le sujeta los muslos entre las rodillas" (138). Consciousness (Elia) must intervene by repressing the confrontation of these two antagonistic components of her unconscious: "Es ahora imprevistamente Elia la que lo golpea y le desmonta y aparta a Clara hasta el extremo más remoto de la cama" (138). We thus arrive at the understanding of what *El amor es un juego solitario* is about: the conscious awareness of the binary make-up of all things and the natural tendency, although arduous task that it is, to transcend the oscillating One and the Other.

It becomes clear that socially conditioned values and attitudes, carried well into adulthood, not only establish a bi-polarity between the two sexes, but they also create a bipartite division within the female psyche into the self, or what is "natural," and into the other, or what is "unnatural," but socially expected and, therefore, culturally taught and reinforced. In truth, the forbidden passage "naturally" awakens in males and females alike a deep, dark, primal force, resulting in a heightening of the senses and an upsurge of all of the instinctual energies and desires emanating from the human id. Whereas in nature males and females alike live completely in response to their basic instincts, in society males are permitted to express, and even to act upon (within reason, of course) these impulses, while females are required to repress them or else suffer socio-religious condemnation. Consequently, women are psychologically conditioned by society, by the Catholic Church, and by their families, to repress sensual desire, to abstain from sexual pleasure, and to regard themselves solely as objects of male desire and as mechanisms of reproduction. Because women are so discouraged from experiencing themselves as subjects of desire—sexual and otherwise—and from realizing their full human potential, they are estranged from the wholeness and completeness of their own sex, and simultaneously trapped in an ambivalent relationship with the other sex. While on the one hand women are dependent upon men to validate them since male approval forms the basis of the female identity, at the same time they deeply resent dependence upon a source of acceptance that lies outside themselves, but which they have internalized as their own through years of social and religious conditioning.

From the very outset of her novel, Tusquets establishes the three planes of narrative development that ultimately will be intertwined and rendered indistinguishable: Elia's erotic adventure with Ricardo (literal plane); the springtime mating call of jungle simians (creationistic plane), and an inner urge or calling (*"llamada"*) stemming from the dark (*"oscura"*) realm of protagonist's unconscious (psychic plane) which sets the individuation process into motion. The solitary context in which Elia creates and plays out her erotic fantasies throughout the novel is consistent with the first of the four stages of the individuation process: the recognition of one's divided nature. The prelude to individuation begins with a conscious awareness that the image of one's Self that one projects to the outside world is quite distinct from, if not diametrically opposed to, one's inner nature. Jung refers to this protective outer cover, or "mask," as the persona. It has two functions: first of all, it serves to create a specific impression on other people, and, secondly, it hides the inner Self of the individual (*Man and His Symbols* 287). Outwardly, Elia has more than fulfilled the two expectations drummed into her since early childhood, "de muy niña" (64) by her family and social class: "el matrimonio y la cultura general" (64). She is married to a man who, by her own admission, loves her, and she is the mother of two children, all three of whom are conspicuously absent from the action of the novel. She is well-read, well-traveled and has seized every opportunity to visit museums, to take in art exhibits, and to attend concerts and the theater. Inwardly, however, she feels empty and unable to achieve a *joie de vivre* at any level of her existence. Of Elia and her entire social class, Barbara Ichiishi observes that "while the adults who act out the grotesque masquerade of social life seem to be irrevocably cut off from their childhood selves, their self-alienated behavior is on the deepest level evidence of their very subjugation to that early childhood state" (93). Despite the privileged status and wealth in which Elia was raised and into which she married, her social prestige and material comfort have never filled the void left by the emotionally distant, neglectful parents whom we met in the previous novel; there, as here, both are described as being unavailable to their daughter, "inaccesibles como los dioses" (67). The protagonist is emotionally subjugated to her inner child (personified by Clara) who keeps her stuck in an unresolved Electra complex that was the result of the young girl's inability to identify and bond with her same-sex parent. Because Elia continues to yearn for the comfort of her mother's unconditional love, she is unable to offer to her own children the maternal nurturance of which she has been deprived. She is unable to give to another what she herself has never had. Although she believes that she loves them, she is saddened by the recognition that she feels lost and empty inside, that they have not fulfilled her as her social class had led her to believe that they would: "acaso sea cierto que Elia los ame, pero es asimismo seguro de que no han logrado colmar nunca su vida (vida de mujer ociosa, de niña consentida, diría seguramente Ricardo, pero Clara sabe bien que no es esto, o por lo menos que no es tan sólo esto"—51). In order to mask the emotional pain that continues to haunt the deepest levels of her inner child being (personified by Clara), she unknowingly relies upon the indifferent bravado provided by her compensatory *animus* (personified by Ricardo).

As previously stated, the second novel not only follows, but likewise is enclosed within, the first insofar as Elia's age bisects that of the anonymous protagonist at the time of her autobiographical narration of *El mismo mar...* (fifty) and the age at which she claims her psychological maturation to have ceased due to Jorge's unexpected suicide (seventeen) which, (not) coincidentally, is her interlocutor's, Clara's, age (and likewise the age of the sexual apprentice, Ricardo). Therefore, if in accordance with the Demeter/Kore archetype elaborated upon in the previous section, the narrator and Clara are aspects of one female Self, then Elia would be situated midway along the Clara/narrator continuum of the uninterrupted chain of female generations.

Not only in relation to *El mismo mar de todos los veranos*, but also at each and every level of its own internal narration, *El amor es un juego solitario* dramatizes metaphorically, symbolically, and archetypally, the oscillatory polarity of the female psyche about to embark upon the individuation voyage that the previous first novel completed. From the point of view of the individuation process, then, the second novel is the first novel of the series. From the perspective of chronological publication, however, it is the second, by virtue of which it begins to chart the psychologically journey at whose destination we previously arrived at the close of *El mismo mar...* and once again will reach at the end of *Para no volver*. It is not until the third novel, *Varada tras el último naufragio*, however, that the rhythmic fluctuation generated by the *El mismo mar/El amor...* duality is released and surpassed, and movement toward psychic growth can be perceived. As we shall discover—and in accordance with the symbolic quality of three— *Varada*... "represents the solution of the conflict posed by dualism" (Cirlot 222) that the thesis/antithesis juxtaposition of *El mismo mar...* and *El amor...* (from the point of view of the tetralogy) and of Clara/Ricardo (constituting Elia's most irresolute unconscious interaction in *El amor...*) have laid out.

In addition to its internal structural dynamics that are played out by Elia (consciousness), and Clara and Ricardo (unconscious archetypes), the very title, *El amor es un juego solitario*, constitutes a miniature replica of the relational tension between the first and the second novels. The commonly understood meanings of "love" and "game" mutually repel and attract one another. The repellence is explained by the fact that "love" implies a deep affection and warm, personal attachment that one person feels for another, while a "game" suggests a competitive activity governed by pre-established rules in which two or more people are engaged in a battle to outmaneuver the other(s) and thus achieve victory. The attraction, on the other hand, is the result of the inherent contradiction, which produces the effect of arousing the reader's curiosity about what possible relationship might exist between these two ostensibly irreconcilable concepts. Furthermore, if "love" is a "game," and the "game" is a "solitary" one, that is to say, played alone, then "love," not only is a "game," but it is a "game" played in isolation. Each term negates the other because of mutual exclusivity; quite simply, the totality cannot be. Each term also lures the other because the tension arouses a question for which curiosity mandates a response: Might there by a higher, synthetic meaning and, if so, what is it? The reading of the text thus is propelled by a need to decipher the meaning of its title. In the process, the reader is confronted with the arduous task of "decoding" not only the complex nature of the relationship between the second and first texts, but likewise the even more ambiguous relationship between Elia and the Clara portion of her unconscious, between Elia and the Ricardo aspect of her unconscious, and between Clara and Ricardo, two incompatible splinter personalities whose vociferous co-existence has brought Elia to the troubled state of internal conflict (equated with the earliest stage of the individuation process) that forms the *raison d'être* of the second novel.

Just as the terms of the title cancel one another out, rendering unattainable an integrated totality, Elia, Clara, and Ricardo analogously constitute three sides of a potential, but never constituted, triangle (Elia + Clara; Elia + Ricardo; Clara (not +) Ricardo), whose symmetric unity is well anticipated but unrealized due to Clara's unequivocal rejection of Ricardo. Hence, the (non-)triangular relationship is no more than a time-restricted process of attachment, detachment, reattachment, and, ultimately, unattachment; that is, fragments of wholeness never wholly assembled to transcend the sum of its parts. In the end, the love-starved Clara (el amor) is consumed with jealousy over Elia's erotic interlude with Ricardo which he has constructed and played out as a skillfully calculated game (*un juego*) in which he uses Elia as a means to his real pursuit. In the end, Ricardo's premeditated ploy miserably betrays him, casting the lonely Elia into yet another abyss of boredom and despair (*solitario*), "peor que muerta, mucho peor que muerta" (150), comforted solely "por la esperanza de que pueda surgir todavía algo exterior capaz de devolverle el movimiento... y que le dé, durante otra breve etapa, la ilusión de existir a través del existir de otros" (150).

In summation, the painfully love-starved Clara, although unquestionably embarrassed, "inequívocamente avergonzada" (13), playfully arranged, "riendo y al parecer divertida" (13), the unlikely encounter between her male classmate and her surrogate mother. Ricardo, like Clara, has spent his entire childhood and adolescence awaiting a loving word or gesture from his rigid, austere, embittered mother. Therefore, inasmuch as Clara/Ricardo display a vast system of diametric oppositions (female/male; prey/predator; homosexual/ heterosexual; passive/aggressive; emotional/stoic; insecure/self-confident, etc.), they do in fact share a single common denominator with Elia: all three have been deprived of maternal love, acceptance, and meaningful bonding since early childhood. Furthermore, recalling that Elia's age is twice that of Ricardo, and Ricardo and Clara are the same age, the laws of mathematics tell us that Elia's age equals Clara's plus Ricardo's. To put it another way, Elia's psyche is comprised of the sum total of the Clara/Ricardo unity (common denominator) of paired opposites (the inherent binary structure of the psyche). Hence, inasmuch as *El amor...* gives every appearance of dramatizing an erotic love triangle involving three distinct individuals, Jungian theory offers a key which unlocks quite a different reading. In the same way that sensual play is a mere vehicle by means of which each of the three characters attempts to satisfy a narcissistic need—sexual initiation for Ricardo, maternal nurturing for Clara, and an escape from depression and boredom for Elia—the erotic triangle offers a secondary allegorical meaning when read from the Jungian perspective of the individuation process. This is not to imply that Tusquets intended to write such an allegory, nor even that she was/is aware that one existed/exists. It is meant to suggest that each of the three characters has been infused with universal archetypal attributes (of which the author may or may not have been conscious during the writing of the novel, or of which she may have been only partly conscious) whose interaction narrates a psychological tale that deviates from the literal one. In this archetypal drama, the bisexual Elia represents the central regulating and mediating archetype of the self, Ricardo represents the *animus*, or unconscious masculine counterpart to Elia's female consciousness, and Clara represents the *anima*, or unconscious feminine counterpart to Elia's masculine consciousness. When read from this perspective, *El amor es un juego solitario* either is a conscious fictional rendition, or even more plausibly, an unconscious projection, of the bisexuality of its creator: Esther Tusquets. Hence, it might well be argued that in this, her second novel, the author appears to be grappling with the discovery and meaning of her own bisexuality (psychological and/or physical), while at the same time redressing female estrangement from her true nature on an archetypal as well as socio-historic level.

3. *Varada tras el último naufragio*: Three as Synthesis and Transcendence

The third novel of the series, *Varada tras el último naufragio*, has received far less critical attention than the other three novels comprising the original trilogy, and later tetralogy. As a matter of fact, we are not aware of a single study that has been done exclusively on *Varada*.... In the handful of instances where the 1980 novel has been the subject of critical analysis, it invariably has been within the context either of the trilogy (Bellver, Gould Levine, Vásquez), or of the tetralogy (Dolgin, Gil Casado, Ishiisi), or within the scope of Tusquets' narrative fiction as a whole (Molinaro). The author herself was astonished by the sharp contrast between the paucity of critical interest on the one hand, and the overwhelmingly positive response by her reading public as evidenced by the hundreds of laudatory letters she received (primarily) from women throughout the western hemisphere.

The reemergence in the third novel of Elia and Clara, in addition to references to the protagonist's cat, Muslina, immediately link it to the preceding two. Elia, however, is ten years older than in the previous novel, *El amor...*, is married to a philanderer named Jorge, and is the mother of one teenage son, Daniel. Following the yearly custom of spending the summer months on the Mediterranean coast with Elia's and Jorge's married friends, Eva and Pablo, the novel opens at the beach in the early days of June. Unlike all previous summers, however, Elia for the first time has joined her friends unaccompanied by her husband who, weeks before, had announced to his wife that he no longer loved her. Consequently, Elia has been under the care of a psychiatrist and friend, Miguel, who has supplied her with anti-depressants and tranquilizers to help her survive the shock of a failed marriage with Jorge, upon whom she had been totally dependent throughout her adult life. Frightened and insecure about the prospect of having to spend the rest of her life alone, Elia is catatonic and unable to sleep, socialize with her friends, or to write even a single word despite spending the majority of each day in front of her typewriter staring at a blank sheet of paper. Throughout the majority of the novel, Elia teeters between a nervous breakdown and committing suicide, offering the reader little evidence that she will be able to avoid one or the other or, ultimately, both.

Shortly after Elia's arrival, the self-confident attorney, Eva, brings an emotionally disturbed, orphaned teenage girl named Clara into the house to live with her, Pablo, and Elia. While attempting to help Elia acknowledge her share of responsibility for the break-up of her marriage, as well as to be a surrogate mother to Clara (she fails miserably at both), Eva is stunned to learn of her own husband's marital infidelity when Clara witnesses Pablo in his and Eva's bedroom having an affair with a young, attractive redhead whom he had met at the beach. After Clara informs Eva of what has transpired one evening in her absence, Pablo terminates the affair in order to try to save his marriage. Meanwhile, Eva banishes Clara from their home in order to rid herself of anything or anyone that might remind her of Pablo's indiscretion, "porque la imagen de Clara ha quedado ligada... a aquella revelación para ella monstruosa" (246-47). In the midst of Eva's and Pablo's marital crisis, Elia receives a letter from Jorge who is hopeful of being permitted to return home to his wife. In an ironic twist of fate, the ostensibly independent, invincible Eva suffers from a mental breakdown from which she emerges prepared to forgive and forget her husband's infidelity so that "en toda esta tormenta de verano, al terminar habrá salido su matrimonio con Pablo malparado pero en pie, habrá salido su amistad con Elia debilitada pero indemne, y habrá sido en definitiva Clara la única expulsada, sacrificada, elegida como chivo expiatorio o como víctima" (247). Conversely, the seemingly needy, dependent Elia refuses her husband's request for a marital reconciliation upon arriving at the heart-wrenching realization that she possessed no identity of her own in the absence of Jorge's love for her, and that her "happy" marriage had been nothing more than a romantic farse which she and Jorge had invented and been acting out for decades. Elia's identity as a wife, mother, and poet has been so confusingly intertwined with the storybook fantasy of happily-ever-after with her knight-in-shining-armor whose interests, ambitions, feelings, likes and dislikes, and hers, were one-and-the-same, "como si nada fuera de Jorge pudiera interesarme como si no existiera nada que desligada de él pudiera yo tener interés en visitar o conocer o experimentar o descubrir como si todo me llegara a través de él en función de él" (251-52). Every aspect of Elia's life had been an extension of

Jorge, including her creative writing and her son: "no hubo otro camino ni otra forma superior a la escritura hasta que llegaste tú hasta que te inventé a ti para mejor amarle a él" (259), both of which exalted him in the present and ultimately served to immortalize him for all eternity. The plot of the fictional tale takes an unexpected turn, however, when Elia finds the inner strength to accept the responsibility for having authored a fairy tale that she erroneously came to identify as her life. The problem was that her own fiction did not correspond to what was real or true from the points of view of her husband and son. In the final pages of the novel, her illusory happiness is supplanted by a truthful confrontation with the previously unknown positive as well as negative portions of the Self referred to by Jung as the shadow. At the close of the novel, Elia's happily-ever-after fiction is transformed into her open-ended autobiography, setting her on the tortuous, but ultimately self-rewarding, path of individuation.

In diametric opposition to the Elia of *El amor...* who was resistant to seeing herself within the context of her family, the forty-year-old Elia of *Varada...* wrestles with her inner conflicts precisely within the structural dynamics of her role as wife and mother. In Jungian analytical psychology, this progressive differentiation within the personal unconscious signals greater proximity to the *animus* of the collective unconscious which is, as we know, the theme of the fourth novel. As discussed in the introduction, in his clinical practice Jung had identified the conscious confrontation of the contra-sexual archetype to be most arduous phase of the individuation process for men and women alike, but nonetheless indispensable if access to the archaic images of the collective unconscious were to be reached. Identical to the emotional plight of the narrator/protagonist of *El mismo mar...* who has been emotionally "abandoned" by her philandering husband, as well as geographically "abandoned" by her narcissistic mother and professionally self-absorbed daughter living in the United States, the Elia of *Varada...* likewise finds herself left emotionally stranded (hence, the title of the novel) and psychologically shipwrecked by her husband, not to mention physically forsaken by her son who is spending the summer at a sleep-away camp. At this juncture, the plot bifurcates. In addition to serving as the causal unfolding of the story at the literal, plot level of meaning, it simultaneously becomes the springboard from which the narrative plummets the depths of Elia's psyche and explores the neuroses harbored there. From page 97 to Elia's direct interior monologue which begins on page 250, the component parts of the protagonist's unconscious psychological conflicts are projected onto Eva, Pablo, and Clara who, in addition to dramatizing the actions of the plot, at one-and-the-same-time are projections of the restructuring process in which Elia's fragmented psyche is engaged. In Elia's final twenty-one page direct interior monologue, narrated in the first-person and devoid of any punctuation in its entirety until the final period with which the novel ends, her psyche progressively builds bridges connecting her personal unconscious to consciousness. In the last few pages, her psyche expresses itself as an integrated, fluid whole which has succeeded in identifying, working through, integrating and transcending the conflicts which Jorge's shocking announcement had activated within the realm of her personal unconscious.

Since the novel opens with a depiction of Elia's emotional crisis and ends with its triumphant resolution, it is reasonable to call her its protagonist. The third-person narration moves from a physical description of Elia lying on the beach, basking in the July sun like a tired, aged lizard, to the inner world of her childhood memories (reminiscent of those that are relived by the narrator/protagonist in the opening novel of the series), a time when she felt as equally dispensable and unloved by her mother, "una mujer espléndida y arrogante" and her father, "un padre siempre ausente" (10), as she does now by her perfidious husband. The fortysome-year-old protagonist feels ravaged, hopelessly alone, and trapped in a time warp: "Elia la despojada, Elia la sola, la que ha sido exiliada del devenir del tiempo, la que yace en la arena y no tiene siquiera un pasado que desee recordar, un futuro que pueda asumir, sólo un paréntesis" (15). Stretched out almost lifelessly near the water's edge, perceiving herself to be at death's door, she imagines what it would be like to become transformed into a green stone: "Sería un fin hermoso, piensa Elia, un bonito modo de terminar, tendida aquí, al sol tibio de la mañana de julio, como un lagarto perezoso, un lagarto muy viejo y quizás sabio, tanto que de puro sabio lo ha olvidado ya todo, y sólo aspira a convertirse un día, perdido su existir apenas vegetal, en una hermosa piedra verde" (17).

A number of symbols in this paragraph foreshadow the birth-death-rebirth individuation theme. As will be discussed subsequently, the positioning of Elia's body is highly symbolic of the transitional state in which she is. For the present, we will point out the fire/water dichotomy symbolized by the sun and the ocean, respectively. As elaborated upon in great detail in the introduction, the sun is the primary universal symbol of light and warmth, and also of masculine spiritual consciousness, rational discrimination, and creative energy. Its identification with the fire element makes it a unifying and stabilizing force. It is the element with which most alchemical practices begin and end, and is symbolically depicted by "an upward-pointing triangle, which signifies rising flames, and hence solar power and life" (Gibson 75). The alchemical opposite of fire is water; hence its alchemical sign is that of fire inverted (Gibson 75), which is the downward-pointing triangle. Whereas fire is solar and, therefore, inextricably linked to masculine consciousness, water is lunar and associated with the feminine unconscious and its correlative non-discriminatory irrationality. Since it was believed by many ancient cultures that the Earth was created from primeval waters, water has come to be regarded in analytical psychology as a metaphor for the birth of ideas in the unconscious mind.

The two organizing principles, or *leitmotifs*, that structure the underlying (but, in actuality, the level of meaning of primary importance) plot development of the third novel are the sea (water), symbolizing the feminine unconscious, and the sun (fire), symbolizing masculine consciousness. Although the two metaphoric family triangles (elements of water and fire) remain apart throughout the third-person omniscient narration (through page 250), it is within the context of Elia's first-person, direct interior monologue that they converge into dynamic fluidity corresponding to a heightened state of consciousness. Gibson states that "when the two opposing symbols are interlocked, the union of the contrasting elements of fire and water is attained, creating 'fluid fire' or 'fiery water'." It is of further relevance to the individuation theme of *Varada...* that the "alchemists considered the elemental pairs of triangles as representing the *forma* (essence) and *materia* (substance), and hence the spirit and soul of everything in existence" (75). It seems hardly coincidental that the six characters in the novel embody two oppositional, intermingling ternaries (like the triangular symbols of fire and water) which take the form of contrasting family triangles, one constituted by Elia, Jorge and Daniel (masculine-dominated), and the other by Eva, Pablo and Clara (feminine-dominated). The triangle, as we know, symbolizes a multitude of significant triads, including life-death-rebirth and father-mother-child. In the third novel, the elements contained within each of the two triadic sets as well as the unity of one triangle *vis-à-vis* that of the other, contrastingly complement, integrally overlap and, ultimately, inseparably interpenetrate to form the alchemical image of the *filius philosophorum*, the philosopher's son, meaning the spirit born out of the art (here both psychic and literary) of alchemy. Elia's spiritual rebirth at the close of the novel signals the synchronicity of the transcendental syntheses both of the protagonist's feminine consciousness with her masculine unconscious, resulting in a higher level of consciousness and, with respect to the completion of a trilogy, the third novel as a synthesis ($1 + 2 = 3$) and transcendence ($1 + 2 + 3 = 6$ or $1 \times 2 \times 3 = 6$) of the first two.

In *Psychology and Religion*, Jung offers a psychological description of the qualitative significance of the three-continuum, placing particular emphasis on the all-important transition from two to three and on the relationship between three and the unity of the One:

> Every tension of opposites culminates in a release, out of which comes the 'third.' In the third, the tension is resolved and the lost unity is restored.

Unity, the absolute One, cannot be numbered, it is indefinable and unknowable, for the 'Other' which is required for this act of knowing is lacking in the condition of the One. Three is an unfolding of the One to a condition where it can be known—unity become recognizable; had it not been resolved into the polarity of the One and the Other, it would have remained fixed in a condition devoid of every quality. (Quoted in Franz, *Number and Time...* 180)

First and foremost then, the function of *Varada...* as part of, and as responsible for, the creation of a trilogy, is to mobilize the characteristic impasse symbolized by the oscillatory quality of the number two, or diametrically-opposed duality, with which the preceding novel, *El amor es un juego solitario* ends. Regarding the symbolic importance of the number three, Cirlot has the following to say: "Three symbolizes spiritual synthesis, and is the formula for the creation of each of the worlds. It represents the solution of the conflict posed by dualism... It is the harmonic product of the action of unity upon duality. It is the number concerned with basic principles, and expresses sufficiency, or the growth of unity within itself" (222). There also exists a transcendental significance to the one-two-three continuum, for not only do one, two, and three yield the number six when added together, but also when multiplied by each other. Due to the fact that the number six is equated with the number of days of creation and to the six directions of space (Cirlot 222), it has distinctive temporal and spatial connotations. Since the original act of creation took six days, the number six also is equated with the cessation of movement and, hence, "is associated with trial and effort." Finally, and of unquestionable relevance to the structural dynamics of the six characters constituting the two "families" in *Varada...*, the number six also comprises "the union of the two triangles (of fire and water) and hence signifies the human soul" (Cirlot 222). Fire being an active element associated with transmutation, regeneration, energy, fecundity, and libido, it is symbolic of the masculine. Hence, the masculine-dominated Elia-Jorge-Daniel family triangle functions as its symbol in the novel. Water, on the other hand, connotes the feminine as mediator between life and death, death and rebirth, creation and destruction and as a universal symbol of the unconscious and human potentialities. In this case, it is the feminine-dominated Eva-Pablo-Clara triangular structure that which symbolizes the feminine principle in the novel. As we shall discover, each and every one of these symbolic qualities associated with the number three, and its transcendental multiplicity of six, reveals the rhythmic pattern of psychic development undergone by Elia in the third novel. Ultimately, Elia will discover, and make the conscious decision to act upon, the full range of potentialities within her own personality, bringing about the symbolic union of the two "family" triangles within her own reborn soul.

Let us first take a look at how Tusquets handles the transition from the second to the third novel, as well as the intertextual elements that render the third novel an integrative synthesis of the first two. At the close of the second novel, Elia is not afforded any kind of psychic movement other than a predictable rhythmic back (solitude) and forth (a temporary sexual affair) that is intended to replicate the tension of diametric opposites structuring her psyche at that point in its immature development. In her moments of estrangement from the world, Elia can do no more than fantasize about, or anticipate, an inevitable forthcoming affair. When engaged in an erotic adventure, she obsesses over the inevitability of its end, stirring up within herself such a high level of anxiety that she must retreat from the relationship in order to regain some semblance of mental and emotional equilibrium. More often than not, however, her thought process and her physical circumstances, her conscious ego and unconscious complexes, her external persona and inner psyche, all are dangerously out of synchronization. Elia seldom lives in the here-and-now. When she "plays" the traditional role of wife and mother, she yearns for the isolation that will enable her to withdraw into the "fictional" world of her erotic fantasies. When alone, she is consumed by loneliness and boredom and seeks to convert her erotic fantasies into real-life adventures. Accomplishing the latter, she painfully experiences a deeply-rooted desire for the real intimacy and inner fulfillment that she knows is not attainable in any relationship in which she selfishly uses another human being to satisfy her own narcissistic tendencies. As we saw in the previous section, the gross physical and emotional incompatibility between Clara and Ricardo is but a psycho-literary projection of the psychological incompatibility of the "little girl" or "inner child" (personified and dramatized by Clara) and young, volatile *animus* (personified and dramatized by Ricardo) complexes inhabiting Elia's unconscious. This unresolved unconscious warfare has rendered the protagonist's conscious life dysfunctional. With a frightened, insecure little girl and unfulfilled creative potential vying for her conscious attention, it is no wonder that she is incapable of performing her roles as wife and mother without a certain degree of bitterness. It is only natural that she should resent caring for others when she neglects and ignores significant aspects of her own Self.

In typical Tusquetsian fashion, the beginning of the third novel sets the stage for the two-tier literal/symbolic development of the plot. The carefully crafted juxtaposition of the physical macrocosm and of the psychic microcosm prefigures the psychological forces to be mobilized within the protagonist, Elia, via the meaningful dynamics of the unfolding of the plot. The opening narration, while spatially and temporally referential on a descriptive plane, has profound psychological implications on a symbolic level of interpretation:

> Apoya la cabeza de lado sobre la toalla, y el sol le llega tamizado a través de su cabello oscuro, como filtrado por los tallos sombríos de una selva en miniatura, la tupida enramada de una jungla minúscula, tan oscuros ahora—un castaño denso, con mechones canos—los tallos y el ramaje, en los que pone el sol leves motitas de oro, y antes fueron sus cabellos de un caoba cálido con reflejos de miel, y antes de un rubio evanescente, líquido, y antes aún, todavía más lejos en el túnel del tiempo, de un amarillo que se ponía en verano con el sol casi albino, tan claro. (7)

The first image is of a head resting on a towel with beams of sunlight penetrating its dark strands of hair. This description situates the individual at the beach at a spatially symbolic intermediary place. Vertically, she is located between heaven and earth, the former being symbolic of the active principle related to masculinity and to spirit, and the latter symbolic of the passive principle related to femininity and to matter. Horizontally, she partakes of the ocean water and of the land on which she rests. Literally and metaphorically, physically and symbolically speaking, she occupies an unmistakable central position where, at a far-off distance, heaven and earth appear to meet while the ocean tides bathe the sand at rhythmic intervals. The image of centrality, the common meeting place of multiple points of convergence, is reinforced by the head-symbol which "coalesces with that of the sphere as a symbol of Oneness" (Cirlot 134) whose center is simultaneously everywhere and nowhere. In just a few lines, Tusquets depicts a macro- and a microcosmic image of an *unus mundus* which, in fact, anticipates the goal toward which the female psyche will develop throughout the third novel. Subsequently, Tusquets introduces the richest of all spheric symbols, the Sun, which "is the astral body of immutable constancy, and hence it reveals the reality of things—not their changing aspects as the Moon does" (Cirlot 305). Since the principle terms of solar symbolism are "as an heroic image (Sol *invictus*, Sol *salutis*, Sol *iustitiæ*), as the divine eye, the active principle and the source of life and energy" (Cirlot 304), Tusquets' allusion to it provides a further symbolic elaboration of the head at rest on one of its sides on the towel. The specific reference to her hair, "because it grows on the top of the human body, symbolizes spiritual forces" while hairs, generally speaking, "represent energy, and are related to the symbolism of levels" (Cirlot 129). There exists an analogous relationship between the levels of height and depth assigned both literally and figuratively to heaven and earth, to the Sun and the Moon, and to consciousness and the unconscious, by virtue of the fact that the first element of each pair (heaven, the Sun, and consciousness) symbolizes the "higher" (but no more essential to the integrative totality of the *unus mundus*) active masculine principle, while the second element of the three pairs (earth, the Moon, the unconscious) symbolizes the "lower" (but no less essential to the integrative totality of the *unus mundus*) passive feminine principle. Inasmuch as these equations "are certainly not constant... the exceptions do not invalidate the essential truth of this symbolism. Even physically speaking, the Moon merely fulfills the passive role of reflecting the light which the Sun actively diffuses" (Cirlot 303). Cirlot also reminds us of an important secondary meaning derived from hair color: "Brown or black hair reinforces the symbolism of hair in general, that is, dark, terrestrial energy; golden hair is related to the sun's rays and to the whole vast sun-symbolism; copper-coloured hair implies a Venusian or demoniacal characteristic. Hairs, then, come to symbolize the concept of spiritualized energy" (129-30). Returning to Tusquets' narrative, while one half of the head is exposed to and illuminated directly by the solar rays which are identified with "purification and tribulation, the sole purpose of which is to render transparent the opaque crust of the senses so that they may perceive the higher truths" (Cirlot 305), the other half is shaded by nothing more than its own being and, like the Moon, would remain in complete darkness if not for what it received indirectly from the Sun. The relationship between the "heights" of consciousness and the "depths" of the unconscious partakes of an analogous dependency; contents of the unconscious can be fathomed and assimilated into consciousness only after first being "illuminated" by it. Reciprocally, the conscious masculine principle is dependent upon the feminine passive principle in order to keep it at bay. If this relationship falls out of synchronization, the result is excessive vanity, egotism, narcissism, and/or idealism that are incompatible with reality.

The evocation of darkness in juxtaposition to the bright, sunny, summer day, is reinforced by the image of tall, leafy, shady trees characteristic of a jungle or forest, for which her dark, thick hair is a simile in miniature. Among the most complex of symbols, the forest "is connected at all levels with the symbolism of the female principle or of the Great Mother" (Cirlot 107). Equally significant to a symbolic reading of *Varada*... is that the forest stands as a symbol of the unconscious, since "the female principle is identified with the unconscious in Man" (107). Throughout their writings, Jung and his disciples, most notably Marie-Louise von Franz, equate the repeated appearance of sylvan horrors in children's fairy tales with the dark, frightening, unknown realm of the unconscious which threatens to obscure reason and drive one to madness. Time and again, literature portrays an abandoned young maiden who is forced to overcome, against seemingly insurmountable odds, the cold, dark demons of the woods as a test of her worthiness to join the adult community, symbolized by the marriage ceremony that inevitably follows her victory over evil. As discussed in the introduction, the marriage ceremony is a symbol of the union of opposites. For this reason, Jung refers to the psychic integration of the conscious and the unconscious as a marriage of complementary opposites. Such a union is, as we recall, the goal of individuation which, in fact, is the theme of Tusquets' third novel.

The gray locks of hair that are intermingled with the dark brown ones signal yet another transitional, or intermediary, point which is temporal: that between youth and old age. There follows a retroactive journey through the time tunnel depicting the increasingly more youthful stages of the character's life. In each phase of life the protagonist's hair was lighter in color than in the subsequent one, so that the changes in hair color signify a shift in dominance from "un amarillo que se ponía en verano con el sol casi albino" (7), symbolic of the light and clarity of consciousness, to "un castaño denso, con mechones canos" (7), symbolic of the dark realm of the unconscious. This signifies that as the character has aged, her unconscious life has come to play a more active role in her total psychic activity. At the point in time when the third novel begins, her psyche is equally influenced by the conscious and the unconscious. It is, in a manner of speaking, caught in the rhythmic oscillation of the two-polarity. As the plot of *Varada...* unfolds, the protagonist will be cast into the deepest, darkest layers of her unconscious, which progressively will become illuminated to her by the solar consciousness of her *animus*.

The co-presence of solar light, energy, and warmth (symbolic of the masculine principle of *logos*, or differentiation, and consciousness) on the one hand (or side, as the case may be), and the pale, delicate nature of lunar light, associated with female passivity and coldness and, hence, the ocean waters (symbolic of the feminine principle of *eros*, or relatedness, and the unconscious) on the other, establish the conscious/unconscious incompatibility to be revealed, reckoned with, reconciled, and transcended by the protagonist. Cirlot writes that "the broadest and most authentic interpretation sees the Sun as the cosmic *reductio* of the masculine force, and the Moon of the feminine. This implies that the active faculties (of reflection, good judgment or will power) are solar, while the passive qualities (imagination, sentiment and perception) are feminine, with intuition possibly androgynous" (303). Both the active solar and the passive lunar faculties are required for the integrative wholeness of the physical universe, of a coherent, self-contained literary work of art, and for psychic health and wholeness of being. In fact, it is the discovery of the equilibrium of this diametric duality that renders possible any type of cosmic totality, be it physical, literary or psychic.

In order to bring about a release from the oscillatory duality that immobilizes her psychological development in *El amor...*, Elia's psyche is about to set a third element into motion which ultimately will enable synthesis and transcendence. This task constitutes the plot of the third novel, *Varada...*, and is accomplished on both the psychological and literary planes of development of the trilogy, ultimately to become a tetralogy. Whereas in the previous novel, the thirty-something-year-old protagonist, Elia, projects her psyche in terms of irresolute binary oppositions that are personified by Clara and Ricardo, "estos dos adolescentes que la inventan" (*El amor...* 148), she now appears in the third novel nearly a decade older and with the components of her psyche further differentiated to form a psychological triad comprised of Clara (*Luna*, linked to sea-water and salt), Pablo (*Sol*, linked to fire and sulphur) and *Eva* (Mercury, linked to air and quicksilver). As projections of Elia's unconscious, Clara would correspond to the needy, abandoned, orphaned inner child inhabiting Elia's personal unconscious; Pablo would correspond to her *animus* situated at the entrance to the universal collective unconscious of all women; and Eva would correspond to the "social" frontier of the unconscious, located mid-way between the personal and the universal, for it refers collectively to Spanish women who were brought up during the height of the Franco years. Among Elia's three unconscious projections, Eva is the changeable, erratic one; hence, her mercurial nature. In accordance with the alchemical body of formulas and procedures purported to create invaluable substances (such as gold) from base matter, Jung believed that the activities of burning (*calcinatio*), dissolving (*solutio*), drying (*coagulatio*) and evaporating (*sublimatio*) that were performed in a sealed, hermetic vessel, were the substantive correlative of psychic transformation, a projection of the psychological experience of personal growth that, as we know, he called individuation. Each of the four stages of the alchemical process moves the *prima materia* through a procedure governed by each of the four elements: fire, water, earth and air. According to Jung, each alchemical step represents a stage of psychological transformation or phase of the individuation process. Within the hermetic vessel (a metaphor for the Self on the psychic plane), distinct elements (fragments of the psyche) are collected in order to be fused into one. As a result of this process, the many are transformed into a new creation (rebirth on the psychological plane), within which the union of opposites—the *coniunctio*, or marriage—has taken place as synthesis (integration) and transcendence (a newly conceived, higher, more valuable form). In *Alchemy in a Modern Woman: A Study in the Contrasexual Archetype*, Robert Grinnell explains the manner by which Mercurius facilitates the integration into Oneness of the oppositional/complementary forces of the masculine and the feminine:

Fire works on air and brings forth sulphur. Air works on water and brings forth Mercurius. Water works on earth and brings forth salt. Fire is active, worked on by nothing, and earth is passive and works on nothing. Fire and earth can unite only through Mercurius. Hence, male and female are produced from three principles: the male emerges from the sequence fire, air, sulphur; the female from water, earth, salt. Mercurius is the uniting factor, coming form the union of air and water. Thus, sulphur and Mercurius produce the male; salt and Mercurius produce the female. Male and female therefore represent the prime opposites, while male, female, and Mercurius, with their inner conjunctions, produce the Incorruptible One—the *quinta essentia*. The final union of male and female is the achievement of art and conscious effort, resulting in self-knowledge, in which the active principle is sulphur and the passive principle is salt. (Grinnell 20)

From a psycho-literary perspective, *Varada...* both *is* and *is about* psychological rebirth. Not only is it a transcendental synthesis of *El mismo mar...* (birth) and *El amor...* (death). It is at one-and-the-same time a hermetic vessel containing the intra-subjective life-death-rebirth drama of Elia's psyche as her consciousness is transformed *vis-à-vis* the aspects of her personal, social, and collective unconscious that are personified by Clara, Eva and Pablo, respectively. With respect to the author's perception of the triadic relationship among the three texts, we would posit the theory that *Varada...* does not merely summarize the two earlier novels; it fuses (synthesizes) and surpasses (transcends) the irresolute thesis/antithesis posed by their sequential juxtaposition. While the forty-year-old Elia of the third narrative does represent a synthesis of the female protagonists in the preceding ones by virtue of her age equaling the average of their ages (fifty and thirty), at the same time the novel is greater than the sum of the two parts; in other words, Elia's age is of more symbolic significance than the mere average of the ages of the previous two protagonists. In terms of chronological age, the Elia of *Varada...* sets into motion the profound contact with the personal and collective unconscious experienced by the unnamed fifty-year-old protagonist of *El mismo mar...*, while simultaneously releasing the thirty-year-old Elia of *El amor...* from the psychological as well as literary impasse that has left readers feeling so uneasy with the second text. In the sequel, on the other hand, every dualistic structure, be it the married couple, Eva and Pablo, or the mother-daughter relationship suggested by Eva and her "adopted" daughter, Clara (the former approaching the middle of her life and the latter an adolescent) is mediated by a third element (by Clara in the former and by Pablo in the latter). This factor, in addition to the obvious units of three comprised of the family units of Elia-Jorge-Daniel and of Eva-Pablo-Clara, call attention to the symbolic importance of the triad or triangle. In its natural position with the apex pointed upward, the triangle symbolizes "the aspiration of all things towards the higher unity" (Cirlot 332). In psychological terms, this third novel, with its emphasis on triangular structures and dynamics, symbolizes a striving toward—and the ultimate attainment of—spiritual synthesis and a higher level of consciousness by Elia. From the analogous perspective of literary creationism, the publication of the third novel within three years from the first establishes the three narrative units as a meaningfully-ordered series in which *Varada...* recapitulates the psychological and literary issues raised in *El mismo mar...* and *El amor...* while, at-one-and-the-same time, the first two undergo sublimation by the third. Hence, their classification as a trilogy.

Elia's new state of consciousness, symbolized by the hermaphroditic *filius philosophorum* (the spiritual rebirth for which her son serves both as symbol and as catalyst) recalls the statue of the chthonic, androgynous Mercurius who greeted the narrator/protagonist of the incipient novel of the trilogy/tetralogy as she made the symbolic descent from the light of consciousness to the realm of psychic differentiation that is to take place in her unconscious underworld. The cold, musty confines of the abandoned home of her childhood, in conjunction with the return (accompanied by Clara) to her grandmother's home by the sea (who not coincidentally dies shortly before the protagonist's rebirth), set the stage for the multifarious phases of union of the feminine and the masculine enclosed within the squared circle. This is to imply that, although Mercurius makes a physical (statuesque) appearance only in the first novel, as the arcane substance he is the transforming link throughout, conferring meaningful structure to an ostensibly chaotic group of novels. All of the psychological problems portrayed throughout the tetralogy are conjoined by a single common denominator: transformation from psychic fragmentation to wholeness, for which is required the integration of feminine consciousness with its masculine unconscious counterpart (*animus*). This union of consciousness with the unconscious "carries within itself the mysterious drama of death and rebirth and the immemorial human emotions which collide in the problem of bringing the feminine and masculine backgrounds of men and women into harmony with the principle of spirit" (Grinnell 20). Central to this mysterious phenomenon of psychic transformation—whose nature is, by definition, inconceivable—is the figure of Mercurius. Grinnell describes him as

> the essence or seminal matter of both men and women: *Mercurius masculinus* and *Mercurius foemineus* are united in and through *Mercurius menstrualis*, which is the divine *aqua*. Mercurius personifies the collective unconscious which surrounds consciousness on all sides and which can be

expressed only indirectly through its manifestations. He appears as an original *unus mundus*, as *agnosia*, as a primordial unconscious state of absolute undifferentiation; and yet, as the subjective factor traceable through a whole range of differentiations, he appears in the discriminating consciousness working to recreate again a *unus mundus*, the redeemed world of the shadow. Mercurius is fundamental to the union of opposites, and without him no combination results. (21)

Elia's quest for a hermaphroditic psyche is realized in the final pages of *Varada*... when she makes a conscious commitment to her maternal-filial relationship with Daniel (feminine function) and to the fullest exploration of her creative potential (her *animus*, or contra-sexual masculine archetype) which takes place in *Para no volver*. Her transcendence thus is a two-fold Oneness: the end of the trilogy is identified with a synchronous psychic and literary synthesis and transcendence. Within this context, the rising sun such as the one alluded to in the above-quoted passage from the novel, anticipates rebirth, since it is, according to Gibson, "a symbol of hope and new beginnings" (90). Likewise the lizard, "because it sheds its skin... is a clear symbol of rebirth"(106). But perhaps the symbol that most illuminates the meaning intended to be gleaned from the Elia's psychological odyssey toward the *coniunctio* (the integration of consciousness with its contra-sexual unconscious archetype) is that of the green stone into which Elia hopes to be reborn after death. In general terms, the stone is a universal symbol of being, "of cohesion and harmonious reconciliation with self" (Cirlot 299). With reference to the philosopher's stone in alchemy, "it represents the 'conjunction of opposites', or the integration of the conscious self with... the unconscious side" (Cirlot 300). The fact that she wishes for it to be green is consistent with the goal of uniting the feminine lunar and the masculine solar to form a new, higher level of consciousness. Not only is green the color of the springtime annual renewal of life and the color of the sea, it is also the color of mediation between the red of hell-fire and the blue of the sky. According to Becker, green plays the dual role of sometimes being the antagonist of the color red while at other times, as the color of life, acting as a substitute for the color red" (133). This is due to the fact that, in many mythologies, there exist intimate connections and transformations between green and red. In alchemy, frequent transformation processes took place as a result of the interaction between feminine green and masculine red. In nature, green is to be found in the rising and the setting of the sun when it occasionally appears as a manifestation of light known as the green ray.

Consistent with the playfully deceptive quality of the New Novel, a more in-depth look at the function of the five secondary characters (Jorge, Daniel, Eva,

Pablo and Clara) reveals that they are not altogether what they appear to be. As in the traditional novel, their actions aid the protagonist in mobilizing the plot into its cause-and effect development; however, quite distinct from the typical function of secondary characters, their role in *Varada*... does not end there. At a secondary—which turns out to be the more significant—narrative level, their roles become identified with functions or aspects of Elia's conscious/unconscious, masculine/feminine, mother/child psychodynamics. Their duplicitous presence in the novel is a narrative paradox; while functioning as secondary characters on one narrative plane, they are, simultaneously, either catalysts for the mobilization of the individuation process of Elia's psyche, or else dramatize shadow facets of the protagonist's unconscious psyche. Although giving every indication of being a novel about six characters, or two triangular (archetypal) family units, the interfacing of the two families is mere smoke and mirrors, disguising an obtuse sub-text of far greater significance: the process of psychic differentiation, or individuation, in which Elia's psyche is engaged. The novel is about Elia, and only about Elia, whose psychological trials and tribulations are a fictional projection of those of her demiurge. Let us take a look at each of the five secondary characters for the purpose of determining the part that each plays in setting the stage for the psychological conflict that is the necessary prelude to Elia's discovery of the path of self-knowledge and psychic wholeness.

Jorge, who never makes a physical appearance in the narrative present, is the catalyst that throws Elia into the depressed, almost catatonic state in which we find her at the beginning of the novel. Everything she does is perfunctory, including stationing herself day after day for hours on end in front of the typewriter with a blank piece of paper staring her in the face. In his physical absence and feeling emotionally rejected by her husband of approximately twenty years, Elia's entire being has turned inward and shut down. He has precipitated Elia's mid-life psychological conflict. It is evident from the circumstances of their separation that Jorge is going through a mid-life crisis of his own, weighing his hopes and dreams against his actual accomplishments, and perhaps realizing (as does his best friend, Pablo) that he has fallen short of where he intended to be in the waning years of the first half of his life. During the course of the summer, he becomes aware that his personal discontentment has nothing to do with being in or out of love with his wife. Rather, it is rooted within his own being; consequently, his attempts to fill the inner void from without are to no avail. It is within this context that we are meant to understand his desire for a marital reconciliation at the end of the novel, an offer which Elia refuses for reasons which will become abundantly clear when we look at the circumstances surrounding Eva's and Pablo's "marriage."

Moving on to Daniel, Elia retrieves her only child from camp at the end of the summer, on a magnificent fall-like August afternoon, "la tarde pacífica, soleada, realmente espléndida de finales de agosto, casi ya una tarde otoñal" (218). Associated with the transitional period from one season (summer) to the next (fall), Daniel is a correlate of Elia's transition from the second to the third quarter of life to which the end of summer/beginning of fall seasonal reference is analogous. His "timely" appearance serves a two-pronged function; he is both a catalyst and mirror for Elia's self-revelation (217-71). As she prepares Daniel for the break-up of the family unit, Elia assumes that she will be the one to move out of their home and that Daniel "naturally" will remain there with his father while visiting Elia on a regular basis. As she explains the new arrangements to her son, he interrupts her monologue with "yo quiero vivir contigo" (219). These most unanticipated words elicit an expression of such disbelief on Elia's face, that Daniel can only chuckle and ask her if it really seems that unbelievable to her that he wants to live with her, his own mother: "¿tan raro te parece que yo quiera vivir contigo, que yo quiera vivir con mi madre?" (219).

In his innocence and naïveté, Daniel is instrumental in making Elia realize that they have a meaningful one-to-one mother/son relationship that is capable of standing on its own merit independently of the father-mother-child (archetypal) family triangle of which their mother/child relationship is one of its three angles. Daniel's startling words are catalytic in Elia's recognition that she completely lacked an identity of her own, that she always had viewed herself as an appendage to Jorge, and everything in her life—including her poetry and her son—as fueling that husband/wife bond. She woefully explains to her son that

> lo que yo fuera o dejara de ser no tenía ninguna importancia ya desde el momento en que tu padre me había cogido al pasar como quien arranca una rosa y me había elegido como suya y la escritura se me metamorfoseó entonces en otra forma de amar otro camino por el que aproximarme a Jorge porque él ha sido para mí durante años el único camino por el que me llegaba todo y a mí me parecieron durante años pocos todos los caminos para llegar hasta él y para más amarle y no hubo otro camino ni otra forma superior a la escritura hasta que llegaste tú hasta que te inventé a ti para mejor amarle a él para poder amarle en unas zonas que no había conseguido alcanzar jamás. (259)

Elia, like so many other women of her social class, has been conditioned to understand and fulfill the needs of their husbands while repressing any of their own, "adiestradas y constreñidas y forzadas desde niñas a poner nuestro personal vivir en función de otro" (263). Instead of making love the center of her life, she mistakingly has reduced the entire world to the central focal point of her love. Consequently, in the absence of Jorge's love, Elia's world is an immense void, a vast nothingness in terms of personal identity or self-realization. As the protagonist tells her son, "al perder el amor desligada de todo incapaz de escribir incapaz en cierto modo lo lamento Daniel incapaz de pensarte a ti en ti mismo de disociar mi amor por ti del amor que había sentido por Jorge... tampoco era capaz de proyectar mi propia imagen en un futuro inverosímil en el que estaría sola y sin él expulsada" (262-63). The novel ends with the widening of Elia's horizon of consciousness as she acknowledges her fear as well as her ability to face the future as a single woman. Uncertain of "lo que será de mí si lograré establecer nuevos lazos con el mundo abrir también nuevos caminos, si reencontraré como te (a Daniel) he reencontrado a ti mi escritura si amaré yo de nuevo alguna vez... no sé nada de nada pero... sabes Daniel estoy contenta de verdad contenta" (271). From a Jungian perspective, the admission of a life of self-sacrifice and a resulting non-existent self-identity, coupled with a willingness to embrace change, signals an important step on the path of individuation for Elia. The end of the novel finds the protagonist on track, having withdrawn many of her projections, and prepared to confront the second half of her life with greater maturity and sense of purpose.

The remaining secondary characters—Clara, Eva and Pablo—personify shadow aspects of Elia's personal, social and collective unconscious, respectively. The orphaned Clara forms a generic coherence with the "huerfanita envejecida" *leitmotif* with which the aging protagonist in *El mismo mar...* refers to herself. Unlike the unattractive physiognomy of the homely Clara appearing in *El amor...*, which underscores the ugly duckling complex that has shaped the protagonist's self-perception since childhood and been one of many factors contributing to her low self-esteem, the Clara of *Varada...* is quite attractive: "tan guapetona, con unos ojos profundos y oscuros, casi tan grandes y hermosos como los de la propia Eva, y una boca carnosa y roja, y un cabello denso y perfumado que le desciende por la espalda, y esa carne prieta y dorada, y unos pechos soberbios, agresivos... y unas piernas finas y unos muslos largos, increíblemente buena moza la tal Clara" (73). She is, as a matter of fact, exotic and alluring like Clara, the student from Colombia, with whom the narrator/protagonist has an intense one-month affair in the opening novel of the tetralogy. When Eva brings her to the beach house, Clara does not let her surrogate mother out of her sight, "muchacha tímida y huraña que acompañaba a Eva como una sombra, que la seguía como su sombra, sombra que parecía extraer de la otra su corporeidad" (36), thereby making her reminiscent of the shy, awkward, pathetically insecure Clara who clings for dear life to Elia in the second novel. Whereas in the previous two novels Clara is seventeen-years-old, the Clara of the third, "una muchacha que pasados ya los veinte años aparentaba apenas diecisiete" (36), only appears to be seventeen, suggesting that her level of maturity, like that of her adult counterpart, has not caught up with her chronological age. In all three cases, it is clear that Clara incarnates the protagonist's inner child struggling to make the transition from adolescence to young adulthood. As divulged in the first novel, it corresponds to the exact time in the collective protagonists' life when psychological development became obstructed.

Whereas the Clara of *El amor...* has a cold, aloof mother (not unlike that of the female protagonists who is the target of bitter criticism in all four of the texts), in the third novel we have progressed a step deeper toward approaching the underlying negative mother complex that we know to be at the root of Elia's thwarted psychological development. As we move through the analysis of the secondary characters, it will become evident that it is Eva who personifies Elia's negative mother complex. The fact that, biologically speaking, Clara is motherless, explains the intensification of the insecurities, neediness, possessiveness and lack of social skills that we witness in this "muchacha que se azaraba ante la presencia de extraños, absurdamente incómoda y temerosa ante el mundo exterior" (36). Likewise, it places yet greater emphasis on an emotional issue that runs throughout the psycho-emotional make-up of the four protagonists comprising the collective female psyche for which the tetralogy is a symbol: intertwined with the feeling of being unloved, and of being unworthy of receiving the love of another person, is an intense fear of being abandoned by an individual upon whom she is emotionally dependent. This is precisely the predicament in which Elia finds herself in *Varada...* Therefore, it is no wonder that Elia re-visits her early relationship with her mother in the opening pages of the text, specifically recalling her mother's habit of placing into doubt the genetic relationship between her and Elia—¿a quién habrá salido esta chiquilla? (9)—since the two did not resemble one another in the least (we recall that the narrator-protagonist of *El mismo mar...* elaborates extensively on the psychological effect that this had on her). As she rummages through her childhood photos, she comes upon one, and only one, which causes her to experience an ephemeral mother-daughter bond and to ruminate over what it might have been like to have felt like the apple of her mother's eye. It is a picture of Elia dressed for school, in which her mother stands back from her daughter, conveying a facial expression of pride and joy at her daughter's appearance:

> (tan maternal su madre en esta fotografía), apartándola un poco de sí para verla mejor, mirándola de hito en hito y sonriendo con orgullo, en un gesto muy tierno y en el fondo casi desvalido, con una belleza suave, ensoñada, melancólica, porque la madre ha sido siempre, hasta donde alcanza sus

recuerdos, una mujer espléndida y arrogante, y sólo en esta fotografía surge y sobrevive inesperada la imagen de una mujer muy joven, frágil, que sonríe para sí en un gesto tímido, con un encanto tierno y escondedor que en la realidad Elia no le ha visto jamás. (9-10)

There is an unmistakably analogous relationship between Elia and her mother, and between Clara and Eva. Clara yearns for the same sense of connectedness to Eva that was absent from Elia's relationship with her own mother. Eva is unnerved by the orphan's clingy, needy possessiveness because, as we witness in Eva's childlike behavior when she learns of her husband's extramarital affair, her extreme bravado is but a compensation for her own deeply rooted emotional insecurity. Eva is both drawn to and repulsed by Clara (as most of us are in the presence of someone who stirs within us negative aspects of our own shadow), whose visible lack of self-confidence and self-esteem is so like Eva's when put to the test by Pablo's indiscretion. Eva's banishment of Clara from the house—not at all unlike the discharging of Sofía from her domestic employment in *El mismo mar...* when the narrator's mother learns of the housekeeper's trysts with her husband—is, in fact, a dramatization of a profound psychological reality: it models the manner by which consciousness attempts to rid itself of anything with which, or anyone with whom, conscious confrontation is too hurtful. It is the very stuff of which the personal unconscious is made. Eva's reconciliation with Pablo and disenfranchisement of Clara from the family unit has psychological repression as its motive; clearly, she is determined to obliterate anything or anyone that would remind her that she has conferred greater importance upon the maintenance of social appearance than upon facing up to the reality of her failed marriage.

The relationship between Elia and Eva is symbiotic, personifying the mutual attraction and repulsion, and potential unity of opposites housed within the psyche. As Pablo reminisces over the first time he met the two inseparable friends, his impression of them was, and still is, as conjoined opposites, as two sides of the same coin:

fundidas ambas para Pablo en una realidad en cierto modo indivisible y única, tal vez porque eran entre ellas tan amigas cuando las encontró, en la noche de aquel remoto estío de hace ya dieciséis o diecisiete años, y quizás ayudó la coincidencia de haberlas casi juntas conocido, caras complementarias aunque opuestas de una misma moneda, Eva solar y prepotente, Eva fuente de vida, Elia selénica y acaso secretamente embrujadora y lúdica. (41)

Although for completely different reasons, Pablo is equally enamored of Eva and Elia, referring to them collectively as "mis mujeres" (41) because "les destina extrañamente un amor contrapuesto y compartido" (42). The psychodynamics of his relationship with his wife and her best friend sheds enormous light on the overall structure of Elia's psyche. Pablo is married to his physical opposite, Eva, whose solar, *animus*-possessed personality has eclipsed her femininity, making her seem more like a male friend to Pablo than his heterosexual marital partner. This situation has activated Pablo's unconscious contra-sexual lunar *anima*, which feels more comfortable relating to the masculine-dominated Eva than does his masculine consciousness to which it is so similar that no attraction of opposites exists. While Pablo's *anima* is magnetically drawn toward Eva, it also identifies itself intimately with Elia, with whom it shares fundamental feminine, lunar qualities. Hence, a curious alliance between Pablo and Elia exists with respect to Eva, the two being "cómplices en una misma devoción, planetas apagados de un universo solar en el que Eva les confiere y comparte con ellos la luz propia, unidos ambos quizás en el orgullo de admirarla, en el afán de comprenderla y secundarla, en el vago temor a perderla" (42).

Elia and Eva—opposite sides of the same coin—represent a state of female ambivalence in which the female psyche is torn between allegiances to feminine/matriarchal and masculine/patriarchal forms of consciousness. She is indecisive as to whether she is to play the *anima* in relation to a masculine mentality or else manifest a dedication to the *animus* in a feminine world (Grinnell 6). The result is something like a shadow-effect in the *anima* character of her archetypal femininity where she becomes increasingly overshadowed by the *animus* in her contra-sexual side. As we know, Elia is *animus*-possessed, due largely to the negative mother-complex in which her entire psychic being is enshrouded. Her contra-sexual side is personified by Eva, whose feminine consciousness—which under normal circumstances would be ruled by the feminine principles of human relatedness and bonding—has been overrun by a masculine un-relatedness and aloofness towards others, in particular those who are most in need of her empathy and nurturance.

Elia'a *animus* possession is compatible with the negative mother complex that co-dominates her ego personality insofar as they share a personality that is more characteristically masculine than feminine. According to Jung, the etiology of the mother-complex is derived from two sources: "(1) those corresponding to traits of character or attitudes actually present in the mother, and (2) those referring to traits which the mother only seems to possess, the reality being composed of more or less fantastic (i.e., archetypal) projections on the part of the child" (*The Archetypes*... 83). There is no doubt that the unified female protagonist of the tetralogy has projected a great deal of the archetypal negative mother attributes onto her human mother, thereby giving her a "mythological background that invests her with authority and numinosity" (*The Archetypes...* 83). As we recall, the negative mother-complex usually produces the atrophy of the maternal instincts as we see personified by Eva, whose feminine *eros* is contaminated by a masculine *logos*, resulting in irritability whenever feminine attributes are tapped into by another. It is hardly a wonder that caring for Clara and empathizing with Elia are virtually impossible tasks for Eva, whose adult life attests to the resistance-to-the-mother manifestation that Elia's negative mother-complex has taken. Unlike the traditional Spanish woman born in the 1930s, Eva is an accomplished attorney who has climbed the ladder of success and made her way to the pinnacle of a male-dominated profession. Her unconventional professional pursuits would appear to be the result of her resistance to be anything like one's own mother, whose flamboyant bourgeois lifestyle is as professionally unaccomplished as a life can be. Jung explains how resistance to the mother can result in the daughter's creation of a sphere of interest in which the mother neither does nor can participate: "Resistance to the mother can sometimes result in a spontaneous development of intellect for the purpose of creating a sphere of interest in which the mother has no place... Its real purpose is to break the mother's power by intellectual criticism and superior knowledge, so as to enumerate to her all her stupidities, mistakes in logic, and educational shortcomings. Intellectual development is often accompanied by the emergence of masculine traits in general" (*The Archetypes...* 91).

Psychologically, Elia experiences her husband's having fallen out of love with her in much the same way that she was affected by her mother's inability to be emotionally demonstrative during those critically formative years of ego development when she was impressionable and highly vulnerable to becoming emotionally scarred for life. Her neuroses are the result of a clash between her masculine-dominated consciousness (personified by Eva) on the one hand, and her emotionally needy and demanding inner child (personified by Clara) on the other. To complicate matters further, co-habitating in Elia's unconscious along with her repressed inner child reside two of the most positive of all *animus* aspects (personified by Pablo): the *logos* principle of rational discrimination and a full expression of her creative talents, both of which have been eclipsed by her emotionally needy, clamoring inner child (personified by Clara). To state matters more plainly, due to the unconscious interference of her frightened inner child, Elia is unable to live out her life in a mature, satisfying way either as a feminine consciousness supported by unconscious masculine attributes, or as a masculine consciousness with compensatory feminine qualities. Her psyche functions partially out of both realms, partaking of the least desirable attributes of each. The result is an inability to ground her identity in a coherent, secure sense of Self. Elia manifests all of the following characteristics of possession as enumerated by Grinnell: "a predominating contra-sexuality, a forcible intrusion of the unconscious, a predominance of the shadow, and a contra-sexual consciousness—that is, the exclusion of the consciousness specific to a given sex and the predominance of the consciousness appropriate to the opposite sex" (9). The needs of her inner child are so overwhelming that she must expend large quantities of energy forcing them back into the sphere of the repressed personal unconscious. Her interactions with Eva are both alluring and painful in that they often trigger recollections of her hurtful relationship with her own mother to whom Eva's character is akin. Similarly, Jorge's physical absence reverberates within her recollections of her father's infrequent presence at home and the profound sense of yearning that is all too familiar to her inner child. When Clara is brought into the home, Elia is compelled to re-visit some of the most profound inner voids stemming from her childhood: feeling unloved, unwanted, dispensable, abandoned, orphaned.

Elia faces before her two monumental life tasks: 1) she must exhume from the depths of her female collective unconscious her repressed feminine *eros*, particularly the positive maternal qualities of loving, caring and nurturing, attributes which she then could use to begin the healing process of her inner child, and 2) having accomplished that, she must activate the positive *animus* features of the universal archetype, most notably those of rational discrimination followed by the creative faculties which would harness and stabilize the feminine process of the integration of opposites both within her own psyche and within her literary cosmos. The events of the novel mobilize Elia's psyche in pursuit of these goals towards which the archetype of the self compels the Self to be oriented. Eva's egregious treatment of Clara reconnects Elia to her archaic, archetypal femininity, precipitating within her an awakening of her repressed maternal instincts. Eva's inability to cope with anyone whose emotional needs are greater than her own affords Elia an opportunity to view her own mother's relationship to her in a new, more realistic way. The Eva-Clara interaction objectifies for Elia the causes of her own neuroses stemming from her earliest relationship with her mother; specifically, she is able to see that it is not she who is unlovable but, rather, her mother whose limitations impede her from being emotionally demonstrative. Here begins the process of discrimination between human mother and the universal mother archetype. As Eva's godliness is demythified before Elia's eyes, so too is the deification of Elia's mother by her repressed inner child. As the inner child begins to view her mother as less than what her image of her had been, she simultaneously begins to regard herself as more than what her self-perception had been. This transformation is represented in the novel when Elia allows herself to empathize with Clara's impending estrangement from the family unit (a feeling not at all unfamiliar to Elia within the dynamics of her own family-of-origin) and to cradle her (her own inner child) in her arms as only a mother can do.

Although Pablo's infidelity to Eva ostensibly has devastating consequences for Clara, it is an estrangement that is absolutely essential to Elia's psychological development in terms of re-positioning herself on the individuation continuum. The symbolic "death" of Clara in *Varada...* forms a generic coherence with the rupture between the narrator-protagonist and Clara in *El mismo mar...*, which served to facilitate the psychic integration of the former. Consistent with the structural dynamics of all rites of initiation, the child must die in order for the adult to progress to the next stage of development in his/her life. Rebirth is possible only after a death has first taken place. Clara's disclosure of Pablo's extra-marital affair with a girl half his age, followed by the forced departure of the orphan from the familial nest, paves the way for Elia's psychological rebirth. In an attempt to explain the reasons for his infidelity to Eva, Pablo probes, with Elia as his interlocutor, the reasons for his mid-life dissatisfaction. His recognition of all the ways in which he betrayed himself throughout the first half of his life by settling for less or for something other than that to which he truly aspired, serves as a catalyst for Elia's second and most difficult psychological task. Subsequent to her conversation with Pablo, she is able to pull apart and differentiate from among the distinct facets of her being in relation to her husband, son and fiction. Scrutinizing the first half of her life with Daniel as interlocutor, Elia is able, for the first time, to extricate the different areas of her life from her adoration of Jorge:

> la literatura se me metamorfoseó entonces en otra forma de amar otro camino por el que aproximarme a Jorge porque él ha sido para mí durante años el único camino por el que me llegaba todo y a mí me parecieron durante años pocos todos los caminos para llegar hasta él y para más amarle y no hubo otro camino ni otra forma superior a la escritura hasta que llegaste tú que te inventé a ti para mejor amarle a él. (259)

Consistent with the symbolic qualities of the number three, *Varada tras el último naufragio* is about a woman's task of calling upon the strength of the *animus* to assist in pulling apart and discriminating from among the multitude of facets of the psyche (manifested in the novel as the significant aspects of Elia's life—husband, son, fiction, reality—which are indistinguishable from each other until she is reunited with Daniel at its conclusion), followed by the fullest utilization of the feminine principle of integration. From Elia's decision to terminate her marriage is born a marriage quaternio of her psyche, whereby a process of discrimination, synthesis and transcendence of the paired opposites takes place. Her negative mother complex/*animus*-possessed consciousness (personified by Eva), her unfulfilled creative potential as a poet (personified by Pablo who secretly had always aspired to be a literature teacher and poet instead of the business man which he became), and her neglected inner child (personified by Clara) all are transformed throughout the course of the development of the novel. Eva's and Pablo's characteristic masculinity, manifested as unrelatedness, is transformed by the presence of Clara who is the catalyst for their marital crisis. Although it easily could be debated whether or not their marriage merits further effort, the essential point is that, as a result of the ensuing tragedy and their decision to remain together, each acquires a heightened sense of awareness of the needs and vulnerabilities of the other. This newly-acquired knowledge could strengthen their union in the future. Furthermore, Eva's and Clara's mother-resistant/mother-needy impasse is torn asunder by Pablo's affair and Eva's near mental breakdown. Elia's archetype of the self orients her toward the discovery of the wholeness of her Self. Both sets of paired opposites objectify not only Elia's situation with her husband but, more significantly, the structural dynamics of Elia's psyche. The critical detachment—a function of the masculine principle of *logos*—provides Elia with greater insight into herself. It also affords Elia contact with her repressed maternal femininity. In caring for Clara, she nurtures her own inner child which, in turn, has a calming, soothing effect on her volatile *animus*.

The *coincidentia oppositorum* comprised of Elia, Eva, Pablo and Clara dramatizes the *Sol-Luna* archetype of consciousness expressing the transformational function of the self. Within this schemata, Elia represents *Luna*, the symbol of feminine consciousness. Eva incarnates *Sol*, the symbol of Elia's contra-sexual masculine consciousness. Pablo represents *Sol* as the contra-sexual *animus* figure to Elia's lunar consciousness, while Clara represents *Luna* as the contra-sexual *anima* figure to Eva's solar consciousness. *Varada tras el último naufragio* dramatizes the resistance-attraction-conjunction of these four figures, symbolizing the union of the conscious personality with the unconscious.

In typically Tusquetsian fashion, the reemerging theme of individuation is presented under the guise of anything and everything but what it is, in this case within the ostensibly relevant, highly distracting context of the ethos of the Catalonian bourgeoisie to which, as we already know, Tusquets and all of her fictional protagonists belong. Apart from the banal, materialistic, hypocritical existence of this all-too-familiar social group, under particularly severe microscopic scrutiny in *Varada*... are two prevalent attitudes among the upper socio-economic echelon of Catalonian society: the first is the tendency of individuals to seek from family members and/or friends—that is, from outside the confines of one's own being—the answers to one's own personal contentment and self-definition, and the second is the custom of criticizing in others what one cannot help but fall victim to in one's own life. The Eva-Pablo-Clara triad comes to be viewed as a projection of the structural dynamics of Elia's present family (Elia-Jorge-Daniel) on a personal level, which in turn comes to be viewed as typifying the upper-middle class Catalonian bourgeoisie to which all of the characters belong. The particular as well as social implications of the plot open the door to an allegorical reading of the dynamics of Elia's unconscious. This secondary reading is two-tiered as is the primary literal one; just as the individual comes to be viewed as representative of the collective at the plot level, Elia's personal unconscious (unresolved conflicts with her own parents) awakens and interfaces with universal female archetypes, specifically with the young maiden, the *animus* (both of which she already encountered in the previous novel, but unsuccessfully merged with consciousness), and the Great Mother, the third element that will bring about the transformation of the unresolved duality of the other two. Elia's conscious recognition at the end of the novel of the importance of the mother-child bond, of which she had been deprived by her own mother at great cost to her psychological development and with which she had unknowingly neglected to provide her son, simultaneously enables her to heal the scars from her own painful childhood and to meaningfully bond with Daniel. In a world devoid of the nurturing power of the maternal principle such as Tusquets portrays it in *Varada...*, the personal path of individuation on which Elia walks as Daniel's mother and as a creative writer at the end of the novel (evidenced by the termination of her marriage to Jorge and her self-alienation from her socio-economic group) heralds the triumph of the feminine maternal principle in the universe.

4. *Para no volver*: From the Four Comes the One

The fourth novel of the series depicts the four months of psychoanalysis undergone by Elena, an upper-middle-class Catalonian woman who has been married for thirty years to a filmmaker named Julio. They have two grown sons, Pablo and Jorge. Suffering from severe depression, she meets with her Argentine analyst four times weekly at five o'clock. With her promiscuous husband once again traveling abroad, accompanied by his latest mistress, and her sons too self-absorbed to recognize that their mother is on the verge of an emotional breakdown, Tusquets' female protagonist, identical to the preceding three, feels useless, dispensable, hurt and angry. As if the situation were not trying enough, Elena's impending fiftieth birthday seems more than she can bare: "Lo cierto era que ahora, en ese preludio otoñal en que iba a cumplir cincuenta años y en que la habían dejado sola, lloraba Elena por cualquier nimiedad y sin saber siquiera por qué lloraba, y quizás estuviera llorando por sí misma, por el paso del tiempo, por la juventud ahora sí irremediablemente perdida" (43). Not surprisingly, she transfers this sea of conflicting emotions onto her poised, self-controlled analyst, whom she wittingly refers as "el Mago," "el Impasible," "Forastero," "Cara de Palo," "Cara de Póker," and "Papá Freud." Frustration mounts as she not only is unable to elicit any type of reaction from him, but cannot even see him once they enter his inner office where treatment takes place, for he insists that she lie down on the therapeutic couch with him seated on a chair behind her. The mere positioning of analyst and analysand awakens within Elena feelings similar to those that she experiences with other men in her life, most notably her husband and sons: "Father Freud," as she refers to him, seems cold, aloof, insensitive, uncaring, and disturbingly in control: "el Mago no responde a nada, no pregunta nada, no comenta nada. La ha dejado sola en el diván, naufragando en el océano revuelto y proceloso de sus propias palabras, hundiéndose en la viscosidad de este mar como en un pantano... cada vez más deprimida y más ansiosa—más agresiva también, aunque acaso se negaría ella a reconocerlo" (28).

Such profound feelings of need, mistrust, idealization, and defiance toward her husband and sons—and transferred onto her analyst—are intricately intertwined with a lifetime of harboring resentment toward her unloving, non-nurturing mother, and her practically non-existent father who seldom spent any time at home when Elena was growing up: "una infancia triste, o que ella recuerda como triste, una adolescencia conflictiva—¿qué adolescencia no lo es?—, unos sueños de juventud, individuales y colectivos, realizados unos, frustrados la mayoría, en lugar de insistir en ese padre ausente, esa madre en exceso brillante y desamorada" (57). Consequently, Elena's sense of estrangement toward those to whom she has devoted her entire life—vivir enteramente o en parte a través de los demás, en función de los demás" (192)—and from whom she most profoundly feels deprived of genuine affection and understanding, results in sarcasm and feigned indifference during her analytic sessions as protective mechanisms of defense "que debía atribuirse a sus múltiples y complejísimas resistencias, enormes resistencias" (121).

During the course of psychoanalysis, as a way of filling what seem to her to be countless hours between sessions, she maintains two concurrent extramarital affairs: one with Eduardo and another with Arturo, both of whom are painters.

Despite countless personality differences among her husband and two lovers, Elena feels magnetically lured toward the one and only attribute shared by them all: their artistic creativity. When counterpoised to Julio's, Eduardo's and Arturo's gift for creating complex, thought-provoking works of art "que rezuman ambivalencias y complejidades y se prestan a múltiples interpretaciones, porque es ésta una de las características de todo arte" (185), Elena's inability, or lack of self-confidence, or absence of desire, to complete a single one of the numerous books of poetry and short stories that she had begun, acquires significant psychological meaning. Among Elena's psychological issues is an attraction to men who possesses the very quality that she has repressed within herself—split off from her conscious personality—namely, confidence in and respect for her ability as an artist. The inferiority complex from which she discovers she has been suffering throughout the first half of her life, coupled with deeply-rooted insecurities stemming from her childhood, indeed have immobilized her artistic talents. Consequently, she has spent her adult life projecting her own creativity onto her husband and male friends, which has resulted in a distorted, inflated view of them on the one hand, and a devaluation of her own self worth on the other.

The day prior to her husband's return from the United States, Elena assumes the role of initiator and aggressor in a lovemaking session with Arturo. Startled by her most unusual behavior, the painter asks his friend and mistress what she is doing. Elena's reply—"Te estoy amando" (194)—signals a marked shift in behavior from passive participant to active initiator as she reaches an orgasmic climax unlike anything she recalls ever having experienced before, "como si se tratara de un rumor oscuro y confuso que procede de las más hondas cavernas de los más intricados laberintos de ese total desconocido que es para Elena su propio cuerpo, un temblor imperceptible, casi ilocalizable, apenas detectable, pero que anuncia sin posible error la proximidad creciente e incontenible de la tromba marina o el huracán—, la presencia incuestionable del deseo, ese deseo tan poco frecuente en ella desde hace años" (194). The symbolic episode further suggests that her defensive wall has come crumbling down and that she has freed herself from her resistant, self-defensive posture so evident in all of her relationships with males. Subsequent to her erotic interlude with Arturo, she assembles all of her and Julio's friends at their house in honor of her husband's homecoming. Surveying each of them, one at a time, she realizes that they are not who or what she previously had thought them to be. Even more significantly, it begins to dawn on her that perhaps she is not either. As she withdraws her *animus* projections from them while simultaneously considering her potential as a writer from a positive vantage point, they come to be regarded as aspects of her own psyche. Consequently, she makes the decision to break the news to her analyst—yet another projection that she has withdrawn—the following day that she has decided to discontinue treatment. Elena opts to tell him at the threshold leading to his inner office, a passageway which she has no intention of ever crossing again: "Sabés una cosa, Mago, me voy a psicoanalizar" (217), the words with which Tusquets brings her narrative cycle to a close.

Para no volver (1985) did not appear until five years after *Varada tras el último naufragio* closed the trilogy (1980), for whose appearance seven years earlier with the publication of *El mismo mar...* it paradoxically sets the stage. Just as the number three and the geometric figure of the triangle are recurring images in the third novel, and binary oppositions qualify the structural dynamics of the second novel, and an integrated, undifferentiated One embraces the psychological meaning of the first novel of the series, in the fourth novel the number four and the geometric figure of the square serve as structurally thematic *leitmotifs*. Elena is at the end of her fourth decade of life, about to turn fifty years old; is part of a four-member family constituted by herself, her husband, and their two sons; frequently expresses her outrage (concealing jealousy and resentment) toward her two sons and the two women with whom they have chosen to share their lives; attends psychoanalytic sessions four times weekly, spends four months in psychoanalysis and has four significant male figures in her life throughout the temporal enclosure of the narrative, all of whom, as previously stated, are *animus* projections[15] that Elena withdraws and subsumes within her increasingly integrated Self.

Indeed, the 1985 novel plays a complex role with regard to the previous three: it shares countless similarities with *El mismo mar...*, it is a "natural" or "logical" sequel to *Varada...* and the trilogy which the third novel synthesizes and transcends; it performs as a prelude to the preceding trilogy which chronologically it follows; and like *El amor... vis-à-vis El mismo mar...*, it is contrapuntal with respect to its relationship with the trilogy. Recalling Franz' explanation of the difficult passage from three to four elaborated upon in the theoretical section of this study, *Para no volver* has the ultimate effect of producing a novelistic tetralogy; that is, of enclosing the circular meaning of the quaternity structure of wholeness offered by the sum total of the four texts by virtue of portraying "the inclusion (no longer avoidable) of the observer in his *wholeness* within the framework of his process of understanding" (*Number and Time* 122). Let's examine each of these roles that the fourth novel plays with respect to the wholeness it creates and within which it paradoxically is enclosed.

---

[15] We recall from the introduction that a woman's *animus* more often than not appeared in collective form.

When the almost-fifty-year-old protagonist of *Para no volver* seemingly avows not only to initiate a career as a professional writer, but also to terminate psychoanalytic treatment with her Argentine doctor and herself assume the role of analyst of her own self—"Sabés una cosa, Mago, me voy a psicoanalizar" (217)—it would seem that she has triumphed over the *animus* possession that has beguiled her throughout the tetralogy. The statement is ambiguous, to be sure, given that it has two possible and divergent meanings. "Me voy a psicoanalizar" could be taken to mean "I am going to undergo psychoanalysis"; in other words, that Elena has completed the first phase of analysis—the shedding of the defensive wall of defiance and animosity toward her analyst—and that only now is she prepared to initiate the second phase of treatment with her doctor. In accordance with this interpretation, the orgasm that she reaches while assuming, for the first time, the superior, aggressive top position in her lovemaking with Arturo, signifies that Elena has been psychologically liberated from her emotional impasse and is open to a fuller, more profound exploration of her unconscious. The problem with this interpretation, however, is that it does not explain her unwillingness to be ritually escorted the following day by her doctor to the inner room where treatment takes place. This leads us to the second possible meaning. "Me voy a psicoanalizar" could be interpreted as Elena's intention to quit traditional psychoanalysis in the belief that the discovery and exhumation of her own repressed creative potential is the answer to all of her problems. From this point of view, through the writing of the tetralogy whose reading we as readers have just completed, Elena, Elia, the autobiographical "I" of *El mismo mar...*—ultimately, Esther Tusquets—has reconciled the numerous diametric aspects of her being and given material, objective form to the wholeness of the Self. This is, after all, Elena's therapeutic goal as defined by her: "reunir de nuevo las partes dispersas en un todo armonioso" (32). The mental invocation of her analyst with which the novel concludes as Elena stands in her home and in the physical presence of Julio, Arturo and Eduardo, signifies the all-important passage from three to four which symbolizes the transcendence of a conflict insofar as "a psychological problem of considerable importance is constellated between the numbers three and four" (Franz, *Number and Time* 126). Paradoxically, this finale also serves as a prelude to Tusquets' first novel, *El mismo mar...*, given that Elena's *animus* complex, portrayed by "the young poet," Ricardo in *El amor...* and by the artistically unfulfilled Pablo in *Varada...*, had manifested itself as an inability to express herself artistically, a problem which the publication of Tusquets' first novel needless to say has resolved. This is not to imply that

Elena and Esther are one-and-the-same[16] (or are they?); it is, rather, meant to suggest that the anonymous fifty-year-old first-person narrator/protagonist of *El mismo mar...*, the thirty-something-year-old Elia of *El amor...*, the forty-something-year-old Elia of *Varada...* and the almost-fifty-year-old Elena of *Para no volver* are projections[17] of Esther Tusquets' psyche. Moving from the abstract to the concrete, the neurosis that is overcome by the fictional character in *Para no volver* coincides with Esther Tusquets' debut as a novelist... seven years earlier.

We recall that, in *El mismo mar...*, we meet an anonymous middle-aged wife and mother who has been abandoned by her husband, Julio, who, like the Julio that we meet in *Para no volver*, is a cinematographer with a penchant for having affairs with young, attractive women. As the narrator/protagonist autobiographically narrates her descent into her personal and collective unconscious in an attempt to set her psychological development into motion after what she, like Elena, perceives to have been thirty years of stagnation, we also learn that, like Elena, she too bares the scars of an unloving, overly-critical mother and an absent father. And like Elena in relation to her two sons, she feels forsaken by her daughter, Guiomar, who is a college math professor living and working in the United States.

Curiously enough, the hurt, scared, insecure, fifty-year-old "huerfanita envejecida" (*El mismo mar...* 16) that we encounter in the opening pages of the first novel is none other than the almost-fifty-year-old "niñita tarada... que no ha sabido, no está sabiendo, correctamente envejecer, al borde de la menopausia y sin haber superado en ningún momento la adolescencia, sin haberse convertido para casi nada en una mujer adulta" (*Para no volver* 27) whom we meet in the fourth. *El mismo mar...*, then, plays the ambiguous role of setting into motion a psychological journey of self-discovery which dubiously is terminated—while

---

[16] Tusquets does make the point, however, that Elena's birthday not only occurs, as we know does the author's, during the transitional period between summer and fall—"ese preludio otoñal en que iba a cumplir cincuenta años" (43)—, but also that she, like Tusquets herself, was born during the first year of the Spanish Civil War: "la propia Elena, nacida, como tantos de sus compañeros de universidad, de sus amigos, en el primer año de la guerra civil, una madrugada en que bombardearon la ciudad los alemanes y no pudo, por miedo, por falta de transporte, por descuido, acudir a tiempo la comadrona, que llegó cuando ella ya había nacido" (48). One cannot help but wonder if the circumstances of Tusquets' birth were identical or similar.

[17] We recall that a projection is an "unconscious, that is unperceived and unintentional, transfer(s) of subjective psychic elements onto an outer object" (Franz, *Projection...*" 3).

at the same time prefaced— by *Para no volver*. Furthermore, the 1978 publication of *El mismo mar*... gave birth to what many critics—and even the author herself—would come to identify as a trilogy, with the almost immediate publication thereafter of *El amor*... one year later (1979) and *Varada*... just one year after that (1980). The relationship between and among the four novels indeed is complex, for not only do we find ourselves confronting a circular structure in the relationship between *Para no volver* and *El mismo mar*..., but also a triangular relationship formed by the first three novels which must be reconciled with the emergent square produced by the fourth text since we already have seen how intimately related the first and fourth novels are.

Whereas the first three novels—the trilogy—appeared within three years, it was not until four years after the completion of the third that there came a fourth which so closely resembles the first: "It is... not surprising that the step from three to four involves particular difficulties, for it is bound up with painful insights. The step is portrayed in alchemist tradition"... by the famous axiom: "Out of the One comes Two, out of Two comes Three, and from the Third comes the One as the Fourth" (Franz, *Number and Time* 129). Hence, a tetralogy emanated from a trilogy, three plus four equals seven, and so it is that between 1978 and 1985 Esther Tusquets completed a novelistic cycle: the One. Regarded as a symbol of perfect order and of a complete period or cycle, the number seven likewise comprises the unity of the ternary and quaternary, not to mention the "the reconciliation of the square with the triangle by superimposing the latter upon the former (as the sky over the earth) or by inscribing it within" (Cirlot 223).

The threshold at which Elena pauses at the close of the fourth novel coincides circularly with the threshold to the unconscious over which the unnamed fifty-year-old protagonist crosses at the opening of the first novel: "Cruzo la puerta de hierro y cristal, pesada, chirriante, y me sumerjo en una atmósfera contradictoriamente más pura" (Tusquets, *El mismo mar*... 7). Furthermore, in addition to its literal meaning that Elena does not intend ever to return to the psychoanalytic couch, the title, *Para no volver,* echoes the well-known verses by Rubén Darío, "Juventud, divino tesoro, ya te vas para no volver," with which Tusquets introduces her fourth novel. Recalling that Tusquets prefaces the beginning of *El mismo mar*... with the highly significant words of J.M. Barrie's *Peter Pan*, "...Y Wendy creció," words which Elena, like the narrator-Clara protagonist of *El mismo mar*..., read and re-read over and over again as a child, "debajo de la mesa del comedor, casi sin luz, leyendo por milésima vez *La Sirenita* o las últimas páginas de *Peter Pan*" (*Para no volver* 34), it would seem, then, that the title of the fourth novel, like the final sentence that brings it to a close, "me voy a psicoanalizar," have implications that are far more germane to the *corpus* of Esther Tusquets' novelistic production than they are to the particular text in which they appear. They connote both a cyclic meaning and a circular structure within which there is no identifiable beginning or end insofar as each and every point along the circumference simultaneously is an end and a new beginning. It should be remembered that the same is true of the individuation continuum which, although linear, ultimately is circular insofar as each "death" is identified with a "rebirth."

Turning to the all-important transition from three to four represented by the *Varada...*/*Para no volver* narrative sequence, Elena is approximately a decade older than Elia in the preceding novel, *Varada...*, who is approximately a decade older than Elia in the preceding novel, *El amor....* The progressive increments of about ten, from thirty-something in novel two, to forty-something in novel three, to the eve of her fiftieth birthday when Elena opens the fourth novel, establish a rhythmic pattern of development which situates the fourth novel as part of a temporal continuum. At a more subtle level of meaning, the unnamed, first-person autobiographical "I" from whose perspective *El mismo mar...* is narrated, when added to Elena's three syllable name, yields a total of four syllables ($1 + 3 = 4$), as does the sum of the two Elia's in novels two and three ($2 + 2 = 4$). But perhaps the most compelling argument that supports the assertion that *Para no volver* is a "natural" continuation of *Varada...* (and, by implication, of the trilogy) is that it picks up the individuation process of the female psyche precisely where it was left at the close of the third novel: with the acknowledgment of the existence of the *animus* archetype and the intention to explore its full range of complementation to female consciousness. Recalling that the final twenty-one page portion of *Varada...* (pages 250-71) is narrated as a first-person direct interior monologue, in contrast to the rest of the novel which is told from the third person omniscient point of view, we witness the early stage of the inclusion of the observer (omniscient narrator) in his/her wholeness (the Self = I) in the process of understanding that in which one has been involved (the writing and publication of *Para no volver*). It is our contention that the so-called "double-voiced discourses" of which Robert Spires speaks in his analysis of *Para no volver*,[18] attest to this very duality of the positioning of the both within as subject and outside as object. We will return to this matter shortly.

Distinct from, and in compensation to, the predominance of females in the first three novels of the tetralogy, is the male framing of the female protagonist's quest for integrative wholeness in *Para no volver*. The three artists—Julio, Eduardo and Arturo—with whom Elena has an antagonistic love/hate relationship, symbolize her ambivalence toward her repressed *animus* that is engaged in the dynamic process, albeit a reluctant one, of becoming conscious. All that is needed is a fourth element—the *logos* principle of rational discrimination and comprehension—in order for the *animus* to complete its ascent into the conscious life of the protagonist. Eduardo says as much at the cocktail party honoring Julio's return from New York: "Nos has reunido aquí a los tres, sólo falta... tu psiquiatra" (207). In the final pages of the narrative, Elena has an epiphanic moment when she realizes that her anger and resentment toward Julio in fact have been projections of her own disappointment in herself "porque no ha tenido nunca el coraje de apostar, de terminar sus poemas y sus cuentos e intentar publicarlos," (216) "dispuesta y hasta feliz de haber renunciado lo que pudo haber sido su vida profesional independiente para vivir" (101).

The animation of the *animus* archetype further signifies that the protagonist possesses at her disposal all of the resources needed to cross over into the second half of life with self-confident optimism: "Elena dispone pues su instrumental, sus armas, y sonríe" (217). Elena had been, but no longer appears to be, caught in the grips of what Jung terms the most trying stage of the individuation process for women: recognition, acceptance and integration of the *animus*: "The conscious attention a woman has to give to her *animus* problem takes much time and

---

[18] In his article, "The Dialogic Structure of *Para no volver*," Spires writes: "Although the novel seems simple enough in summary, it is constructed around a complex series of double-voiced discourses. Since it is Elena's story, the first and most obvious level of discourse consists of her interior monologue. Yet it is apparent from the very beginning that her thought processes are motivated more by her frustrations with the analyst than by the infidelity of her husband, that nearly everything is in one way or another a reply to her doctor. The discourses, therefore, are really dialogues, come recreated and others merely imagined, between the two. But this example in which a monologue is also a dialogue does not end the process of double-voicing. Although her thoughts are focalized, she is not the origin of the focalization or of the narrating voice. A narrator standing somewhere above and beyond Elena's world is responsible for the narration. As a result, the Elena/analyst relationship is a refracted image of the narrator/reader relationship; the dialogue sustained by Elena within the fictitious world is double-voiced and leads us to the dialogue sustained by the narrator outside the world" (94).

involves a lot of suffering. But if she somehow can turn the stranglehold that the unconscious *animus* forces have on her into the invaluable conscious tools for living that they have the potential of becoming, she will possess for life an inner companion who endows her with the masculine qualities of initiative, courage, objectivity and spiritual wisdom" (Jung, *Man and His Symbols* 194). In the closing scene of the novel, after her husband's less than successful United States tour, Elena for the first time discriminatorily observes her friends and lovers: Eduardo, "tan derrotado... que no ha llegado en opinión de los otros, en el público sentir, a nada" (216) and Arturo, "que no ha conseguido echar raíces en nada ni en nadie ni en ninguna parte," (216), as well as her husband, Julio, who "no ha de alcanzar ya nunca la cima de la ambición: por mucho que los demás le vean en la cumbre, existirá siempre un oscuro crítico de provincias que asegure que es un bluff o que está como creador exhausto y agotado" (216), all as failures. As she acknowledges all three for who they truly are, she recognizes that her inflated views of them are but projections emanating from her own being, that her aggrandizement of their worth proportionately had yielded a minimizing of her own. They are, in other words, aspects of her own Self that she had repressed during the first half of her life: "si no ha perdido nunca es porque nunca ha tenido el coraje de apostar, de terminar sus poemas y sus cuentos e intentar publicarlos" (216). With this newly acquired perception of Self, Elena avows to assume control of her own destiny" "cuando el Mago le abra la puerta de la consulta, le cogerá la mano que él le tienda y no se la soltará, no dejará que inicien el tortuoso camino hacia el prostíbulo-santuario" (217). There, at the threshold (the same one that she symbolically crosses in the opening line of *El mismo mar...*), "en el mismo umbral" (217), she will verbally assume the synchronous, dual roles of subject and object (the inclusion of Elena in her wholeness within the framework of her own process of understanding): "me voy a psicoanalizar" (217), words which, as we know, escort the reader to the beginning of the tetralogy.

From a Jungian perspective, the complete activation of the *animus* function as the fountain from which spout forth the "masculine" capacity to discriminate, energy to create, wisdom to guide, and spirit to inspire, with which *Para no volver* concludes, is prefigured by the recurrent *leitmotif* of tears. The unwritten verses which follow those quoted in the epigraph— "cuando quiero llorar, lloro, y a veces loro sin querer"—describe Elena's behavior during the early phase of her psychoanalytic treatment, when she would uncontrollably cry over everything:

> Algo en su interior ha sido dinamitado y han sido catapultados los pedazos a los más remotos extremos del universo, y nada ni nadie, tampoco el psicoanálisis, podrá ir a recuperarlos ni mucho menos reconciliarlos, y el

mismo estallido ha abierto al mismo tiempo, parece, un amplísimo cauce para las lágrimas, de modo que llora Elena a todas horas y por los motivos más disparatados. (33)

The tears that Elena interminably sheds are linked to the sustained image of ocean water within which the first and third novels are engulfed by virtue of the common property of salt that they share. Salt is among the most symbolically endowed of all of the arcane substances employed by the alchemists in their *opus*, without which the work cannot be successfully completed. As Jung quotes from the alchemists, it is "not without good reason" that "salt has been adorned by the wise with the name of Wisdom" (*Jung on Alchemy* 162). The wisdom of which Elena is in pursuit throughout the fourth novel—and which also may be identified as the *raison d'être* of the entire tetralogy—is self-knowledge, the wisdom to understand and appreciate the complexity of the Self.

As identical points on the circle symbolizing the female Self (from the four comes the One), novels one and four share novels two and three in the formation of two triangles. The ensuing image is the following:

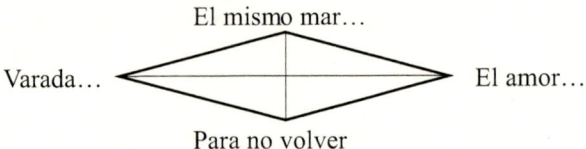

What we have is a squared circle comprised of two triangles (one that includes novels one, two and three and a second that includes novels four, three and two), that is bisected vertically by novels one and four (1 + 4 = 5) and horizontally by novels two and three (2 + 3 = 5), adding up to the all-encompassing number ten (5 + 5 = 10), which raises all things to a spiritual unity. Furthermore, each triangle adds up to one hundred eighty degrees; the two of them equal three hundred sixty degrees, the number of degrees of a circle, all of which is regulated by the central and centralizing archetype of the self.

Returning to what Spires has termed the "double-voiced" discourse from which *Para no volver* is narrated, for the first time in the tetralogy a clear separation can be established between the "internal" protagonist, Elena, and an unidentified, but nonetheless existing, "external" narrator. In the preceding three novels, virtually no distinction can be made between the voice of the author, the narrator and the protagonist, irrespective of whether the text is narrated from the first person autobiographical or the third person omniscient point of view, or a combination of the two as in *Varada*.... This is consistent with the general characteristics of the New Novel, in which the voice of the author is indistinguishable from that of the character(s).[19] The heteroglossa of *Para no volver* is quite distinct, however, in that it is particularly refined and complex due to the fact that the narrative voice, although omnipresent at all levels of the narrative as is typical of the New Novel, simultaneously is refractory, thereby setting up a dialogic relationship between the text and the reader (as a representative of culture) and, on a more subtle internalized textual level, between the protagonist's consciousness and the masculine aspects of her unconscious towards which she is resistant: her *animus*. Although the majority of the narrative discourse is either a recapitulation of a situation in which Elena has been, is, or in which she is anticipating being, engaged with another character—usually her psychoanalyst—there exists a higher, omniscient voice whose use of "humor, impertinence and parody" ("Through the Mirror..." 139), to quote Elizabeth Ordóñez, places her (the "external" narrator) in the authoritative role of understanding more and better than Elena what is transpiring in the text, and of sharing this knowledge, and its not readily apparent significance, with the reader. This is due primarily to the fact that, in dramatic opposition to the novels comprising the trilogy, *Para no volver* is inscribed within the strict parameters of Freudian psychoanalysis and the allegiance to patriarchal supremacy that this closed-system model implies.[20] The eponymous adjective "Freudian" entails many principles, the most

---

[19] According to Pablo Gil Casado, "lo típico de la novela deshumanizada es que la voz del personaje se confunda con la voz del autor. No se considera ya necesario el establecimiento de una diferencia entre la lengua propia del personaje y la privativa del autor. El personaje ya no dialoga; informa, discursea... lo mismo que tradicionalmente venía haciendo el autor. Pero ahora, el autor se entromete en la ficción, hasta el punto de asumir el papel del personaje. En particular, en las novelas creacionistas donde existe un intra-autor y un extra-autor, el personaje es a la vez actor y creador, y el escritor es simultáneamente creador e intérprete. Al borrarse las diferencias entre el mundo exterior y el interior del relato, predomina la imprecisión de que es el autor quien sostiene una conversación con el lector, anulando así al protagonista. El resultado es un conjunto narrativo, indiferenciado e indiferenciable, cuyos componentes tienden al recambio mutuo" (54).

[20] Borrowing from Jung's writings and lectures, Dr. Joseph L. Henderson explains the methodological distinction that the depth psychologist had made between psychoanalysis and psychotherapy as the following: "Analysis implied intensive work involving patient and doctor over a long period of time with frequent sessions. Psychotherapy implied an alliance between therapist and patient that was not binding as to time or as to frequency of sessions, and that could be adjusted to meet immediate needs for psychological insight or crisis intervention; it could, however, turn into an analysis at any time." Of particular relevance to our intentional choice of the term "Freudian psychoanal-

important of which and those which are most relevant to *Para no volver* being: 1) a focus on the role of unconscious processes as motivators of behavior; 2) an abiding concern with the cognitive and the symbolic; 3) a preoccupation with the biological progenitors of human behavior; 4) a strong presumption that there exists a profound cause-and-effect relationship between early experiences and later behaviors; 5) a penchant for deep interpretation, for rummaging down through the layers of the psyche to seek understanding and explanation; and 6) the elaboration of the methods of psychoanalytic therapy as a means for producing changes in behavior, thought and feeling" (Reber 287). The ultimate parodying of the Freudian psychoanalytic model results from the "surprise" ending of the novel when we discover that the source of Elena's personal unfulfillment has absolutely nothing to do with the founding principles of the psychoanalytic method in which she is engaged. As Spires, Navajas and Ordóñez all have convincingly demonstrated, Tusquets situates the origins of female dependency on the patriarchal social hierarchy, of which Elena is a quintessential example, squarely within the parameters of western culture and, more specifically, within the reigning years of the Franco regime during which her social being—not to mention that of all of her female characters—was molded. As Ordóñez perceptively observes, "like many women of her generation and class, Elena has a tendency to measure herself by the achievements of her spouse. And according to official ideology, Julio's record does not appear insignificant. She has exalted him as 'Julio the great victor, innate leader, paladin of anti-Francoism and democracy, Julio, conqueror of the West Indies' (124) and has accepted her own self-sacrifice in the name of her husband's higher, nobler exploits" ("Through the Mirror…" 146-47).

ysis" in describing the type of treatment that Elena receives in the novel is that "Jungian analysis, no less than Jungian psychotherapy, departs from the Freudian model of closed-system analysis, in which the analyst maintains an impersonal and essentially passive position *vis-à-vis* the patient." Jung, on the other hand, conceived of a dialectical procedure that was based on an open-system theory in which the patient and analyst shared an interactive relationship. Henderson goes on to articulate the fundamental point on which the Freudian and Jungian psychoanalytic models overlap insofar as both provide patients with "a protective setting in which to regress to early childhood in order to reexperience and correct disorders in their object relations." Distinct from the Freudian treatment of regression, however, "the Jungian treatment of regression, following Jung's theory of the role of the Self, goes further; it expects to find regression occurring not just in the service of the ego, but also in the service of the Self" (15-16).

Whereas the Freudian school assumes that unconscious complexes are the causes of all female neuroses and therefore works deductively, the Jungian school assumes nothing and proceeds inductively towards an identification of the multifarious aspects of the Self and their harmonious integration. As evidenced by Jung's numerous studies in which he analyzes the effects of culture on the human psyche, the Jungian analytic/therapeutic model naturally would deem the political ideology of the Franco years to be potentially significant inhibitors of the psychological development of women who grew up during that time. In other words, whereas Freudian psychoanalysis operates from the perspective that the causes of neuroses lie repressed in the unconscious, a Jungian therapist assumes that they make their presence known within and throughout the entire constitution of the Self. For example, while Elena "buys into" the necessity of participating in this type of socially sanctioned psychoanalysis in order to relieve her depression in the short run, she has doubts about whether or not it will assist her in accomplishing her long-term goal: "tal vez el análisis le ayude, no está segura, a vislumbrar, pero no existe análisis en el mundo capaz de reunir de nuevo las partes dispersas en un todo armonioso, teme ahora Elena, desolada y resignada" (32). Her internal conflict is shrouded within a larger questioning of the efficacy of the Freudian method being used as echoed by the counterpoised Jungian concern with the totality of the Self.

In equally sharp contrast to the Jungian Self-orientation of the original trilogy, the fourth contrapuntal novel of the tetralogy is satirical[21] in tone as well as extra-narratological perspective as it parodies[22] the Freudian psychoanalytic model with its emphasis on the impersonal role of the analyst. The dehumanized relationship between analyst and analysand is graphically depicted on the front cover of the novel where the top half of a large green shoe foregrounds a Freudian couch. Indeed, Elena has a difficult time communicating her innermost thoughts and feeling to a shoe: "es un poco ridículo, la verdad, andarle contando según qué cosas a un zapato" (47). The Freudian psychoanalytic model is made a mockery of by the brightness of the shoe that seems to be cut in half, signifying that this is all of the analyst that the patient is able to see during treatment. Within the narrative, the parody is extended as Elena, not even convinced that "the

---

[21] By "satirical" we are referring to the Tusquets' use of irony, sarcasm, ridicule, and the like, for the purpose of exposing and denouncing the ineffectualness of the Freudian "closed" psychoanalytic model, as well as of the homage to patriarchy that it implies.

[22] It is our contention that *Para no volver* is a parody of Freudian psychoanalysis, that is, a satirical imitation of the Freudian closed-system model.

Wizard" really is there, assumes the dual role of doctor and patient: "Elena, representando alternativamente el papel de los dos: yo digo y tú dirás y entonces yo replicaré... Hasta que pierda el Impasible la paciencia—harto tal vez de que le hagan decir aquello que no dice, harto de esta representación teatral, con un solo personaje y un también único espectador, en que convierte algunas veces, o la mayoría de las sesiones, Elena el diván, un diván escenario, le dijo en cierta ocasión el Mago, y ella representando sobre él todos los papeles de la farsa" (47).

The aloof superiority of the doctor is complemented by the Freudian school's strict adherence to the principle of the male sexual origin of female neurosis, specifically, penis envy. Although Elena is certain that the source of her depression is neither an Œdipal nor a castration complex—both of which her Freudian analyst assumes to exist at the core of her unconscious, "porque andan locos los dos, el Mago y ella, desde hace semanas, casi desde el mismo inicio del análisis, a la caza del complejo de edipo y del complejo de la castración, y venga abrir cajones y revolver arcanos de la memoria perdida" (76)—she dismisses her doubts as she reminds herself that if she were conscious of the presence of these complexes, not to mention the much sought after penis envy, then they would not be unconscious complexes: "poco importa que a nivel consciente no haya sentido nunca envidia del pene, ya que ¿cómo se demuestra que no la ha sentido tampoco a nivel inconsciente, cuando lo que caracteriza al inconsciente es precisamente que permanece para nosotros oculto?" (76). The point to be made here is that it will always be assumed by a Freudian analyst that these male-oriented unconscious complexes reside at the core of all female neuroses. Since it never can be proven that they do not, countless years of analysis may be spent looking for that which is never to be found, either because it is inherently unconscious and, therefore cannot be rendered visible to consciousness without ceasing to be that which it is, or because it never existed to begin with. The external narrator is drawing the reader's attention to the absurdity of a process in which the female patient is treated as an appendage to male sexuality which is deemed to be superior and, therefore, secretly envied and desired by her. This is the explanation offered for the wall of ambivalent resistance that Elena puts up in the early phase of psychoanalysis: she resents wanting what she cannot have (penis envy) and feels equally resentful that her emotional well-being requires that she partake of a relationship in which she must accept a dependent, submissive role, always at the mercy of a game devised and controlled by men. It goes without saying that she has transferred her still unconscious self-neglect accompanied by subservience to her husband onto her analyst. As Catherine Bellver comments, "the epithets alluding to the analyst's authority are symptomatic of the dialectic tension persisting throughout the novel between submission and subversion, between acceptance and resistance. The ambivalent, contradictory stance of the protagonist before psychoanalysis is demonstrated especially in her habit of referring to Freud as 'Papá Freud.' Freud is, to be sure, the father of psychology, but the diminutive form and its feigned intimacy serve to demythify and even to trivialize psychology's pioneer and the patronizing paternalism implicit in his methodology" (Intertextuality..." 110-11).

The New Novel being what it is, however, deceptive appearances never are far away. With female homosexuality conspicuously absent, the final novel of the series appears to be about the protagonist's distinct, yet complementary, relationships with four men: her husband, Julio, her two friends and lovers, Eduardo and Arturo, and her Argentine Freudian analyst. As the reading progresses, it becomes increasingly evident that the novel is not really about Elena's relationship with these four significant men in her life. Rather, it is about the dynamics of the female psyche as it grapples with the positive and negative attributes of the contra-sexual *animus* archetype housed within: his attitude of superiority with respect to women; his detached, rational, dispassionate, ostensibly insensitive approach to life's challenges, his demeaning trivialization of female need and desire; his discriminating, analytical method of conflict resolution, his goal of being viewed as successful in the eyes of society; his physical, sexual and intellectual superiority; his creative energy and his spiritual wisdom. Since many of these so-called "masculine" traits operate in an adversarial role to women and perpetuate their subordination, it is no wonder that women have such a hard time reconciling feminine consciousness with their "inner man."

Each of the four male characters dramatizes a distinct aspect of Elena's *animus* which, in unison, pull her out of the creative and spiritual lethargy that has immobilized her throughout the first half of her life. Julio has learned to live with the combination of professional successes and failures that he has endured:

> Este regreso que tan frívolamente están celebrando todos como un éxito ha tenido por lo menos tanto de fracaso como de éxito genuino, y Elena piensa que no existe remedio tampoco para Julio Welles, Julio da Vinci, Julio el Maravilloso, Julio el Triunfador, porque va a sentirse él siempre, por lo menos en sus períodos de depresivo desencanto—que suceden y preceden a los períodos de euforia desatada, en los que sigue creyendo posible comerse el mundo—, tan derrotado como Eduardo. (215-16)

He also comes to symbolize for Elena a delicate balancing act of independence and dependency, for it is only she who really knows how needy her husband is of having someone to inflate his ego and fill him with a sense of self-worth that he is unable to muster on his own. Eduardo, on the other hand, is the romantic genius whose commitment to his art always has outdistanced his accomplishments. As Elena acknowledges that perhaps it has been her fear of failure that which his prevented her from developing her own artistic talents, Eduardo becomes a role model that can assist her in assuaging her self-doubt just enough to be able to mobilize her creativity and be willing to take the risk that her efforts might yield personal reward. It also is the feminist Eduardo who compels Elena to confront the reality that she has been both victim and perpetrator of male superiority/female servility:

> En el sucio juego, tan femenino, de adorar a su hombre como si se tratara de un dios y protegerle como si fuera un niño, dispuesta y hasta feliz de haber renunciado a la que pudo haber sido su vida profesional independiente para vivir—lo reconozca o no, y por mucho que lo condene en las demás mujeres—en función de otro, sin llegar a terminar jamás ni uno solo de sus libros de poemas, ni uno solo de sus relatos, y, lo que es muchísimo peor, sin que parezca importarle o lamentarlo demasiado, Elena (según Eduardo) en permanente arrobo, haciendo a un tiempo de madre, de esposa, de secretaria, de enfermera. (101-02)

If the solitary, introspective Eduardo represents the perfect balancing act of masculine discrimination and female/maternal nurturance, "Eduardo-mi-queridísima mamá—no una madre como las que habían tenido ellos dos, claro está, sino una madre auténtica y genuina" (93), the gregarious, fun-loving Arturo provides a return, albeit temporary and artificial, to the lost youth whose passage Elena so profusely laments: "esta adolescente que pretende haber descubierto Arturo en ella, porque sólo una Elena jovencísima podría devolverle a él a su vez, como un espejo reflectante, esa juventud que se ha ido para no volver" (158). An Argentine like her analyst, Arturo shares with Elena horrific stories of political unrest in his homeland, and the pain and suffering that he has had to endure as a result. Consequently, she discovers for the first time that men have feelings and vulnerabilities too, a conscious awakening which further lowers her resistance to her own inner masculinity as the female psyche comes to feel less threatened by what it had perceived as adversarial masculine insensitivity.

Elena's analyst, of course, is a symbol of masculine wisdom and spirituality. He possesses the ability so lacking in Elena to position himself above and beyond the chaos of the present and confer order and meaning to it. This explanation seems to provide the most plausible explanation for the closing words of the novel: Elena no longer is in need of psychoanalytic treatment because she has incorporated the *animus* attributes provided by her male analyst into her arsenal of skills which will serve as a helpful companion to her throughout the second half o her life.

To summarize, in *Para no volver* Tusquets cunningly utilizes a parody of Freudian psychoanalysis as a springboard from which she dramatizes the activation of the *animus* archetype as discussed in the introduction and analysis of *El mismo mar*... Hence, the Freudian model is treated as a satire of the culturally masculine-dominant principle of *logos* which has all but dismissed the feminine principle of human relatedness—*eros*—as a necessary component of cultural and universal equilibrium. As Gonzalo Navajas aptly states, "one important effect of civilization is that it grounds human relations in power and, consequently, thwarts the possibility of equality between human beings. Civilization justifies the establishment of structures of hierarchy and subordination of one subject to another, maintaining that they are needed in order to preserve the balance and peaceful development of social relations" ("Civilizations..." 124). Civilization, to be sure, is an unfair game. It is, however, the only game in town, and women must abide by its man-made rules if they wish to be included as players. It is within this context that we are meant to understand Elena's resentment of her husband and the role of hero-worshipper in which Spanish society has cast her. The Freudian psychoanalytic model is but a microcosm of Spanish women's more generalized submissive role to men, which not surprisingly Elena transfers onto her analyst. Suddenly, "Julio the Great," "Julio the Magnificent," "Julio the Genius" etc., are transferred onto "Father Freud," "the Wizard" as Elena equates his silence with the silence of culture when it comes to female aspirations.

In the process of seemingly redressing political, cultural and social inequities within Spain in particular, and western civilization in general, Tusquets sets up a narrative game in which she probes the nature of the feminine contra-sexual archetype from the vantage point of parodying the deterministic Freudian psychoanalytic model within the broader Jungian individuation framework. The Jungian model presupposes not merely the inherent bisexuality of all of creation, but a relationship of mutual dependency between masculine and feminine in which neither reigns superior.

The author's inquiry into the nature of (fe)male psychic cohabitation has profound individual (Elena), cultural (Spain) and universal (Esther Tusquets as representative of the universal female psyche) implications. The creation of any discourse for an intended recipient—be it amorous, psychoanalytic or literary, communicated to a lover, an analyst or a reader—is construed as a game in which two adversarial positions comprise its wholeness. Being the New Novel that it is, *Para no volver* as a seemingly psychoanalytic novel, in reality possesses all of the attributes of a game:

Throughout *Para no volver*, the protagonist equates analysis to a game; to a struggle between analyst and patient; to a situation concurrent with, yet not identical to, life; and to a process, albeit slow, aimed toward completion. These conditions—dialectical tension, mimesis, and progression—also constitute the very essence of the game of writing. What we find in *Para no volver* is a game within a game within a game, played in their respective realms by protagonist, writer, and reader... Within the novel, the protagonist is not only subjected to the rules of analysis enforced by her psychologist, but she also invents her own private game in an attempt to destroy his impassive anonymity... The relationship between Elena and her analyst, like that between reader and author, must define itself through an arduous process of opposition and unity, of subversion and cooperation." (Bellver, "Intertextuality..." 114-15)

The nature of all games played by adversarial opposites is the hallmark of the New Novel, which forever challenges the reader not only to be victorious at decoding its obtuse meaning, but also to decipher the rules of the game as part of that understanding. In *Para no volver*, as well as throughout the tetralogy that it both foregrounds and culminates, Tusquets sets up a narrative game in which the most notorious of all female adversaries—masculinity—becomes her most loyal, devoted companion as she embarks upon the creation of the novelistic tetralogy whose final page we have just concluded.

III. Conclusion

THE RE-EMERGENT, ALMOST SIGNATURE point of departure for a vast number of Tusquets' narratives, is the plight of women who have been abandoned by narcissistic lovers or husbands, who respond by turning inward to probe the depths of their soul in an attempt to understand the reasons for their solitude, and who ultimately opt for reconciliation. Those of us who work with Esther Tusquets' fiction are all too familiar with this recurring theme of female abandonment and reconciliation. A literal reading and interpretation of novels such as *El mismo mar de todos los veranos* and *Para no volver*, both of which end with the reconciliation of the protagonist with her estranged husband, leaves the majority of female readers angry and frustrated with Tusquets' middle-aged protagonists who resignedly allow their husbands to get away with repeated incidents of marital infidelity. It indeed is understandable that their obsequious tolerance of such emotional abuse would leave female readers disappointed in these protagonists—and perhaps even in the author herself—since most of us cannot imagine acquiescing to such an egregious betrayal of commitment and trust from our partners. In the case of *El amor es un juego solitario*—a novel with which the author herself was disappointed due to its harsh pessimism—the female reader is left dismayed and disillusioned with the very principles that constitute the hallmark of "the feminine," namely, nurturing relationships, motherhood in particular, and a steadfast commitment to those whom she loves, all of which are disturbingly absent from the text. With regard to its continuation, *Varada tras el último naufragio*, the oscillating duality of binary oppositions within the thirty-something-year-old Elia are mediated here by the transcendent function—the protagonist's recognition that everything that she needs to feel whole and complete lies within her Self—at work in the same female psyche a decade later.

If, as demonstrated by all great works of art, form and content comprise two sides of an inseparable whole, then Tusquets' intensely baroque style should forewarn the reader that the content cannot, and should not, be taken at face value. Wholly consistent with the baroque esthetics foregrounding the New Novel is the notion that content is subservient to form and that appearances are deceptive, that they do little more than shroud a different, often unrelated and at times contradictory, underlying meaning. Tusquets' particular contextualization of the theme of abandonment in *El mismo mar de todos los veranos*, *El amor es un juego solitario*, *Varada tras el último naufragio* and *Para no volver* is a unifying principle of these four novels. Insofar as the novels are read literally, they reveal little more than a dismal view of woman's role in Spanish patriarchal society. When, however, they are read as an elaborate, intricate system of female archetypes and universal symbols, they reveal a positive, healthy, coherent pattern of psychic growth that the Swiss analytical psychologist, Carl Jung, termed individuation. Throughout his writings, Jung describes individuation as a dialectical process involving harmonious unity with another, followed by a devastating separation which, after a period of despondency and self-pity, eventually propels the individual to embark upon an inner quest for the "lost object." Once the light of the inner spirit is rendered visible to the individual, he or she arises anew like the phoenix soaring towards heaven from the death of his own ashes with greater splendor than ever before.

Individuation is a lifetime process of "abandonments" which trigger "deaths" and "resurrections." This dialectical procedure is absolutely essential for psychological growth for, in its absence, an individual stagnates, ceases to mature psychologically. In this sense, the individuation process is analogous to rites of initiation, or "tests" of endurance against the darkest evils and the most profound solitude, by means of which an individual must prove his or her worthiness to move to a higher level within the social order and to a broadening of consciousness in terms of his/her personal psychological development. Our most beloved fairy tales dramatize this painful dialectical process from innocence to adulthood.

According to Jung, the most life-altering stages of the individuation process emerge in mid-life when one becomes conscious of his or her own divided nature and, in particular, begins to understand and wrestle with the complex nature of the interrelationship between conscious and unconscious life. Tusquets' dramatizes this very dawning of awareness of the binary make-up of the psyche in *El amor...* Although the author's second published novel is a logical continuation of the "uroboric" introduction of the preceding *El mismo mar...*, *El amor...* just as compellingly behaves as the first novel of the series from the point of view of the chronological age of the projecting psyche of the female protagonist who is embarking upon the individuation process. The systolic/diastolic energy forces that keep Elia trapped in an oscillating duality of binary oppositions that are portrayed in the novel as male/female, adult/child, *logos/eros*, Apollonian/Dionysian, static/dynamic, depression/euphoria, prey/predator, fiction/reality etc., while ostensibly contradictory and potentially conflictive, can, if wrestled with long enough, become useful complements and compensations to the human psyche, comparable to the dynamic interplay of opposing elements constituting the make-up of the universe. In the psyche as well as in the universe, when one element gains too much control at the expense or repression of its compensatory complement, an unhealthy, often destructive, imbalance ensues. If not corrected in an individual, dissociation of the personality brought about by the conflict of incompatible tendencies occurs. The result is the formation of an autonomous splinter personality, thereby promoting a psychic imbalance—a neurosis—which, if not treated, thwarts a healthy, integrated Self. The Self, according to Jung, is the sum total of the conscious and the personal as well as collective unconscious. While the personal unconscious is made up of all individual experiences that have been forgotten or repressed, the collective unconscious houses universal archetypes. Among those inhabiting the female unconscious are the Demeter/Kore rebirth journey, and the *animus*, which is the unconscious, masculine side of a woman's personality. The ultimate goal of individuation during the second half of life is to integrate as much of the unconscious into conscious awareness as possible. This often involves the troublesome confrontation of dichotomies at war with each other in the psyche. If, however, the psyche can weather the storm, an integrative synthesis takes place and the psyche transcends to a higher level of consciousness. As a result of the individuation process, the individual acquires more and more tools with which to live a more satisfying, productive second half of life.

Such is the case with our collective female protagonist(s). Her unconscious is caught between two incompatible splinter personalities: a frightened, insecure, emotionally abandoned "inner child"—personified by Clara in the trilogy—and an overbearing, insensitive *animus*—personified by Ricardo in *El amor...*, by Pablo in *Varada...*, and collectively by Arturo, Eduardo, Julio and the Argentine psychoanalyst in *Para no volver*, all of whom are prefigured by the symbolic content with which the bronze statue of Mercurius that greets the protagonist in the opening pages of *El mismo mar...* is endowed. Both splinter personalities have developed in response to the negative mother complex that dominates the protagonists' personality. As the protagonist ages throughout the tetralogy, the spillover of the two discordant personalities into her conscious life becomes increasingly pronounced. It is therefore her distinctly mid-life task to obliterate the negative mother stranglehold so that her inner child and *animus* can be harnessed, each one by the other, and ultimately transformed into positive inner companions to a healthier, more integrated psyche.

It has been our objective to demonstrate that these are the very forces at work in Esther Tusquets' four novels, *El mismo mar de todos los veranos*, *El amor es un juego solitario*, *Varada tras el último naufragio* and *Para no volver*. We have justified our classification of the four novels as constituting a tetralogy by demonstrating their form-content indivisibility from the point of view of Jungian psychoanalytic theory. Read symbolically, the novels reveal a form-content indivisibility. As a narrative *opus*, they collectively embrace the theme of the search for, and discovery of, an individual and the universal female Self. The theme is embedded in the dialectically transcendent process of individuation that the unfolding of the cumulative content of the tetralogy imitates. At the level of graphic symbolism, the structural relatedness of the four novels intimates a mandala-like design, or squaring of the circle. This circular structure of the tetralogy is framed within a symbolic square comprised of two pairs of *coincidentia oppositorum*, whose two sets of mutually dependent opposites describe the structural and thematic interrelatedness of the four novels. *El mismo mar de todos los veranos* and *Para no volver* oppose each other by similarity in that both novels deal with the exhumation from the unconscious of two distinctly universal female archetypes: the Great Mother/Daughter unity linking all female generations, and the *animus*, respectively. We already have seen the crucial role that the *animus* archetype played in unleashing Elena's artistic potential. In *El mismo mar...*, the lesbian relationship between the middle-aged protagonist and the adolescent Clara is a symbolic reenactment of Demeter's rescue of her daughter, Kore, from the rapist, Pluto, who had abducted her while she was gathering flowers. The cycle of initial unity of mother and daughter, Pluto's violation of that unity, and its eventual restoration "represents psychologically an internal conjunction of woman and woman, a woman's integration of her own parts, or... a re-membering or a putting back together of the mother-daughter body" (Pratt 113). Similarly, *El amor...* and *Varada...* stand in relational opposition to one another as textual embodiments of nature and culture, respectively. The Dionysian frivolity, or return to basic instincts, that characterizes the three binary relationships in the second novel of the series is juxtaposed to the two sets of father-mother-child archetypal triangles constituted by Elia-Jorge-Daniel, on the one hand, and the Eva-Pablo-Clara projection, on the other. The novel takes a critical view of the marital infidelities that disrupt these seemingly happy upper-middle class Catalonian families while scrutinizing their obsessive preoccupation with public opinion, or *el ¿qué dirán?*

In the macrocosm the square corresponds to the four elements making up the earth while the circle is, of course, the great cosmic symbol of heaven. Tusquets' magnificently constructed novelistic tetralogy is a literary microcosm which equates the circle with the square. Cirlot describes the aim of "squaring the circle" as achieving "unity in the material world (as well as in the spiritual life) over and above the differences and obstacles (the static order) of the number four and the four-cornered square" (293). This higher synthesis is what is meant by the whole being greater than the sum of its parts. As we hope to have demonstrated, Tusquets' narrative *unus mundus* indeed is greater than the sum of *El mismo mar de todos los veranos*, *El amor es un juego solitario*, *Varada tras el último naufragio* and *Para no volver*. The circular confluence of omniscience and autobiography, of narrative object and narrative subject, of analysand and self-analyst, of literary character and author and, ultimately, of creation and creator, that characterize the structural-thematic dynamics of the tetralogy, captures the mid-life journey of the female psyche toward Self and its artistic expression, a journey which culminates in their synchronous, indistinguishable realization of wholeness.

Bibliography

BOOKS:

Abel, Elizabeth *et al*, eds. *The Voyage In: Fictions of Female Development*. Hanover: New England UP, 1983.
———, ed. *Writing and Sexual Difference*. Chicago: Chicago UP, 1982.
Adler, G. *The Living Symbol: A Case Study in the Process of Individuation*. New York: Bollingen Foundation, 1961.
Arcana, Judith. *Our Mothers' Daughters*. Berkeley: Shameless Hussy Press, 1979.
Bakhtin, M. M. *The Dialogic Imagination*. Translated by Caryl Emerson & Michael Holquist. Edited by Michael Holquist. Austin: Texas UP, 1981.
Barrie, J.M. *Peter Pan*. New York: Bantam Books, 1981.
Bataille, George. *Death and Sensuality*. New York: Walker and Company, 1962.
Beane, Wendell C. & William G. Doty, eds. *Myths, Rites, Symbols*. Vol. I. New York: Harper & Row, 1975.
Becker, Udo. *The Continuum Encyclopedia of Symbols*. Trans. by Lance W. Garner. New York: Continuum Press, 2000.
Birkhäuser-Oeri, Sibylle. *The Mother: Archetypal Image in Fairy Tales*. Edited and with a Forward by Marie-Louise von Franz. Toronto: Inner City Books, 1988.
Blair, Nancy. *Goddesses for Every Season*. Rockport (Mass.), Shaftsbury, Dorset (Great Britain) & Brisbane, Queensland (Australia): Element Books, 1995.
Bolen, Jean Shinoda. *Goddesses in Everywoman: A New Psychology of Women*. New York: Harper & Row, 1984.
Brewi, Janice and Anne Brennan. *Celebrate Mid-life: Jungian Archetypes and Mid-life Spirituality*. Crossroad: New York, 1990.
Bruns, J. Edgar. *God as Woman and Woman as God*. New York: Paulist Press, 1973.
Campbell, Joseph. *The Masks of God: Primitive, Oriental, Occidental, and Creative Mythology*. 4 vols. New York: Viking Press, 1959.
Carlson, Kathie. *In Her Image: The Unhealed Daughter's Search for Her Mother*. Boston & Shaftesbury: Shambhala Publications, 1989.
Castillejo, Irene Claremont de. *Knowing Woman: A Feminine Psychology*. New York: G. P. Putnam's Sons, 1973.
Chesler, Phyllis. *Women and Madness*. New York: Avon, 1973.
Chodorow, Nancy J. *Femininities, Masculinities, Sexualities: Freud and Beyond*. Lexington: Kentucky UP, 1994.

———. *The Reproduction of Mothering: Psychoanalysis and the Sociology of Gender.* Berkeley & Los Angeles: California UP, 1978.

Ciplijauskaité, Biruté. *La novela femenina contemporánea: Hacia una topología de la narración en primera persona (1970-1985).* Barcelona: Anthropos, 1988.

Cirlot, J. E. *Dictionary of Symbols.* Second Edition. Trans. from the Spanish by Jack Sage. New York: Philosophical Library, 1971.

Dolgin, Stacey L. *La novela desmitificadora española (1961-1982).* Barcelona: Anthropos, 1991.

Dowling, Colette. *The Cinderella Complex: Women's Hidden Fear of Independence.* New York: Summit Books, 1981.

Downing, Christine. *The Goddess.* New York: The Crossroad Publishing Co., 1981.

Eagleton, Terry. *Marxism and Literary Criticism.* London: Methuen, 1976.

Edinger, Edward. *Anatomy of the Psyche: Alchemical Symbolism in Psychotherapy.* La Salle (Illinois): Open Court, 1985.

———. *Ego and the Archetype: Individuation and the Religious Function of the Psyche.* Baltimore: Penguin Books, 1973.

———. *The Living Psyche: A Jungian Analysis in Pictures.* Wilmette (Illinois): Chiron Publications, 1990.

Ellenberger, Henri. *The Discovery of the Unconscious: The History and Evolution of Dynamic Psychiatry.* New York: Basic Books, 1970.

Fincher, Susanne F. *Creating Mandalas: For Insight, Healing and Self-Expression.* Boston & London: Shambhala Publications, 1991.

Fischer, Lucy Rose. *Linked Lives: Adult Daughters and Their Mothers.* New York: Harper & Row, 1986.

Fordham, Michael, Rosemary Gordon, Judith Hubback & Kenneth Lambert, eds. *Technique in Jungian Analysis.* 2nd ed. London: Karnac Books, 1989.

Franz, Marie-Louise von. *The Feminine in Fairy Tales.* Revised Edition. Boston & London: Shambhala Publications, 1993.

———. *Individuation in Fairy Tales.* New York: Spring Publications, 1977.

———. *An Introduction to the Interpretation of Fairy Tales.* Dallas: Spring Publications, 1970.

———. *Number and Time: Reflections Leading Toward a Unification of Depth Psychology and Physics.* Evanston: Northwestern UP, 1974.

———. *Projection and Re-Collection in Jungian Psychology.* La Salle & London: Open Court, 1980.

———. *Psyche and Matter.* Boston & London: Shambhala Publications, 1992.

———. *Shadow and Evil in Fairy Tales.* Dallas: Spring Publications, 1974.

Freud, Sigmund. *Beyond the Pleasure Principle.* Trans. and Ed. by James Strachey. New York & London: W.W. Norton & Co., 1961.

———. *The Ego and the Id.* Trans. by Joan Riviere. Ed. by James Strachey. New York & London: W.W. Norton & Co., 1960.

———. *New Introductory Lectures on Psychoanalysis.* Trans. and Ed. by James Strachey. New York & London: W.W. Norton & Co., 1964.

Frey-Rohn, Liliane. *From Freud to Jung.* New York: J. P. Putnam's Sons, 1974.

Friday, Nancy. *My Mother, My Self.* New York: Delacorte Press, 1977.

Gibson, Clare. *Signs and Symbols: An Illustrated Guide to Their Meanings and Origins.* New York: Barnes & Noble, 1996.

Gil Casado, Pablo. *La novela deshumanizada española (1958-1988).* Barcelona: Anthropos, 1990.

Gilbert, Sandra & Susan Gubar. *The Madwoman in the Attic: The Woman Writer and the Nineteenth-Century Literary Imagination.* New Haven: Yale UP, 1979.

Gilchrist, Cherry. *The Elements of Alchemy.* Rockport (Mass.), Shaftsbury, Dorset (Great Britain) and Melbourne, Victoria (Australia): Element Books, 1991.

González-del-Valle, Luis T. and Catherine Nickel, eds. *Selected Proceedings of the Mid-America Conference on Hispanic Literature.* Lincoln: Society of Spanish and Spanish-American Studies, 1986.

Goodwin, James. *Autobiography: The Self Made Text.* New York: Twayne, 1993.

Grinnell, Robert. *Alchemy in a Modern Woman: A Study in the Contrasexual Archetype.* Dallas: Spring Publications, 1973.

Guénon, René. *Fundamental Symbols: The Universal Language of Sacred Science.* Trans. by Alvin Moore, Jr. Cambridge: Quinta Essentia, 1995.

Greene, Gayle and Coppélia Kahn, eds. *Making a Difference: Feminist Literary Criticism.* London & New York: Methuen, 1985.

Gunn, Daniel. *Psychoanalysis and Fiction: An Exploration of Literary and Psychoanalytic Borders.* Cambridge: Cambridge UP, 1988.

Haddon, Genia Pauli. *Body Metaphors: Releasing God-Feminine in Us All.* New York: Crossroad Publishing Co., 1988.

Hall, James. *Clinical Use of Dreams: Jungian Interpretations and Enactments.* New York: Grune & Stratton, 1977.

———. *Jungian Dream Interpretation.* Toronto: Inner City Books, 1983.

Hannah, Barbara. *Encounters with the Soul: Active Imagination.* Santa Monica (California): Sigo Press, 1981.

———. *Striving Towards Wholeness.* Boston: Sigo Press, 1988.

Harding, M. Esther. *Woman's Mysteries: Ancient and Modern.* New York: G. P. Putnam's Sons, 1971.

Hawkes, Terence. *Metaphor.* London: Methuen, 1972.

Hirsch, Marianne. *The Mother/Daughter Plot: Narrative, Psychoanalysis, Feminism.* Bloomington: Indiana UP, 1989.

Hodgson, John. *The Search for the Self: Childhood in Autobiography and Fiction Since 1940.* Sheffield: Sheffield Academic Press, 1993.

Ichiishi, Barbara F. *The Apple of Earthly Love: Female Development in Esther Tusquets' Fiction.* New York: Peter Lang, 1994.

Infusino, Giampaolo. *El extraordinario poder de los mandala.* Trans. by M. Àngels Pujol i Foyo. Barcelona: Editorial De Vecchi, 1999.

Jacobi, Jolan. *The Psychology of C.G. Jung.* London: Kegan Paul, Trench, Trubner & Co., 1942.

———. *The Way of Individuation.* Trans. by R. F. C. Hull. New York: Harcourt, Brace & World, 1967.

Johnson, Barbara. *The Critical Difference: Essays in the Contemporary Rhetoric of Reading.* Baltimore: The Johns Hopkins UP, 1980.

Johnson, Robert A. *SHE: Understanding Feminine Psychology.* Revised Edition. New York: Harper Perennial, 1989.

Jones, Margaret E. W. *The Contemporary Spanish Novel, 1939-1975.* Boston: Twayne, 1985.

Jung, Carl G. *AION: Researches into the Phenomenology of the Self.* C.W. Vol.9, Part 2. Trans. by R. F. C. Hull. New York: Pantheon Books, 1959.

———. *The Archetypes and the Collective Unconscious.* C.W. Vol. 9, Part I, 2nd ed. Trans. by R. F. C. Hull. Princeton: Princeton UP, 1969.

———. *Aspects of the Feminine.* From C.W. Vols. 6, 7, 9i, 9ii, 10, 17. Trans. by R.F.C. Hull. Princeton: Princeton UP, 1982.

———. *Aspects of the Masculine* From C.W. Vols. 4, 5, 7, 8, 9, 10, 13,14. Trans. by R.F.C. Hull with an Introduction by John Beene. Princeton: Princeton UP, 1989.

———. *Contributions to Analytical Psychology.* London: Routeledge & Kegan Paul, 1928.

———. *Man and His Symbols.* Garden City: Doubleday, 1964.

———. *Modern Man in Search of a Soul.* Trans. by W. S. Dell and Cary F. Baynes. New York: Harcourt, Brace, & Co., 1933.

———. *Mysterium Coniunctionis: An Inquiry in the Separation and Syntheses of Psychic Opposites in Alchemy.* C.W. Vol. 14. 2nd ed. Trans. by R.F.C. Hull. Princeton: Princeton UP, 1970.

———. *Jung on Active Imagination.* Edited and with an Introduction by Joan Chodorow. Princeton: Princeton UP, 1997.

———. *Jung on Alchemy.* Selected and Introduced by Nathan Schwartz-Salant. Princeton: Princeton UP, 1995.

———. *Psychological Types or the Psychology of Individuation.* 12th ed. New York: Random House, 1964.

———. *The Psychology of the Transference.* From C.W. Vol 16. Trans. by R.F.C. Hull. Princeton: Princeton UP, 1954.

———. *The Structure and Dynamics of the Psyche.* From C.W. Vol 8. 2nd ed. Trans. by R.F.C. Hull. Princeton: Princeton UP, 1969.

———. *Symbols of Transformation: An Analysis of the Prelude to a Case of Schizophrenia.* C.W. Vol. 5. 2nd ed. Princeton: Princeton UP, 1976.

———. *The Undiscovered Self.* From C.W. Vols. 10, 18. Revised trans. by R.F.C. Hull with a New Introduction by William McGuire. Princeton: Princeton UP, 1990.

Kavaler-Adler, Susan. *The Creative Mystique: From Red Shoes Frenzy to Love and Creativity.* New York: Routledge, 1996.

Keyes, M. F. *Inward Journey: Art as Therapy.* La Salle & London: Open Court, 1983.

Knapp, Bettina, L. *A Jungian Approach to Literature.* Carbondale and Edwardsville: Southern Illinois UP, 1984.

Kolbenschlag, Madonna. *Kiss Sleeping Beauty Good-Bye: Breaking the Spell of Feminine Myths and Models.* New York: Bantam, 1981.

Kristeva, Julia. *Black Sun.* New York: Columbia UP, 1989.

Lacan, Jacques. *The Language of the Self: The Function of Language in Psychoanalysis.* Trans. by Anthony Wilden. Baltimore: The Johns Hopkins UP, 1968.

Laing, R. D. *The Divided Self.* New York: Pantheon, 1969.

Landeira, Ricardo & Luis González del Valle, eds. *Nuevos y novísimos: Algunas perspectivas críticas sobre la narrativa española desde la década de los 60*. Boulder: Society of Spanish and Spanish-American Studies, 1987.
Lauter, Estella & Carol Schreier Rupprecht, eds. *Feminist Archetypal Theory: Interdisciplinary Revisions of Jungian Thought*. Knoxville: Tennessee UP, 1985.
Lee-Bonanno, Lucy. *The Quest for Authentic Personhood: An Expression of the Female Tradition in Novels by Moix, Tusquets, Matute and Alós*. Dissertation, University of Kentucky,1984. Ann Arbor: Michigan UP, 1987.
Lipman Brown, Joan, ed. *Women Writers of Contemporary Spain: Exiles in the Homeland*. Newark: Delaware UP, 1991.
López, Francisca. *Mito y discurso en la novela femenina de posguerra en España*. Madrid: Pliegos, 1995.
Lyotard, Jean-François. *La posmodernidad (explicada a los niños)*. Translated from the French by Enrique Lynch. Barcelona: Editorial Gedisa, 1996.
McDougall, Joyce. *The Many Faces of Eros: A Psychoanalytic Exploration of Human Sexuality*. London: Free Association Books, 1995.
Melamed, Elissa. *Mirror Mirror:The Terror of not Being Young*. New York: Simon, 1983.
Miller, Beth, ed. *Women in Hispanic Literature: Icons and Fallen Idols*. Berkeley: California UP, 1983.
―――, Jean Baker. *Toward a New Psychology of Women*. Boston: Beacon Press, 1976.
Mitchell, Juliet. *Psychoanalysis and Feminism*. New York: Pantheon, 1974.
Moi, Toril. *Sexual/Textual Politics: Feminist Literary Theory*. London & New York: Methuen, 1985.
Molinaro, Nina. *Foucault, Feminism and Power: Reading Esther Tusquets*. Lewiston: Bucknell UP, 1991.
Monaghan, Patricia. *The Book of Goddesses and Heroines*. St. Paul: Llewellyn, 1990.
Morgan, Janice & Colette T. Hall. *Gender & Genre in Literature: Redefining Autobiography in Twentieth-Century Women's Fiction: An Essay Collection*. New York & London: Garland Publishing, 1999.
Neumann, Erich. *The Great Mother*. Princeton: Princeton UP, 1955.
―――. *The Origins and History of Consciousness*. With a Forward by C. G. Jung. 11th edition. Trans. by R. F. C. Hull. Princeton: Princeton UP, 1995.
Nichols, Geraldine Cleary. *Des/cifrar la diferencia: Narrativa femenina de la España contemporánea*. Madrid: Siglo Veintiuno, 1992.
―――. *Escribir, espacio propio: Laforet, Matute, Moix, Tusquets, Riera y Roig por sí mismas*. Minneapolis: Institute for the Studies of Ideologies and Literature, 1989.
Olney, James. *Metaphors of Self*. Princeton: Princeton UP, 1972.
Ordóñez, Elizabeth. *Voices of Their Own: Contemporary Spanish Narrative by Women*. Lewisburg: Bucknell UP, 1991.
Ortega y Gasset, José. *La deshumanización del arte y otros ensayos estéticos*. 10th ed. Madrid: Revista de Occidente, 1970.
―――. *Ideas sobre la novela. Obras completas*. Vol. 3. Madrid: Alianza, 1983.
Paz, Octavio. *Los signos en rotación y otros ensayos*. Madrid: Alianza, 1971.
Pérez, Janet W. *Contemporary Women Writers of Spain*. Boston: Twayne, 1988.
―――, ed. *Novelistas femeninas de la posguerra española*. Madrid: Porrúa, 1983.

Pérez Firmat, Gustavo. *Idle Fictions. The Hispanic Vanguard Novel, 1926-1934*. Durham, NC: Duke UP, 1982.
Perkins, Michael. *The Secret Record: Modern Erotic Literature*. New York: William Morrow, 1977.
Philipson, Morris. *Outline of Jungian Esthetics*. Chicago: Northwestern UP, 1963.
Piercy, Marge. *My Mother's Body*. New York: Alfred A. Knopf, 1985.
Pratt, Annis. *Archetypal Patterns in Women's Fiction*. Bloomington: Indiana UP, 1981.
Reber, Arthur S. *Dictionary of Psychology*. London: Penguin Books, 1985.
Robbe-Grillet, Alain. *For a New Novel: Essays on Fiction*. Trans. by Richard Howard. New York: Grove Press, 1965.
Rollo, May. *Symbolism in Religion and Literature*. New York: George Braziller, 1961.
Sjöö, Monica & Barbara Mor. *The Great Cosmic Mother*. San Francisco: Harper & Row, 1987.
Skura, Meredith Anne. *The Literary Use of the Psychoanalytic Process*. New Haven & London: Yale UP, 1981.
Spires, Robert C. *Beyond the Metafictional Mode: Directions in the Modern Spanish Novel*. Lexington: Kentucky UP, 1984.
Stanley, Liz. *The Auto / biographical I: The Theory and Practice of Feminist Auto / biography*. Manchester & New York: Manchester UP, 1992.
Stein, Murray. *In Midlife: A Jungian Perspective*. Dallas: Spring Publications, 1983.
———, ed. *Jungian Analysis*. LaSalle & London: Open Court, 1982.
Stone, Merlin. *When God Was a Woman*. New York & London: Harcourt Brace Jovanovich, 1976.
Tusquets, Esther. *El amor es un juego solitario*. Barcelona: Lumen, 1979.
———. *El mismo mar de todos los veranos*. Barcelona: Lumen, 1978.
———. *Para no volver*. Barcelona: Lumen, 1985.
———. *Varada tras el último naufragio*. Barcelona: Lumen, 1980.
Vásquez, Mary S., ed. *The Sea of Becoming: Approaches to the Fiction of Esther Tusquets*. New York, Westport, CT & London: Greenwood Press, 1991.
Vassi, Marco. *Metasex, Mirth & Madness*. New York: Penthouse, 1975.
Walker, Steven F. *Jung and the Jungians on Myth: An Introduction*. New York: Garland Press, 1995.
Whitmont, Edward C. *The Symbolic Quest: Basic Concepts of Analytical Psychology*. Princeton: Princeton UP, 1969.
Woodward, Kathleen and Murray M. Schwartz. *Memory and Desire: Aging-Literature-Psychoanalysis*. Bloomington: Indiana UP, 1986.
Wright, Elizabeth. *Psychoanalytic Criticism: Theory in Practice*. London & New York: Methuen, 1984.
Yearsley, Macleod. *The Folklore of Fairy Tale*. London: Watts & Co., 1924.
Young-Eisendrath, Polly. *Gender & Desire: Uncursing Pandora*. College Station: Texas A&M UP, 1997.

———— and Terence Dawson, eds. *The Cambridge Companion to Jung.* Cambridge: Cambridge UP, 1997.

ARTICLES AND BOOK CHAPTERS:

Adams, Michael Vannoy. "The Archetypal School" in *The Cambridge Companion to Jung.* Polly Young-Eisendrath and Terence Dawson, eds. Cambridge: Cambridge UP, 1997. 101-18.
Altisent, Marta E. "El erotismo en la actual narrativa española." *Cuadernos Hispanoamericanos* 486 (1989): 128-44.
Bellver, Catherine. "Assimilation and Confrontation in Esther Tusquets's *Para no volver*." *Romanic Review* 81, no 3 (May 1990): 368-76.
————. "Intertextuality in *Para no volver*" in *The Sea of Becoming: Approaches to the Fiction of Esther Tusquets.* Mary S. Vásquez, ed. New York, Westport, CT & London: Greenwood Press, 1991. 103-22.
————. "The Language of Eroticism in the Novels of Esther Tusquets." *Anales de la Literatura Española Contemporánea* 9, nos. 1-3 (1984): 13-27.
Bergmann, Emilie. "Reshaping the Canon: Intertextuality in the Spanish Novel of Female Development." *Anales de la Literatura Española Contemporánea* 12 (1987): 141-56.
Boyer, Agustín. "Lectura del pasado como constructo [*sic*] narrativo: Textualización del 'yo' femenino en dos novelas de Carmen Martín Gaite y Esther Tusquets." *Cincinnati Romance Review* 12 (1993): 92-101.
Bradway, Katherine. "Gender Identity and Gender Roles: Their Place in Analytic Practice" in *Jungian Analysis*. Murray Stein, ed. LaSalle & London: Open Court, 1982. 275-93.
Casado, Stacey Dolgin. "*Para no volver*: Esther Tusquets Brings Her Tetralogy to a Conclusive Beginning." *LA CHISPA '99: Selected Proceedings.* Gilbert Paolini, ed. New Orleans: Tulane University, 1999. 69-78.
————. "The Psychodynamics of Autobiography and Fiction in Esther Tusquets Novels." *Letras Peninsulares*, vol. 13, no. 3 (Winter 2000-2001): 751-65.
Chodorow, Joan. "Introduction" to *Jung on Active Imagination.* Princeton: Princeton UP, 1997.
Cibreiro, Estrella. "*El mismo mar de todos los veranos* y *Nubosidad variable*: hacia la consolidación de una identidad femenina propia y discursiva." *Letras Peninsulares*, vol. 13, no. 2 (Fall 2000): 581-607.
Cornejo-Parriego, Rosalía V. "Mitología, representación e identidad en *El mismo mar de todos los veranos* de Esther Tusquets." *Anales de la Literatura Española Contemporánea* 20, no. 1-2 (1995): 47-63.
Costa, Luis. "*Para no volver*: Women in Franco's Spain" in *The Sea of Becoming: Approaches to the Fiction of Esther Tusquets.* Mary S. Vásquez, ed. New York, Westport, CT & London: Greenwood Press, 1991. 11-28.
Davis, Douglas A. "Freud, Jung, and Psychoanalysis" in *The Cambridge Companion to Jung.* Polly Young-Eisendrath and Terence Dawson, eds. Cambridge: Cambridge UP, 1997. 35-51.

Dawson, Terence. "Jung, Literature, and Literary Criticism" in *The Cambridge Companion to Jung*. Polly Young-Eisendrath and Terence Dawson, eds. Cambridge: Cambridge UP, 1997. 255-80.
Dolgin, Stacey L. "The Æsthetics of Eroticism in *Love is a Solitary Game*" in *The Sea of Becoming: Approaches to the Fiction of Esther Tusquets*. Mary S. Vásquez, ed. New York, Westport, CT & London: Greenwood Press, 1991. 79-92.
———. "Conversación con Esther Tusquets: 'Para salir de tanta miseria.'" *Anales de la Literatura Española Contemporánea*, 13 (1988): 397-406.
———. "Esther Tusquets: Proyección novelística de la psique femenina." *Los Cuadernos del Norte* 44 (1987): 80-85.
Douglas, Claire. "The Historical Context of Analytical Psychology" in *The Cambridge Companion to Jung*. Polly Young-Eisendrath and Terence Dawson, eds. Cambridge: Cambridge UP, 1997. 17-34.
Ferguson, Mary Anne. "The Female Novel of Development and the Myth of Psyche" in *The Voyage In: Fictions of Female Development*. Elizabeth Abel *et al*, eds. Hanover: New England UP, 1983. 228-43.
Flax, Jane. "The Conflict Between Nurturance and Autonomy in Mother-Daughter Relationships and within Feminism." *Feminist Studies*, vol. 4, no. 2 (June 1978): 171-89.
Gardiner, Judith Kegan. "On Female Identity and Writing by Women" in *Writing and Sexual Difference*. Elizabeth Abel, ed. Chicago: Chicago UP, 1982. 177-91.
Gascón Vera, Elena. "'El naufragio del deseo': Esther Tusquets y Sylvia Molloy." *Plaza: Revista de Literatura* 11 (Autumn 1986): 20-24.
Glenn, Kathleen. "*El mismo mar de todos los veranos* and the Prism of Art" in *The Sea of Becoming: Approaches to the Fiction of Esther Tusquets*. Mary S. Vásquez, ed. New York, Westport, CT & London: Greenwood Press, 1991. 29-43.
Gold, Janet. "Reading the Love Myth: Tusquets With the Help of Barthes." *Hispanic Review* 55 (1987): 337-46.
Hart, David L. "The Classical Jungian School" in *The Cambridge Companion to Jung*. Polly Young-Eisendrath and Terence Dawson, eds. Cambridge: Cambridge UP, 1997. 89-100.
Hart, Stephen. "Esther Tusquets: Sex, Excess and the Dangerous Supplement of Language." *Journal of Hispanic Studies* 3 (1991): 85-98.
Henderson, Joseph L. "Reflections on the History and Practice of Jungian Analysis" in *Jungian Analysis*. Murray Stein, ed. La Salle & London: Open Court, 1982. 3-26.
Johnson, Roberta. "On the Waves of Time: Memory in *El mismo mar de todos los veranos*" in *The Sea of Becoming: Approaches to the Fiction of Esther Tusquets*. Mary S. Vásquez, ed. New York, Westport, CT & London: Greenwood Press, 1991. 65-77.
Jones, Margaret E. W. "Del compromiso al egoísmo: La metamorfosis de la protagonista en la novelística femenina de postguerra" in *Novelistas femeninas de la posguerra española*. Janet W. Pérez, ed. Madrid: Porrúa, 1983. 125-34.
———. "Different Wor(l)ds: Modes of Women's Communication in Spain's *narrativa femenina*." *Monographic Review/Revista Monográfica* 8 (1992): 57-69.

Kugler, Paul. "Psychis Imaging: A Bridge Between Subject and Object" in *The Cambridge Companion to Jung*. Polly Young-Eisendrath and Terence Dawson, eds. Cambridge: Cambridge UP, 1997. 71-88.

Levine, Linda Gould. "Reading, Rereading, Misreading and Rewriting the Male Canon: The Narrative Web of Esther Tusquets' Trilogy." *Anales de la Literatura Española Contemporánea* 12 (1987): 203-17.

———. "The Censored Sex: Woman as Author and Character in Franco's Spain" in *Women in Hispanic Literature: Icons and Fallen Idols*. Beth Miller, ed. Berkeley: California UP, 1983. 289-315.

Manteiga, Roberto. "From Empathy to Detachment: The Author-Narrator Relationship in Several Spanish Novels by Women." *Monographic Review/Revista Monográfica* 8 (1992): 19-35.

———. "El triunfo del minotauro: Ambigüedad y razón en *El mismo mar de todos los veranos*." *Letras Femeninas* 14, no. 1-2 (Spring-Fall, 1988): 22-31.

Moix, Ana María. "Frente, contra o en pos del amor: Esther Tusquets." *Quimera: Revista de Literatura* 123 (1994): 58-59.

Morgan, Janice. "Fiction and Autobiography / Language and Silence: *The Lover* by Marguerite Duras" in *Gender & Genre in Literature: Redefining Twentieth-Century Women's Fiction*. Janice Morgan & Colette T Hall, eds. New York & London: Garland Publishing, 1999. 73-84.

———. "Subject to Subject / Voice to Voice: Twentieth-Century Autobiographical Fiction by Women Writers" in *Gender & Genre in Literature: Redefining Twentieth-Century Women's Fiction*. Janice Morgan & Colette T. Hall, eds. New York & London: Garland Publishing, 1999. 3-19.

Navajas, Gonzalo. "Civilizations and Fictions of Love in *Para no volver*" in *The Sea of Becoming: Approaches to the Fiction of Esther Tusquets*. Mary S. Vásquez, ed. New York, Westport, CT & London: Greenwood Press, 1991. 123-36.

———. "Repetition and the Rhetoric of Love in Esther Tusquets' *El mismo mar de todos los veranos*" in *Nuevos y novísimos: Algunas perspectivas críticas sobre la narrativa española desde la década de los 60*. Ricardo Landeira and Luis T. González-del-Valle, eds. Boulder: Society of Spanish and Spanish-American Studies, 1987. 113-29.

Nichols, Geraldine Cleary. "Minding Her P's and Q's: The Fiction of Esther Tusquets." *Indiana Journal of Hispanic Literature* 2, no. 1 (1993): 159-79.

———. "The Prison-House (And Beyond): *El mismo mar de todos los veranos*." *Romanic Review*, LXXV (1984): 367-85.

Ordóñez, Elizabeth. "The Barcelona Group: The Fiction of Alós, Moix, and Tusquets." *Letras Femeninas* 6, no. 1 (1980): 38-50.

———. "A Quest for Matrilineal Roots and Mythopoesis: Esther Tusquets' *El mismo mar de todos los veranos*." *Crítica Hispánica* 6 (1984): 37-46.

———. "*Para no volver*: Through the Mirror and Over the Threshold of Desire" in *The Sea of Becoming: Approaches to the Fiction of Esther Tusquets*. Mary S. Vásquez, ed. New York, Westport, CT & London: Greenwood Press, 1991. 137-55.

Perry, Christopher. "Transference and Countertransference" in *The Cambridge Companion to Jung*. Polly Young-Eisendrath and Terence Dawson, eds. Cambridge: Cambridge UP, 1997. 141-63.

Pertusa, Inmaculada. "*El mismo mar de todos los veranos* y el poder subversivo de la confesión." *Antípodas: Journal of Hispanic and Galician Studies* 11-12 (1999-2000): 125-41.

Rodríguez, Mercedes M. de. "Entrevista con Esther Tusquets." *Letras Peninsulares*, vol. 13, no. 2 (Fall 2000): 609-19.

———. "Motivos mitológicos y del folklore en *El mismo mar de todos los veranos*" in *Selected Proceedings of the Mid-America Conference on Hispanic Literature*. Luis T. González-del-Valle and Catherine Nickel, eds. Lincoln: Society of Spanish and Spanish-American Studies, 1986. 129-36.

———. "Narrative Strategies in the Novels of Esther Tusquets." *Monographic Review/Revista Monográfica* 7 (1991): 124-34.

———. "*Para no volver*: Humor vs. Phallocentrism." *Letras Femeninas* 16, no. 1-2 (Spring-Fall 1990): 29-35.

———. "Talking with Tusquets" in *The Sea of Becoming: Approaches to the Fiction of Esther Tusquets*. Mary S. Vásquez, ed. New York, Westport, CT & London: Greenwood Press, 1991. 173-88.

Rose, Ellen Cronan. "Through the Looking Glass: When Women Tell Fairy Tales" in *The Voyage In: Fictions of Female Development*. Elizabeth Abel *et al*, eds. Hanover: New England UP, 1983.

Salman, Sherry. "The Creative Psyche: Jung's Major Contributions" in *The Cambridge Companion to Jung*. Polly Young-Eisendrath and Terence Dawson, eds. Cambridge: Cambridge UP, 1997. 52-70.

Schumm, Sandra J. "*El amor es un juego solitario*: Loss of Identity Through Metaphors and Provocative Mirrors." *Letras Peninsulares* 8, no. 1 (Spring 1995): 147-67.

Schwartz-Salant, Nathan. "Introduction" to *Jung on Alchemy*. Princeton: Princeton UP, 1995.

Servodidio, Mirella d'Ambrosio. "Esther Tusquets's Fiction: The Spinning of a Narrative Web" in *Women Writers of Contemporary Spain: Exiles in the Homeland*. Joan Lipman Brown, ed. Newark: Delaware UP, 1991. 159-78.

———. "Perverse Pairings and Corrupted Codes: *El amor es un juego solitario*." *Anales de la Literatura Española Contemporánea* 11, no. 3 (1986): 237-54.

———. "A Case of Pre-Œdipal and Narrative Fixation: *El mismo mar de todos los veranos*." *Anales de la Literatura Española Contemporánea* 12, nos. 1-2 (1987): 157-74.

Solomon, Hester McFarland. "The Developmental School" in *The Cambridge Companion to Jung*. Polly Young-Eisendrath and Terence Dawson, eds. Cambridge: Cambridge UP, 1997. 119-40.

Spires, Robert. "The Dialogic Structure of *Para no volver*" in *The Sea of Becoming: Approaches to the Fiction of Esther Tusquets*. Mary S. Vásquez, ed. New York, Westport, CT & London: Greenwood Press, 1991. 93-122.

Stein, Murray. "The Aims and Goals of Jungian Analysis" in *Jungian Analysis*. Murray Stein, ed. La Salle & London: Open Court, 1982. 28-44.

Suñén, Luis. "El mito en el espejo: *El mismo mar de todos los veranos*, de Esther Tusquets." *Ínsula* (septiembre 1978): 5.

Tsuchiya, Akiko. "Theorizing the Feminine: Esther Tusquets's *El mismo mar de todos los veranos* and Helene Cixous's *écriture feminine*." *Revista de Estudios Hispánicos* 26, no. 2 (May 1992): 183-99.

Tusquets, Esther. "Para salir de tanta miseria." *Ojáncano*, 2 (abril 1988): 73-85.

Valbuena-Briones, Ángel Julián. "El camino psicológico de la narradora en *El mismo mar de todos los veranos*." *LA CHISPA '95: Selected Proceedings*. Claire J. Paolini, ed. New Orleans, Tulane University, 1995. 377-86.

———. "*El mismo mar de todos los veranos*: Una novela postmodernista." *Hispanic Journal* 14, no. 1 (Spring 1993): 63-71.

Vásquez, Mary S. "Actor and Spectator in the Fiction of Esther Tusquets" in *The Sea of Becoming: Approaches to the Fiction of Esther Tusquets*. Mary S. Vásquez, ed. Westport, CT: Greenwood, 1991. 157-72.

———. "Esther Tusquets and the Trilogy which Isn't." *LA CHISPA '87: Selected Proceedings*. Alfredo Lozada, ed. Baton Rouge: Louisiana State UP, 1987. 239-43.

———. "Image and the Linear Progression Toward Defeat in Esther Tusquets' *El mismo mar de todos los veranos*," in *LA CHISPA '83: Selected Proceedings*. Gilbert Paolini, ed. New Orleans: Tulane University, 1983. 307-13.

———. "Tusquets, Fitzgerald and the Redemptive Power of Love." *Letras Femeninas* 14, nos. 1-2 (1988): 10-21.

Young-Eisendrath, Polly. "Gender and Contrasexuality: Jung's Contribution and Beyond" in *The Cambridge Companion to Jung*. Polly Young-Eisendrath and Terence Dawson, eds. Cambridge: Cambridge UP, 1997. 223-39.